How I Lived and Loved

A Time to Embrace, A Time to Leave Behind

ANNA VERGHIS

INDIA · SINGAPORE · MALAYSIA

Notion Press Media Pvt Ltd

No. 50, Chettiyar Agaram Main Road,
Vanagaram, Chennai, Tamil Nadu – 600 095

First Published by Notion Press 2021
Copyright © Anna Verghis 2021
All Rights Reserved.

ISBN 978-1-68538-249-0

Dedication

To my beloved grandchildren

Sourabh, Santwana, Srutika, Namith and Shobhith

Contents

Preface

It was June 11 2020, Papa's death anniversary. I wrote a paragraph about Papa and sent it to my children. Prashant's response was immediate. He requested me to write about our ancestors, for they knew nothing about them. I replied that even if I took the pains to write it, nobody would care to read it. But he didn't stop there. Just because he wouldn't give up, I decided to write. In my heart of hearts I had a desire to record all my memories and experiences which still remain in my heart as in a reel. So towards the end of June, I started writing. I wrote those memories just as they came to me, and so the final draft needed more time and effort. I was able to complete it only by the 11th of March. But the whole effort gave me great joy and I got immense pleasure and satisfaction, doing the work. It was a very useful way to spend all the time I got by keeping indoors without any travel because of the virus that has gripped the whole world. A positive outcome indeed, from a very negative experience.

When Kunjuchayan, Mr. K.P. Luke Vydhian, our very close relative wrote his story, "Carried on Eagles' wings", about God's faithfulness in his life, he insisted that I go through it. It was a great inspiration for me. It taught me that age is no barrier to making use of talents invested in us by God.

I have no words to express my gratitude to Sri. Rajan Ittycheria, Manager, CMS Press, who was a great help when I was editor of "Kudumbapriyavadini". He kindly agreed to take care of other skilled work, making use of his invaluable experience.

Sumitra, my dear classmate, and Sri. Govindankutty Menon my dear Chettan were entrusted with finding a title for the book. They took it seriously and Chettan sent me this beautiful title through Sumitra which very aptly expresses the theme of the book itself, for it is all about how I lived and loved.

By writing this book I have been able to pay tribute to so many who loved me and so many whom I loved, who, I still hold in my heart with such precious remembrances. Age cannot wither them or the value with which they are held in my heart.

As I was writing the book I was compelled to re-enter my experiences in life. That gave me a second chance to go through great happiness as well as deep sorrows. I have not been able to include everyone and all events, though they too have an important place in my life.

The day before I was to go for University paper valuation as Chairman of Paper 2 English in S.N. College, Kollam, the verse I read for Bible meditation that day was – "Even there shall Thy hand lead me, Thy right hand shall uphold me." (Psalm 139:10). I wondered why God had given such a promise for an ordinary uneventful paper valuation camp. But when I reached the college I learned that all the leaders who struck work the previous year were allotted to S.N. College with just two lady teachers who were additional examiners, while all the well-behaved teachers were in Fatima college. As soon as I reached the college two leaders came to me, introduced themselves and invited me for coffee to a near-by coffee shop. Of them, Prof. G, a tall, stout, imposing personality, was the leader of the previous year's revels. Anyway, I tried to be as polite and gentle as possible, holding on to God's promise. Everyday, Prof G who was Chief examiner would come late in the afternoon, and very often he had cuts and bruises. The additional examiners complained but I tried to appease them gently. On another day the young clerk who was in charge of the answer papers forgot to bring the keys, and all the examiners stood in the quadrangle, shouting slogans. I stood there with them silently, just clinging to God's promise. The problem was solved after some time.

Prof G used to bring papers to me for re-valuation, and some of the papers were excellent. As soon as he came to me, the other teachers would laugh, remembering what had happened the previous year. Anyway we had a friendly relationship with each other. That year there was strike for two days in Fatima College, but here there was absolute cordiality.

At the end of the valuation, we went our separate ways after collecting our remuneration. The next day we came to the bank to cash our cheques. As I stood there, Prof G walked in. He greeted me warmly and I smiled and greeted him. Then he turned to me and said, "Madam, thank you for your love."

I can never forget his words. Love conquers all. God in His Omnipotence knew what would happen and had given me the promise, and He in His faithfulness led me as I clung to Him.

Jesus said, "If a man loves me, he will keep my words: and my father will love him and we will come to him and make our abode with him" (John 14:23)

God dwells with us in our hearts and homes if we will only keep his words by loving Him and loving one another.

COVID-19 has all the more taught us that God dwells, not in high places, not in institutionalised churches, but in the humble heart of a person who will open the door for Christ.

This book is a very truthful account of my experiences with God and man, though certain things may seem unbelievable, for fact is sometimes stranger than fiction.

Tribute

I lost four jewels one after the other after I finished writing this book —
Ammini of the women's hostel, a very caring friend, Sara John, eminent
principal of Nicholson School, beloved Thankochamma, Thankamma
Varkey and Rajan, Rajan Itticheriya. All four left me during a short span
of four months—Thankochamma and Rajan making a shocking exit. My
love for them is undying, my indebtedness to them is without parallel, and
the void they leave behind can never be filled.

Thankochamma and Saramma were two pillars of Nicholson School,
two valuable gems who belonged to so many who passed through the
portals of the school. All four of them cared so much for me, and their
constant phone calls have now become silent. When God takes away
precious people from our lives, at such a time as this, ours is not to
question why, but yet, with thankfulness comes the pain of deep loss.

My loving tributes.

CHAPTER I

FAMILY ROOTS

Miss. Joan Elliott who taught in the English Department of CMS College, Kottayam, was living in Cheltenham when I went to England on a World Council of Churches scholarship in September 1970. She delighted having overseas students with her wherever she was. I went there to the famous Cotswold region, with Chris and a few others. During our conversation she remembered Professor T.B. Thomas of Union Christian College, Aluva, and his daughter Annu. Annu was then staying in London, married to Brian, an English-man. I knew them very well. So did I know their family connections. Miss. Elliott exclaimed, "Oh, you Syrian Christians!". She very well knew that in Kerala, families were inter-connected and we could easily trace the roots of one another. That brought her remark.

We must know about our roots, traditions, history and genealogy. We may not know where we are going but we know where we come from. Whether we like it or not, we are part of a rich heritage and culture. We do not stand alone.

We have a great heritage through Abraham Malpan, famous reformer of the Mar Thoma Church, for he was Valiammachy's (Thalavady) great-grand father. "Malpan" means, a teacher in the Seminary.

Abraham Malpan became attracted to the reforms that missionaries brought to the church in Travancore. Rev. Joseph Peet especially, was a close friend of Abraham Malpan. Abraham Malpan was captivated by these teachings and so he wanted to do away with the superstitions and blind beliefs that existed in the church. He also decided to translate the Holy Communion (Thaksa) liturgy from Syriac to the mother tongue Malayalam, so that the worshippers could understand what they were saying. Abraham Malpan, himself a scholar of Syriac, recited his personal prayers in Syriac but used only the Malayalam liturgy whenever he led the service.

People from miles around used to walk to Maramon to listen to Abraham Malpan's reforms. They stayed there to hear his teachings. They turned to Abraham Malpan for their doubts and needs. Since a reformed church seemed to be very difficult, they were willing to join the missionaries.

As it was very difficult for Abraham Malpan to bring reform because of the powerful hierarchy of the church, Rev. Joseph Peet requested him to join the Anglicans, and offered him seventy-five rupees as his salary. It was an enormous amount in those days because huge, fertile plots of land could then be bought for forty or forty-five rupees. But Abraham Malpan longed to bring reform to the church from within, however difficult, and he politely declined the offer.

Still, at one point Abraham Malpan felt compelled to join the church of the missionaries. Yet he felt a great responsibility about his own church. His unswerving faith that there was nothing impossible with God, helped him stay persistent. The Maramon Parish was with Abraham Malpan and eminent and scholarly people became his followers. Thus he was a religious stalwart who stood like a rock for his faith.

On his death-bed, even though his nephew Mathews Mar Athnasius who was by his side requested his permission to give him Holy Communion, Abraham Malpan said – "It is hardly forty days since I received Holy Communion. So I shall receive it if Kaithayil Achen comes; otherwise it is not necessary."

He knew that Kaithayil Achen would use only the reformed liturgy. He was not so sure about his nephew the bishop, for even if he used it before Abraham Malpan, Malpan knew he mixed the old and the new "Thaksas" otherwise.

Rev. Joseph Peet who was a constant visitor, came to see Abraham Malpan on his death-bed. They discussed the funeral and other matters. As he departed, he saw people flowing to Maramon to see Abraham Malpan. Rev. Joseph Peet told them – "Your Malpan is going to heaven". Abraham Malpan died soon after Rev. Joseph Peet's departure.

Abraham Malpan was married to Aleyamma, who was the daughter of Tharakan, of Thondemvelil, Thumpamon. She was an expert cook and efficient in managing the household. The Mar Thoma church was a mile away from the ancestral home of "Palakunnathu". Abraham Malpan wanted to stay near the church, and so he bought "Kuzhiyathu", a large plot of land on the banks of the Pamba river. It was on the eastern side of Maramon Church, just next to it. That is how the family name "Kuzhiyathu" became famous.

Abraham Malpan had four daughters and four sons. The daughters were older and were married into well-known families – the eldest Mariamma, was married to Mepral Kaniyanthra house, and later to Kuttickattu house, Aymanam, for she lost her husband while young. Abraham Deacon from Ayrookuzhiyil who was one of Abraham Malpan's disciples, married his second daughter Annamma. The third, Aleyamma was married to Tharakan of Thumpamon, Chakkalamannil, and the youngest daughter Saramma, to Varkey, who was the nephew of Abraham Malpan's intimate friend Edavammelil Oommachen of Eraviperoor.

His eldest son Mathaikunju married from Velliyampally, Mallappally, and his third son Kochukoshykunju, from Puthencavu, Puthenveetil. His second son was Bishop Thomas Mar Athnasius of the Mar Thoma church who died in 1068 (Malayalam calendar) and his fourth son was Theethus Mar Thoma Metropolitan who died in 1085. Thus Abraham Malpan's two sons became bishops of the Mar Thoma church. His brother's grandson later served the church as Theethus II. It is written that Theethus Mar Thoma was closest in resemblance to Abraham Malpan, and had all his true religious fervour. When he was born he was an attractive baby, and Abraham Malpan held him by the legs and said – "These legs will go into the coloured robes of a bishop."

Rev. M.C. George Kassissa, author of the biography of Abraham Malpan was the father of Alexander Mar Thoma. He writes – "When I write this book, Abraham Malpan's beloved son Kochukoshykunju is still alive."

Kochukoshykunju who stayed in Madathil (Changayil), had six children. The eldest was Dr. Abraham who stayed in Ambatt. Mathai the second son, stayed in Mullottil, and the third son Thomas, Valiyammachy's father, was given "Kuzhiyathu house" that belonged to Abraham Malpan. The fourth son was Dethose. He stayed in Kannamvelil. The fifth was a daughter, Mariamma who was married to Poothikottu family, Mepral. The youngest Benyamin (Benjamin) stayed in the tharavadu Changayil.

Kochukoshykunju was a great pioneer of the church, taking after his father, Abraham Malpan. He helped the UC College financially in its early stages and facilitated the construction of the Maramon School. He gave his property for the church in Koodal and also renovated the Maramon Mar Thoma Church when it was in a dilapidated state. The Maramon church was the church of Abraham Malpan, and Kochukoshykunju filed a case in court to prevent the Maramon church too being taken away by the other faction. Thus the Maramon church alone remained with the Mar Thoma Church from the start of the reformation. Kochukoshykunju continued to help the Mar Thoma church in numerous ways, his two brothers becoming the bishops of the church after Mathews Mar Athnasius. This beloved son of the church was like a pillar and was highly respected so that when he died he was buried right in the courtyard of the Maramon Mar Thoma Church.

His sons were all very prosperous and had vast landed property. Abraham Malpan loved farming and had brought new plants and trees from places he visited. It is recorded that when he went to Palayamkottai, he saw a particular breed of plantains with long stalk and fruit. He brought it to Maramon and cultivated it. This was the "Palayamkodan" variety of bananas and was cultivated far and wide in Travancore after that. They all planted nutmeg trees (Jathikka) and other fruit trees that once made Chrysostom Thirumeni who grew up in Maramon to ask Alexi Kochamma, "Is the Jathi that survived the great floods of 1099, still there in Kuzhiyathu?" Some of Abraham Malpan's descendants in proceeding generations have inherited this love of cultivation.

Abraham Apothecary was the oldest among the sons of Kochukoshykunju and lived in Ambatt. He was a flourishing doctor and was very rich, but he had no children. Fortunately I got first-hand information about Abraham Apothecary from a close friend of our family who, as a child had lived near his house.

They were four brothers and four sisters in this family and lived right in Chettimukku main junction next to Ambatt house. The oldest brother was born in 1914. This brother was a very good student. Though they lived at the junction, they had three other plots. The parents decided to send this bright young lad to college when he passed his matriculation in 1930, from the St. Thomas English High School, Kozhencherry. Alexander Mar Thoma, then M.G. Chandy passed out from the same school in 1929.

These two boys were close friends and they used to go to the nearby Kozhencherry Mar Thoma Church every day for prayer during the lunch recess.

The parents decided to mortgage their plot of land in Chettimukku where they stayed, to Abraham apothecary to raise funds to send this son to college. He did his B.Sc Mathematics in UC College, Alwaye, and his father used to take the required money from Abraham apothecary whenever he needed it. Ultimately, the plot was sold to Apothecary to settle their liability. But they continued to stay there till 1938, enjoying all the income of the land. Apothecary was never in a hurry for them to move out and asked them to continue to stay there as long as they wanted.

When their brother passed out in 1934 from UC College, Apothecary sent him to a bank in Thiruvananthapuram with a letter for a job. He got the job and worked there for some time.

The deal with Apothecary was immensely helpful to them as a family. It was a bold decision by both mother and father. Mortgaging and subsequently selling parts of their ancestral property enabled all the children to get the valuable gift of education.

Later this elder brother had an assignment at the United Nations Relief and Rehabilitation Administration Office (UNRRA) in Shanghai, China from 1945 to January 1948. When he returned from Shanghai he had some money. He came straight to Maramon, met Ambatt Apothecary and offered to buy back the plot of land sold by the family, at a price a few times higher than what was paid to them. In fact, Apothecary agreed happily. But this brother discontinued the talk immediately when a dissenting voice was heard from inside the house. It was the Apothecary's wife. "My brother wanted to avoid any embarassment to Abraham Apothecary."

Their eldest sister was married to Yohannachen (John) of Macheril House, Nedumprayar. He was close to Ambatt house since the time of Apothecary. He was looking after their "Illathu Purayidom" near the Maramon Convention Pandal, which incidentally, was close to his house. The brother-in-law took the produce of the land and did not have to pay anything to them at Ambatt, except perhaps the sale proceeds of nutmeg.

Another interesting thing was that when the land-ceiling Act was in the offing they transferred the title deed of one or two of their paddy fields (wetland) in favour of this brother-in-law. This was re-transferred to them subsequently. "How people could trust an outsider so much, so blindly!" he wonders. It shows how people in those days trusted one another and cared for one another.

His eldest sister was born in 1916. She studied only up to primary school std IV, but used to read very well. The Maramon Malayalam School was situated right in front of the Maramon Mar Thoma Church. Chrysostom Thirumeni then was her classmate. She remembers that Thirumeni called Dharmishtan was then staying at Kunnampilly house which belonged to Abraham Apothecary. "Dharmishtan's father, Kalamannil K.E. Oommen Achen was then Vicar of Maramon Mar Thoma Church. He was priest there for thirteen years in different spells."

The children used to visit Dharmishtan's house to drink water. Dharmishtan's mother was very short, and a very good lady. His primary school education was in Maramon and his high school education was in St. Thomas High School, Kozhencherry.

When he was doing his Intermediate course in Mar Ivanios College, Thiruvananthapuram from 1950-1952, their parish priest in the Mar Thoma Church, Paruthippara, was Philip Oommen Achen (Dharmishtan). He was a regular visitor to their college hostels and organised prayer meetings for students on Sundays, in some houses of the nearby parishioners. During that period, Achen planned to renovate the church. So he distributed to the students, donation cards, the size of a post-card with 50 columns each, to be crossed by donors at the rate of half a rupee per column. It was given to them at the start of the term holiday. His mother asked him to go to Ambatt Avarachen and tell him that he was asked to raise donations for Dharmishtan Achen. Avarachen gave him five rupees, a large donation by the standards then. All others donated only half a rupee each and he could hardly raise twenty rupees.

Since Abraham Apothecary, the eldest son of Kochukoshykunju had no children, he adopted Avarachen (Valiammachy's younger brother). That is how Valiammachy's brother Avarachayan came to live in Ambatt.

Valiammachy's father was Thomas, grandson of Abraham Malpan and son of Kochukoshykunju. It was he who inherited Kuzhiyathu house. Kuzhiyathu house had a "chavadi" a separate building for the Bishops. Whenever they came to Maramon they stayed there. Kuzhiyathu was also the house where these two bishops were born and grew up. The "chavadi" had great value and significance because of this. Thomas got married to Kunjandamma from Ooramvelil House, Edathua. Valiammachy's mother was an only daughter among a group of brothers. The brothers when they married came to different families as "dathu", ie, inheriting the wife's property where there is no male heir. One brother thus settled down in Moolamannil, Karackal (near Mepral) and M.O. Koshy Achen was his son. Koshy Achen was later vicar of Chathenkary, Karackal and Mepral parishes and was a devout priest. Another of Kunjandamma's brothers lived in Ooramvelil, Mavelikara.

Of Thomas and Kunjandamma's ten children, the third, Koshykunju died an infant. The eldest daughter was Achyamma who got married to Kottayam Puthuppally, Paloor house, and the second was Aleyamma who was married to Chakkalayil family, Kottayam. Thomachayan (C.C. Thomas) who stayed in Madras and was married to Bishop M.M. John's sister Kunjoonjamma was her son. Both of them were very close to us since we always sailed to Malaya from Madras and Thomachayan was engineer in Binny and Company and worked in the harbour.

Mariamma (Valiammachy) was the third daughter in the family. Next came a brother Chackochayan who later settled down in Koodal. Babuchayan (P.J. Thomas) and Mon (Advocate) are his sons. He had five daughters of whom Kunjochamma, Lisu's mother was the eldest. Kunjoonjamma Kochamma, Ammukutty Kochamma, Susamma Kochamma and Saro are the others. Shoby who became Prashant's friend while in California is Lisu's son.

Avarachayan who was adopted by Abraham Apothecary and inherited Ambatt house was the next. Saramma Kochamma was the fourth among daughters. She was married to Koshykunju, Kadathethu Thumpamon. Kochukunjachayan, Rajanchayan, Sunnychayan, Babychayan, Ammini Ammamma married to Achenkunjachayan who lives in Cherukole, Santhamma who was George Achen's wife and Molly were her children.

The next brother was Mathaikuttychayan who was a dentist and practised in Salem. His wife was a doctor. They both settled down in Pullad.

Dr. Kunjumon and his brother Roy are his children. Dr. Kunjumon and Kunjoonjamma stay in the ancestral property in Pullad.

The youngest of the daughters was Annamma Kochamma married to V.K. Oommen of Vettinilkkunnathil House, Nallanikkunnu. Appachen was a headmaster in different places. Their children are Ammini Kochamma (Trivandrum), Alexi Kochamma (Kumbalampoika) and Babuchayan (Thomas Kurien) who retired from Bishop Moore College.

The youngest was Georgekuttichayan who inherited the famous home, "Kuzhiyathu". Georgekuttichayan has a son and a daughter.

It is this son, Dr. Thomaskutty working in Mar Thoma Hospital, Ranni, and married to a doctor, who recently sold the entire heritage of "Kuzhiyathu" to a real estate agent. It is Indians who don't value history and heritage. In fact Kuzhiyathu house belonged not only to Abraham Malpan but to all who were born there and lived there; all the ancestors including the two bishops of the Mar Thoma church. It also belongs to all Abraham Malpan's descendants in different parts of the world who have this shared heritage. Indirectly the house also belongs to the Mar Thoma church because it is part of the church's history. Dr. Thomaskutty who happened to inherit it was only a trustee of such a heritage. But it was sold for the "Silver Coins" it brought, forgetting the unfathomable riches of such a tradition and heredity. The Bible teaches us to value our heritage. The Bible teaches us to "remember" our forefathers. The present has no value without its link to the past.

This should be a lesson for all who have scant respect for whatever they have inherited from the past. Every tree, every stone, every grain of sand has a story to tell, a story from past ages. Once when Chrysostom Thirumeni came to Nicholson School I gave him my book "Neerum Velakalil" and introduced myself as Kuzhiyathu Mariamma's grand-daughter. Mama was Chrysostom Thirumeni's classmate in Maramon primary school. Chrysostom Thirumeni called me just before leaving and said "you all know little about Kuzhiyathu and Ambatt. Nobody knows as well as I do. As children we were part of these homes and came to Kuzhiyathu kadavu for swimming and bathing".

We must honour and respect our ancestors and their history and try to add something more to enrich the past, not destroy it for our worthless goals. Our children should be taught from childhood to honour the past, their ancestors, the place where they live, their roots and history. Do not measure the worth of everything in terms of money. There are things that money can never buy, things of inestimable worth.

Kuzhiyathu Ammachy, Valiammachy's mother, was a unique lady. She was educated, cultured, efficient and responsible about everything in the household. She used to receive important people with folded hands. Appachen did not have much interaction with people but everyone remembers Ammachy. Papa, when he went with Mama after their wedding to visit Appachen and Ammachy, was greatly impressed by Ammachy. We used to later stay in Maramon as little children, and I remember having "kanji" sitting on a small "kurandi", in the kitchen. I do not remember Ammachy's face but I remember Appachen. He was then blind.

Ammachy, Valiammachy's mother was a very prayerful woman. The Kuzhiyathu house was an "ettukettu" and in the midst of her responsibilities in the kitchen, Ammachy would come to the "Nalukettu" to pray "Yama prarthanakal", ie prayers prayed at different hours of a day. Ammachy had two "valikas" or big ear ornaments each weighing five sovereigns. But she gave them away to the Church for evangelical work and wore only the remaining "mottu" the rest of her life.

She was a great cook too, and Mathews Mar Athnasius Thirumeni of Kurudamannil whose mother belonged to Palakkunnathu family, always said he had an aunt whose cooking was fabulous. Valiammachy looked exactly like her mother, tall, fair, elegant. Kuzhiyathu Appachen was different, and did not have the sociable qualities that Ammachy had. Later he became blind with glaucoma. But as long as Ammachy was alive she "was his eyes" and she looked after him with tender care. But after Ammachy's death his life became a misery.

All who remember Ammachy speak of her with great admiration. Ammachy also looked after the needs of her father-in-law's two brothers, Thomas Mar Athnasius and Theethus Mar Thoma. When the bishops came to the Maramon Mar Thoma Church, they came by "vallom" to Kuzhiyathu 'kadavu' and then stayed in the 'chavadi', next to the house.

Ammachy had a sudden peaceful end. She used to have "thechukuli" or oil baths twice a week. One day, after her bath and evening meals, she went to bed. Then she felt a little uneasy and called her son. She went to the toilet twice after which she came and rested on her bed· In a few moments she was gone. It was December 1950. Ammini Kochamma's wedding had taken place three months earlier and at that time they were in Trivandrum. "By the time we reached Maramon the funeral was over." she says. We were then in Malaya.

It was Georgekuttichayan, Valiammachy's youngest brother who inherited the ancestral home. His wife Aleyamma had been a Malayalam teacher in the primary school next to the church. He fell in love with her and so married her. But it was not at all a match befitting this family. So when Kuzhiyathu Appachan and Ammachy grew old she did not bother to look after their needs. In fact she did not look after her own mother who later stayed with her. Finally, Avarachayan and Ammai sent good food to them every day. It was a "thandan" (a man who climbed their coconut trees) who brought the food from Ambatt to Kuzhiyathu. But this clever bearer used to deposit all the lovely side-dishes in his own house and gave only the rest to Appachen and Ammachy. When Avarachayan discovered it he immediately brought his parents to his own home where they lived till Ammachy's death.

After Ammachy died, the sons decided to share the responsibility of Appachen. So Appachen was to stay one year with each of his sons. Appachen was a healthy man but he suffered a lot this way because he was also blind. At last Avarachayan came to his rescue again and he lived with this son till the day of his death in 1960, ten years after the death of his beloved wife.

Avarachayan's eldest son was Thomaskuttichayan, a brilliant boy according to one who knew him. But after his M.Com from Madras Christian College, "he had to limit himself to their estate in Kanjirappally, thus denying the benefit of his intelligence and brilliance to the betterment of the world outside."

Avarachayan had two more sons, Georgekunju and Koshykunju.

"Georgekunju was my classmate in the primary, in the Malayalam school near the church. After primary I, Georgekunju went to Perumbavoor boarding school. Again we were together in the second form in the Abraham Malpan Memorial English middle school, which later became a high school since 1948." writes our family friend.

"Georgekunju thereafter went to Madras Christian College. They were the first to buy a car in Maramon but Georgekunju had no pretensions. I remember all his siblings and his mother Thankamma." Georgekunju was the only one who married in the family.

Avarachayan's two daughters are Ponnamma, married to Thampi and staying in Trivandrum and Kunjumol the youngest, married to Kunjumon. They stay in Edappally.

Valiappachen, Mama's father, lost his mother at a young age and so we only know that she was Zachariah Master's sister. Zachariah Master was the headmaster of S.C. Seminary High School. Valiappachen had only one sister who was married to Thoppil, Chennithala. T.B. Mathew Vakil, T.B. Thomas who was headmaster in various schools, Anitha's father Keevarchayan, a daughter who was married in Vennikulam, are her children. His father married again and Ilayamma and her daughter Pennamma settled down in Chennithala.

Valiappachen's father and his two brothers lived as one joint-family because they loved one another too deeply to be separated. It was a big and prosperous household. Valiammachy was married here at the time of this prosperity. Each of these three brothers had only one male heir. The sisters were married off. So after their parents' death they moved into separate houses, Valiappachen, to Kandathil Pandamviruthil, Idiculla Appachen in the ancestral home and the oldest of them Ouseph Appachen to Kandathil, Paruvakkal. The Kandathil family in Thalavady is small, consisting only of these three families.

Valiappachen was educated in S.C. Seminary boarding school and he was a gifted singer. He stayed in the boarding school and received prizes for singing. He used to teach Leelamma and me action songs, acting them out with great enthusiasm.

One song was – "Three Jews came from Jerusalem."

The other was – "I'll give to thee a packet of pins

> And that's the way my love begins, will you marry,
>
> will you marry, will you marry me?"

How we enjoyed singing it as little children!!

About Papa's ancestors – a young girl from Vilakkupattathil family was married to a Catholic boy of Chembunthara family, Mambuzhakary, Pulinkunnu. But he died young, leaving her a widow with a small son. Her family brought her back to Mepral and she settled down with her son in a property in Chathenkary. Kunjachayan has later met people from this Catholic family. This son got married and they had two sons. The elder one was Mundakathil Appachen (Kunjen Pappy) who lived to a ripe old age, and the second one was Papa's father.

Papa, Mama, Molly, Leelamma

Both were farmers. Papa's father used to dive to the bottom of the river to catch big fish that was available in plenty in the rich river. But unfortunately, once he caught fever and thus died at a young age. The children always referred to him affectionately as "Achayan". At that time Papa's older sisters Mariamma (Kokkapparambil Valia Ammachy) and Kunjeli (Payalippurathu, Kochammachy) were married. Papa had a younger brother Thomas, who was very affectionately called "Kochachen" by his younger sisters. But he later died of typhoid. Then came Sosamma (Vallimamachy), Kunjamma (Kunjumamachy), Saramma (Kochumamachy) and Kunjachen (Kunjachayan).

Papa's mother Valiammachy, called Kunjannamma was very fair, short, and with a flat nose. Her home was in Vengal. She had only one sister who was older to her, and she lived right behind the Vengal Mar Thoma Church. This Ammachy was tall, and had beautiful features. She had six sons, and a daughter who was married in Kavungumprayar. Pappichayan, Chackochayan, Thomachayan, Johnychayan, Kunjootichayan all lived in Vengal and Perumthuruthy. Thomachayan was a constant visitor to Chathenkary. We used to visit this Ammachy with Valiammachy, going to

Papa, Mama, James, Molly, Leelamma, Alice (left to right)

Vengal by "Vallom." There were many relatives in Vengal. Vallimamachy took us to these homes. I remember her last days very clearly. We went to see her with Vallimmachy. She had slight uneasiness and she asked Thomachayan her pet son named after her father to sing "Samayamam radhathil" a song sung in funerals. Thomachayan laughed and cracked a joke. She died very soon with great hope. We went with Valiammachy for the funeral. When we returned, Valiammachy brought with her, Ammachy's mundu, chatta and neriyathu, saying she wanted her sister's smell. I remember Vengal Appachen too. When he died, Ammachy insisted that the cross on his tomb should be a little high so that she could see it from her bed.

People lived on agriculture and other livelihoods in those days. But money was scarce. Papa, called Unnikunju was Valiammachy's pet son and he was a brilliant student. But after his father's death, the family was in dire straits. He had to be the bread-winner. Valiammachy was a simple, innocent, prayerful woman, very child-like, not familiar with the ways of the world. When Papa finished his high school, he went to Alleppey and made arrangements to migrate to Malaya, which was then a British Colony. He loved his mother very much but he knew he could never leave with her permission. So, sadly, and without informing her, he took leave of her and went to Malaya to save the family from poverty.

Papa worked in the office of the Malayan Railway in Sentul, Kuala Lumpur. He used to get leave only once in six years, for six months. The house in Chathenkary was built by Papa with two rooms, a kitchen, a long veranda and "Arayum Nirayum". The "chavadi" next to it was built years later by Vallimamachy. Papa was only a clerk in the railways, which was a stagnant job without scope for promotion. But Papa looked after all his siblings, got his sisters married and took care of every responsibility in the family.

The bachelors who stayed in Malaya were close-knit friends. They helped one another through thick and thin and nurtured and cherished this lasting bond till the end of their lives. Pillai uncle of Mepral, P.G. Thomas Uncle (Ayroor) and Karippuzha uncle (K.I. Thomas) were especially close. Pillai uncle later married the sister of Vennikulam Gopala Kurup, the poet. P.G. Thomas uncle was married to Mary Auntie of Vadakethu, Kuriannoor, and all her brothers were in Malaya including V.E. Thomas Achen. I remember all of them. The early Malayali immigrants in Malaya lived as one joint family. There were V.E. Chacko uncle, V.E. Varghese uncle, Club Appachen and Ammachy (because they lived near the Golf Club), C.T. Verghese uncle, K.T. Thomas uncle and many others. Thampichayan (P.O. Thomas, the top executive of Rubber Board), Shimochayan (K.I. Simon) and Kochubaby uncle, both brothers of Karipuzha uncle came a little later as bachelors.

Vallimamachy was one day coming back from school and at that very moment the "thandan" who was on the coconut tree threw down his sharp knife (vettukathi). The "Vettukathi" fell right on her knee cutting her blood vessel. She was taken to Kochubaby's (Dr. George Kuruvilla) hospital in Kavumbhagam. But he stitched the wound without suturing the blood vessel. That was how she became lame, her knee losing its pliability. So she remained a spinster all her life.

Kunjumamachy was married more or less at the same time as Papa, for Sunny was a few months younger than me. Uncle married Kunjumamachy because of their friendship. Kochumamachy was teaching with Kunjachayan in Prince Marthanda Varma high school, Peringara, which was a very well-known and disciplined school. Later, she got married to Pappachen (A.C. Cherian, Ambrayil kudumbathu) while he was employed in Singapore.

Kunjachayan, the youngest studied in SB College and later in UC College. He held a very high position in the Scientific Research Institute under the Central government including the Central Leather Research Institute, Madras and finally settled down in Adyar before coming to Tiruvalla. Kochamma is from Kovoor kunnathu, Kavumbhagom.

Papa looked after all his siblings, got his sisters married and took care of every responsibility in the family. Today all of Valiammachy's grand-children the highly educated ones and the not-so educated ones are well-off. So are their generations. "The Lord will not deny any good thing to those who walk uprightly."

The house in Thalavady where Valiappachen (K.M. Kuruvilla) and Valiammachy lived was long and big according to the standards of the day. It had two big rooms, a long veranda, a "nadu muttam" and a "nilavara" (cellar). The back of the house too had a long veranda where we could sit in the afternoons and enjoy the breeze blowing from the paddy fields. Achen uncle who was Mathukutty, was the eldest. He was tall and hefty. Mama who came next was very short. The next was Thankamma resembling Valiappachen and then Kunjoochayan and Amminiammama. Amminiamama too was short and Kunjoochayan was in-between. All these children were well brought up in the fear of the Lord and it was a happy home at all times. All had beautiful voices, except Kunjoochayan who could "make the cow break its rope in fright" as the saying goes. Achen uncle had a booming voice just like his uncle Avarachayan and he stood head and shoulders above everyone else wherever he stood up.

There was a lot of paddy, coconut and fruit trees, cows and chickens. Mama studied in Nicholson school and Aleykutty kochamma used to say, "You have Chinnamma's smile".

CHAPTER II

EARLY CHILDHOOD AND LIFE IN MALAYA

Papa and Mama were married in 1937. As soon as Mama became pregnant Valiappachen and Valiammachy refused to send her in this state to a distant land. So into this house in Thalavady I was born as Valiappachen's and Valiammachy's first grandchild and to the adoration of Mama's other siblings. Amminimama was only eight years old then. I have always heard Valiammachy say that the day I was born Daveed Upadeshi (a Christian from the backward community wearing a pink bush-shirt, whom I too remember) came to the house and sang "Ninte ella nadathippum ente bhagya niravallo" from the popular hymn "Paraparamesa, varamaruleesa neeyathre en rakshadanam." When I grew up I have always wondered how I, a weak tiny creature could have been a stroke of good fortune and blessing for them! According to eyewitness stories, I was dark, very tiny and my legs were tangled together.

Valiammachy wondered if I would survive but she didn't tell Mama about it. Finally, Koshy Achen, Valiammachy's maternal uncle's son, and a devout priest, was requested to come and pray for me. It was after that I survived. Koshy Achen was always there whenever his sister needed him. Later on, for years Achen was vicar of Chathenkary church too. He had amazing talent for singing. Achen and his daughter used to sing "Krusinmel kidakkuvathar? kanka lokame, krusinmmel kidakkuvathar" in our church for Good Friday service. I can still hear it reverberating in the church. He was a great man of prayer and had the spiritual gift of healing. People affected by evil spirits would go to him for healing. He also wrote moving prayers and used them during Holy Communion service. Once during a Sunday school anniversary, when Leelamma and I sang the songs "This is my Father's world," and "Give of your best to the master" which we had learned in the Methodist Sunday school, Achen sang with us.

Finally, after baptism in the St. John's Mar Thoma church in Thalavady, my godmother being Idiculla Appachen's wife, Mama sailed with me to Malaya in early December 1938 when I was five months old. Mama was only twenty-two then, a beautiful young lady with thick hair that touched the ground. Papa has often related his excitement when he first saw me. "I came into the ship and saw a dark thing crying "Mak mak" It was the first excitement of a father. We lived in Sentul and Leelamma was born in December 1939.

The dark clouds of the Second World War (1939-1945) were gathering over Europe and the East, by 1941. Japan was becoming a dangerous ally of Hitler. Just before the Japanese occupation of Malaya and Singapore, the Malayalees sent their families back to India. So Mama, Leelamma and I, Kunjummamachy, Sunny and Baben, Mary Auntie, Geoji and Sunny sailed to Madras. We thus spent our early childhood in Thalavady and Chathenkary till after the war in 1945.

In Thalavady we had Valiappachen and Valiammachy and Achen uncle, Thankamama, Kunjoochayan and Amminimama. In Chathenkary too there were Valiammachy, Vallimamachy, Kochumamachy and Kunjachayan. Kariachayan and Lizyamama too might have been there. So in both homes it was a joint family and we had a host of people to look after us and love us.

Leelamma and I were regarded as twins by all. We were just one and a half year's difference in age, dressed alike and were the same height.

I started learning the Malayalam alphabet on "ola" ie a dried palm-leaf on which the letters were written with "narayam." We sat in a circle before the "aasan" and there was golden sand in front of us. We learned each letter by writing with our forefinger in the sand. So the handwriting was round, clear and steady. Before and after writing each letter 'Aasan' would pronounce the letter clearly and ask " A ennellarum ezhuthiyo?" (Have all of you written A") The kids shouted back in a chorus "ezhuthi" A. Thus there was constant repetition in this manner and we learned the alphabet and its sound correctly. Learning came spontaneously. As we mastered more letters the number of "olas" with us also increased. This basic education in an ordinary setting with an ordinary master imprinted the letters in our minds, and enabled us to write and pronounce correctly all our lives. I must have started very young because when I went back to Malaya in 1946, I was only eight. But by that time I was studying in

Preparatory class in Peringara High School where Kunjachayan and Kochumamachy were teachers. I walked with them to school and used to have lunch from the same plaintain leaf with them in the staff-room. Preparatory class was just before Form I when Middle School started. By that time I had finished stds I to IV in Chathenkary government Primary School.

Kochumamachy too was teaching in the same Primary School, near the "kadavu", then. It was the period when Sree Chithira Thirunal was Maharaja of Travancore. Once, for the birth of a child in the Royal Palace all school children were given "aval pothi."

The school had very efficient teachers and good classrooms. All the teachers carried cane in their hands. We sat on benches and wrote on slates with slate pencils. There were no desks. The marks were written with chalk on the slate itself and children used to go home with these marks written in bold letters. We had to cross a rickety bridge across a "thodu" (a small waterway) to and fro. We had to climb the wooden steps, then cross a long flat wooden portion and again take steps downward. The wooden planks would very often be missing or displaced. So it was a dangerous adventure for children, and passers-by always helped us. One day as Leelamma and I climbed the bridge she slipped and fell into the river and was rescued by people around. I was so frightened that all the slate pencils in my hand fell into the water, while Leelamma was clinging safely to hers when she came out of the water.

Children in those days were infected with sores "chori". It was very common and took long to heal. The only remedy was medicated oil made at home and painful bath everyday, scrubbing the sores with "incha" to clean it.

The medium of instruction was the mother-tongue and I started reading early. We used to sit outside in the courtyard (muttam) at dusk, looking at the moon and stars. Valiammachy told us stories of the wood-pecker, the mosquito and others travelling in a "vallom" when the boat capsized. Ever since, they have been trying to build a new boat. That is why the wood-pecker flies around pecking every tree, testing whether it is good for the boat, and the mosquito murmurs in people's ears seeking help. We played all sorts of games with stones, coconut shells, "vellaka" and leaves of coconut and arecanut palms. Good balls were made from raw coconut leaves and the rest could be used for transport, one person sitting on it and the other pulling it around. Swings were made from ropes and hung, during Onam. There were so many improvised games with things available around and all this helped our imagination and our intellectual growth. There was freedom and security at home and outside.

The main means of transport was "vallom". Relatives came from distant places. But they all walked, and left only after staying at least one night. People did not hesitate to walk long distances. There was plenty of fish in the river and fish would be caught from "meenkulam" also. It was a small pond with a door that could be trapped to catch fish that entered to eat food. The swift flowing river was enough for all our needs, cooking, washing and bathing.

There was no news of Papa or uncle during the war. But before the war was over in the South-East, there were rumours that they were alive. I have clear memory of the day when as soon as the newspaper "Pouradhwani" came home I ran to the courtyard, knelt down and read the headline loudly – "Yudham Theernnu," "the war is over." Papa came only later and then we all got ready to go back to Malaya. Before going back we visited relatives with Papa and one memory that stands out is coming to Karippuzha by "vallom". Since the house is by the side of the road all night we hear the sound of bullock-carts. Karippuzha Appachen arranged for us a "villuvandi" to go to Karthikappally to visit Papa's friend. "Villuvandi" is drawn by a single bullock which goes very fast. It was so exciting. In Karthigappally we ate red cashew-fruit and pineapple. I remember how excited Papa was, enjoying all this, back from a desolate war.

When we sailed back to Malaya, Kunjumamachy, Uncle, Sunny and Baben were with us. We were to catch the train from Kottarakkara to Madras. We boarded a small bus from Tiruvalla to Kottarakara. I have memories of eating "Poori" and potato for the first time in the train. We stayed in a small house in Madras where we played hide-and-seek. One of us got into a neighbouring house and hid behind their clothes.

On board the ship we opted for the European diet and learned to use fork and knife. The food was very good. The only problem was that the day the ship reached Port Swettenham, breakfast was served very early and we missed it. I was crying with hunger and Papa had to request them to give me something. The ship anchored at a short distance from the port and we were taken ashore by boat. Then the ship proceeded to Singapore.

We had to stay in quarantine for a few days where there was a common kitchen. Too much of turmeric in the curries kept our hands yellow.

Before Papa was allotted railway quarters we stayed in an old two-storied bungalow which was rented. It was situated in a nice compound with a huge cherry-tree in front. We plucked cherries and played upstairs. There were no toys but only one or two pieces of wood. But Leelama and I played all sorts of games with these two objects, soaring in our imagination to unknown worlds. Once Papa took us for a haircut to a Chinese barber. When Papa came back, Leelama was crying because all her hair had gone and little remained. The barber apologised to Papa. He said he thought it was a boy. Later we shifted to the quarters in Sentul, very close to Papa's office in the next compound.

All the houses in a row were connected. We made friends with Lalitha and Saro who lived in the next house. Auntie was Malay and she had married an Indian. But their father had died and her present husband also of Indian origin was called "ankunda" by the children. We were thick friends and Mama and Auntie were very close. Even when Papa got promoted to stay in a better quarters right in front of this one, we always played together and went to school together.

Both of us were admitted to Infant Jesus Convent School, Sentul which was a very good school for girls. We were both admitted to standard one. There was a tuck-shop and a church in the compound. We had European sisters and also local teachers. Whenever we wrote answers we were encouraged to draw pictures. Mrs. Campose was a Tamilian teacher and I had a classmate Jacqueline, whose mother was a teacher there. She was Eurasian and they were planning to migrate to Australia. Australia was strictly for "Whites only", in those days and Jacqueline and her mother were lucky to migrate to Australia.

School started very early and we walked to school with Lalitha and Saro. We could eat nothing so early in the morning and our breakfast was just a piece of bread and milk. But we got ravenously hungry at the time of recess. What we brought as refreshment from home was only a small bottle of horlicks which had a deer's picture engraved on it. One person was to drink up to the eye of the deer and leave the rest to the other. Since we were never allowed to buy anything from the tuck-shop, we went back home as hungry as wolves.

We had to cross the Sentul railway line on our way to school. Usually there would be shunting of engines and other things but it was the shortest way to reach school. There would be railway workers ever at work. Once the four of us were so immersed in our conversation on our way back from school, that we did not see a train coming until we reached the railway line. Workers were trying to alert us but we heard nothing. It was a very narrow escape. They reported it to Papa when they met him and we were very careful after that incident.

I got double promotion to Std IV at the end of the year of Std II because unlike in India the syllabus was not taxing and I was first in the class during all the three terms. Miss. Lim Bok Lian was my class teacher in Std IV. She liked me very much and thought I was the brightest in the class. Students who stood top were allowed to go during classes to collect the registers after teachers had marked attendance. It was my duty to collect them and bring them to the office. I was taught to stand at the door and tell the teacher politely, "Please teacher, Madam wants the register." I loved doing it.

Our school motto was – "Simple in my virtue, strong in my duty." – "Simple dans monvirtue Forte dans mondevour." Once when the statue of Lady of Fatima came to Malaya, we went in a procession singing her praises. We sang-

"O Lady of Fatima hail

Immaculate Mother of Grace

Oh pray for us help us today

Thou hope of the human race."

Alice was born on September 6, 1947 in Pudu Hospital. When Mama was in hospital, we stayed with P.G. Thomas uncle and Mary Aunty. Joji and Sunny were there for company. They were studying in the Methodist Boys' school. It was Leelama and I who named her Alice her Christian name being Elizabeth. We loved that name because it was the name of Princess Elizabeth, King George the sixth's daughter who in August 1947 got married to Prince Philip Mountbatten. We admired Princess Elizabeth and Princess Margaret in those days and imitated their smiles. We listened to Princess Elizabeth's wedding live on the radio, with Papa and Pillai Uncle.

The Mar Thoma Church was not yet established in Kuala Lumpur. We attended the Methodist Church close by. Later the Mar Thoma people came together once in a way for worship. There were no sects in the church and all came together. They also started the Sunday School and we were the first sunday school pupils of the Mar Thoma church in Kuala Lumpur. Thampichayan (P.O. Thomas) who had recently come from Karthikappally, was our first teacher. The church was established in a building only much later.

During Christmas we practiced carols and with the grown-ups visited every home for singing. After the carols one of the Sunday School students would loudly announce an appropriate verse from the Bible. C.T. Verghese uncle's son Joy and I were the main announcers. The Malayalis were a very close-knit community, very sincere, loving, caring and helpful. They nurtured friendships to the utmost and had no guile in them. They were like the early churches, governed by love alone. This is such a contrast to what we see now. That was why Uncle and Papa found it difficult to settle down here after retirement. They could easily be fooled by others. In everything they were sincere and straight-forward while it was just the opposite with people at home.

Once the church was established, the priests here were V.E. Thomas Achen and Koshy Achen. They were vicars here all their lives and were an inseparable part of the community.

Papa was not a technical hand. But P.G. Thomas uncle and Karipuzha uncle were. P.G. Thomas uncle held a high position in the railways and so did uncle in the Survey Department. He became the Chief Surveyor of Johore and Malacca States.

Uncle and Kunjumamachy first stayed in Peel Road, and we visited them often. Eappachen was born there. When Kunjumamachy called him "Mon", the Chinese children thought it was "moon". Kochumamachy, by this time, was married and she was staying in Singapore. Uncle was in the PWD and his brother Avarachayen was also there. We had to take an over-night train to reach Singapore.

When we came to Malaya soon after the war, the sight of Japanese prisoners of war being taken in trucks to do work, was a common sight. But when Malaya was under the Japanese occupation, Papa's bosses were Japanese and they learned the Japanese language. There was a bomb in

Pillai Uncle and Family

the compound of Papa's office which had not exploded during the war. It was there for a long time. After the war, the guerillas who had fought from the jungles became a big problem because they would ambush the British and soldiers whenever possible. Months later they started ambushing the railways. Trains got derailed and travel to Penang and Singapore by night became very hazardous. We went to Singapore only by day-train and passed the causeway from Johore Bahru to Singapore during the day.

After many loss of lives and many years of war, the British were finally able to overpower the guerillas and make the country safe. Thus peace prevailed.

The Japanese had tortured many people during the war. They were notorious for their gruesome methods of torture. They would pump water into a man's mouth and then dance on his bloated stomach. Finally, when prisoners were tried and one leader who had tortured many was shot to death, the public jumped on his body and thrust him into the miry clay. Thousands of lives were lost during the war both of civilians and soldiers.

Malaya was a multi-racial country with Malays, Chinese, Tamils and Indians. The Tamils were mainly from Ceylon (Sri Lanka). But all lived together in harmony. The Chinese were merchants and workers and businessmen. They were hard-working. The Malays were lazy because it was their country. Many Indians and Tamils worked in estates. There were places of worship for all these communities. The Chinese temples had big tortoises.

During Diwali, our neighbours would bring sweets while during Christmas, Mama made sweets and sent it through us. We ate ice-cream only after a long time for Papa would not let us eat the local ice-cream that the Chinese brought. So once when the real ice-cream came, Mama bought a bar, cut it into two and gave it to us on a small plate. I still can feel the taste and excitement as we licked the ice-cream for the first time.

Papa used to take us to market with Pillai Uncle. He would buy good fish and meat. Sometimes he bought just the head of a fish called "Koduva" and the curry was very delicious. I still remember standing in the kitchen when meat was cooked. The smell was tempting and Mama would give us a piece to taste. Once when Papa brought a pound of oranges home, they were rotten. The man who sold it had pretended to give him the good ones while he exchanged it for the rotten ones packed earlier. The Chinese were not very honest. Dried frogs, and reptiles were

PG Thomas Uncle and Mary Aunty

a common sight in Chinese shops. Their food was famous and hawkers would go from street to street selling "mee" (noodles) and other attractive things. But we were not allowed to buy anything. Even Tamilians came with Idyappam and a sauce. Mama sometimes had a Malay or Chinese lady to help her with the home. The Chinese washed clothes well and quickly with their hands. When Malays worked there, we would not cook pork in the house. Once we got delicious meat of wild pork. Mama was a good cook and she learned new dishes from her friends. Papa kept ducks in the house. Papa washed their pen every morning and let them out. We would get good eggs everyday.

We used to walk with Pillai uncle and Papa to the village where there was an elderly Malayali couple. They had a "rambutan" in their compound. Papa and Uncle enjoyed chatting with them in Malayalam. We brought guava and rambutan when we came back.

Pillai uncle who was a bachelor then, stayed close by, for he too was working in the railways with Papa. He was a constant visitor to our house and Papa and he together subscribed for the week-end edition of "The

Hindu" which kept a very high standard. That is how I began reading "The Hindu" though we had "Straits Times" coming everyday.

We saw two Malayalam films with Pillai uncle and Papa. One was "Sasidharan." We also saw "Gjana Sundari" in Sentul. On my tenth birthday, Pillai uncle came and made a wonderful payasam. He crushed the coconut and extracted the milk with his own hands, and it was a small celebration at home. Then Pillai uncle said, "You are now ten, and a grown-up girl. So there is no more birthday celebrations". How we were one family!

Mama looked after the home and kept Papa's clothes ready when it was time for him to go to office. Papa was also very punctual. If Mama became a little late for any trip Papa would impatiently say, "Chinnam!". He always called her "Chinnam". Papa was very loving to all of us and very friendly, but he was very strict about our studies. He was happy when I became first in the class. Our study tables had to be kept neat at all times. He had a short temper concerning such disciplines and I dreaded his stick. Leelamma always escaped because she would start crying immediately.

Once when Alice was just a year old, I was sitting on the grass in a cane chair and tried to pick her up. The chair overturned and I broke my right elbow joint. I was ten years old then.

It was a Saturday afternoon and the Kuala Lumpur government hospital was closed. So I had to wait till Monday. By then the elbow was swollen and there was intense pain. Only a sling was tied by a "dresser" to support the arm. On the same day one of our chickens was run over by a car.

On Monday I went with Papa to the Kuala Lumpur General Hospital. I was admitted and Papa went back. No one was allowed to stay with a patient. Finally they decided upon an operation. The surgeon was Dr. Cameron from Scotland. It was the first time I was administered chloroform. I felt like sinking into a deep ocean. While in hospital, the lady in the next bed to mine gave me an English Bible and asked me to learn Psalm 121, and Psalm 23 by heart. She was very pleased when I repeated it to her. What I learned then is still imprinted in my heart.

Papa was always scared that my elbow might become stiff like Vallimamachy's knee. Though the arm has a slight curve nothing like that happened.

I was twelve years old when James was born on June 12, 1950 in Pudu hospital. Again we were with Mary Aunty and P.G. Thomas uncle. Mary Auntie by then was also the godmother of Alice while Leelama's godmother was Kunjumamachy. When he was brought home he looked tiny for he weighed only 4 3/4 pounds while Alice had weighed half a pound more. Papa had always been worried about getting his sisters married, his brother's education and the responsibility of the family. Kunjumamachy also was sent to Nicholson. And when three daughters came in a row he felt greater the burden of his responsibilities. But both Papa and Mama were excited to have a son.

Yet Papa always used to lament – "If my eldest had been a son I could have depended on him to look after the family." I grew up listening to Papa's burdens and regretted I had not been born a boy. Papa was very careful with his money and would get down at an earlier bus stop to save ten cents, for he only had an ordinary job. I grew up with all this. That is how I became a very responsible person, being the eldest child who was not born a son. I had inborn determination that I would never let him down in anything just because I am a daughter. I kept that vow all my life. This sense of duty that I shared with Papa made me capable of doing everything efficiently and with accountability. I obeyed everything my father ever asked me in life, even when he retired and settled down in Kerala.

It was James' baptism and Uncle and Kunjumamachy came to stay with us. Uncle was to be his godfather. Uncle bought a turkey and everything necessary and Mama and Kunjumamachy cooked everything. Uncle was a very generous and sincere person and never allowed Papa to spend money whenever he was here. It was uncle who helped establish the Mar Thoma parishes in Malacca and Johore Bahru. He built churches wherever he was. He loved good food and enjoyed hospitality. Thomas Thirumeni, Thomas Mar Athnasius Suffragen Metropolitan (Panampunnayil Thirumeni) was uncle's close friend. When he visited Malaya he always stayed with uncle. Even when uncle came back to Karipuzha, Thomas Thirumeni was a constant visitor and uncle would not send him back without his great hospitality.

Uncle's table would always be full of good things for every meal. He enjoyed good food and made visitors enjoy it too. Kunjumamachy always fulfilled uncle's wishes. It was a unique experience to have a meal in uncle's home.

Karippuzha Uncle and Ammamachy

It was the end of 1951 and Papa planned to send Leelamma and me back to Kerala, to grow up there, for he feared we would be influenced by the Western culture. In Malaya we would be with parents, getting better education and leading a better life. But he felt girls should grow up on Indian soil, learning Indian culture. It was very sad leaving the school we loved.

CHAPTER III

FINISHING SCHOOL

Thus the four of us and Mama sailed back to India. We reached Chathenkary, and the first priority was school admissions. The medium of instruction was different now and so we had to take a test in Malayalam. I was admitted to Form IV (Std 8) while I should have been in Form V according to the years I studied here. I really had no problem with Malayalam for we spoke the mother tongue at home, read the Malayalam Bible, and every Saturday did two pages of Malayalam copy-writing. Leelama was enrolled in Form II. The headmaster of Prince Marthanda Varma High and Training school was Sri. Kunjiraman Nair, neatly dressed in Khadi clothes. His very presence was enough to impose perfect silence and discipline in the school compound. Not a sound would one hear when classes were going on. He was nicknamed "Kaduva" or tiger because of this imposing personality. He walked around with a cane in his hand.

Every morning we left home with lunch boxes and books and joined other people at Chathenkary "kadavu". We had to cross the river first. The "vallom" that ferried the passengers could never be over-loaded. There were students, teachers and others from places as far as "Muttar" who came to Chathenkary and crossed the river to reach school. So during peak hours the "vallom" would be full and the man who ferried us, who was employed by the government, would carefully take people across the river. One slip was enough to capsize the "vallom" and passengers stood with bated breath till they reached the other shore. Great discipline was necessary when the "vallom" was full, for the river was very deep. Once on the other shore, we walked with our friends to school.

Those were days of poverty, and thrifty living. Neighbours would sometimes come for fire. They would put a piece of hot coal on a dry coconut husk and take it home to keep their fires burning. At times a hungry neighbour would walk in to eat ripe jackfruit that was aplenty in our house. Even a small measure of rice was borrowed to cook at least one meal. We did not experience these things only because Papa sent money.

Today all are self-sufficient and hence pent-up in their homes without any need of a neighbour. But in those days people needed one another for many things and so were always in contact, and willing to help one another.

Once I decided to swim across the river with Molly, my cousin, who did it everyday. We were almost on the other side when somehow, I sank into the water.The river was very deep and I remember finding myself underneath the water. But I was calm and remembered Sunny telling me once that sometimes this happens and then you have to wade forward with your arms, to reach the surface. Cool and calm, I waded to the surface. Valiammachy who was very anxious about her grand-children, was watching and she started crying out loudly. Finally they cut a banana, took the stem and threw it into the river. Molly swam and brought it to where I was. I swam back holding on to it and reached the other side. Valiammachy took a small stick and pretended to beat me, for people believed it would drive out fear. Surprisingly, I did not feel fear at all. I escaped drowning that day because of the prayers of people who loved me.

We had very efficient teachers. Chandrasekharan Nair (English), Thommy sir (Mathematics), T.C. Mathew sir (Biology) and others who were deeply devoted. The last period once a week was for literary debates, essay writing and talent shows.

Chandrasekharan Nair sir once called me to the staff room and read out to me my English composition. He appreciated it openly in front of the other teachers, for after being educated in the Convent in Sentul, I had a good command of the English language. Though it was assumed that I would have difficulty in Malayalam, Malayalam came spontaneously to me. As we were about to leave Malaya, we were given tuitions for Hindi by a tuition master but I have hated that language all my life.

The school anniversary was a very important event and teachers-in-charge would make us take part in various programmes; Leelama and I sang "Old MacDonald had a farm" and the song reverberated for many days after the event. We also took part in a little musical piece where a small sparrow that had broken its leg, seeks shelter of the trees. Every tree refuses except the peepul. And when the rains came and the winds blew, all the trees fell down, but the peepul that had shown kindness stood firm.

All these were very exciting for us. Devaki Amma, Sukumari Amma our neighbours in Chathenkary, and many others, were our great friends.

It was time for Mama, Alice and James to go back to Malaya. So next year we were admitted to Nicholson School, Tiruvalla, Mama's own Alma Mater. This school was started by two missionaries, Mrs. Nicholson and Miss. Mackebin on a hillock near Tiruvalla for the education of girls. It was started independent of the church and only entrusted to the Mar Thoma church later with a clear "Trust Deed". At first they had to go to houses to encourage parents to send their wards to a boarding school. They used to travel to known village families to collect their students. Parents thought it to be a good training for their daughters who would grow up to be house-wives. The expense was not much, but the spiritual and academic training they got there was rich and enduring. That is how Mama studied there. Miss. Aley Thomas, Kovoor Kochachen's daughter, was Mama's teacher. So was Pennamma Kochamma, the journalist P.O. Thomas' sister. Aleykutty Kochamma was headmistress when I joined school, and Pennamma Kochamma was my class teacher in Form V. Chinnama Kochamma, Mr. A. Cherian's sister who had retired, was living close by. She was also Mama's teacher. The school though under the Mar Thoma church, was an independent institution.

We were in the boarding with all the others. There was inspection and marks for everything including the way we arranged our clothes in the cupboard, kept our hair clean from lice and what not! We were divided into houses and each house had a captain. The houses were given the names of precious stones. We were in Saphire. We had balanced diet, starting with 'kanji' 'cherupayar' (lentils) and lime pickle in the morning and in fact all the girls were healthy. There was P.T. in the morning and games in the evening. All these were compulsory.

The teachers, all unmarried, were devoted to the students and stayed in the school. Special mention must be made of Rajamma Kochama, Kunjoonjama Kochama, Kochumariamma Kochamma and Kamala Kochamma. The senior students of Form VI wore "chatta" and "kacha muri", the traditional dress of Syrian Christians, and the juniors wore green skirts and white blouses. We mastered the art of pleating "njori", a fan-like accessory at the back, and learned to wear it elegantly.

No visitors were allowed, and no one was allowed to go home except at the end of the term. Our teachers were strict, industrious, and loving. But we were afraid of Aleykutty Kochamma. If she called anyone "kunju" an affectionate term, we were scared, for we knew she was displeased.

There was a time-table for everything. Every morning at seven o'clock we had half an hour's devotions in the chapel when we sat in perfect silence, reading the Bible, meditating and praying. After half an hour a teacher would come to lead the morning worship. That was the foundation of our quiet time with God throughout life.

There was Holy Communion Service in the chapel once a month, when an elderly Achen would come. We were free on Sundays after the Service. On Saturday evening too we were free from studies. Then Aleykutty Kochamma would call the seniors to her bungalow to tell us stories from classics. We slept on the floor using a "soft methapaya" and a rougher "arippaya" both woven mats, either in the dormitory or in the classrooms, as allotted. We washed our own clothes and were trained to grow up as responsible ladies. That is why even today, it is assumed that if a girl had her education in Nicholson School, she would make a difference wherever she was, whether at home or as a professional. The same could be said of Mahilalayam, Alwaye, Balikamadom, Thiruvalla and Baker School, Kottayam, the fruit of the sacrifice of missionaries. Though these schools admitted day scholars, Nicholson school did not have day scholars except those from Vanitha Mandiram.

Aleykutty Kochamma was our class teacher in sixth form. She taught us English. One day she asked us to speak in class on the subject, "If I were a bird." I stood up to speak. But as I spoke I could not stop laughing. Then she told me, "Stand on your dignity." That was the first lesson I learned about public speaking. Aleykutty Kochamma enjoyed reading and encouraged us to read good books. She introduced us to "Little Women" and other classics. She herself enjoyed books till the end of her life for even when she lost the sight of one eye after a cataract operation, she continued to read with the other eye.

When we came, Miss. Ward and Miss. Viney two elderly English ladies were in the school. Miss. Viney played the piano and chose girls for the choir. That was how I too sang in the choir.

It was in 1953 May, that Rev. M.G. Chandy, Rev. P. Thomas and Rev. Philip Oommen were consecrated as Alexander Mar Theophilus,

Thomas Mar Athnasius and Philipose Mar Chrysostom, Episcopas of the Mar Thoma church. We went to S.C. Seminary compound with Vallimamachy. Achen Uncle with his loud booming voice was chosen to lead the 'Kapyar's, part in the consecration service and Qurbana. His voice filled the place as he recited the responses. Later when school re-opened, a reception was given to the new bishops. We all crowded around them as they stood in front of the school and joked with us. I remember Aleykutty Kochamma saying with great pride, "the youngest Dharmishtan is the most humorous." Chrysostom Thirumeni was in his thirties then.

Our ESLC Examination was held in Government Girl's High School, Tiruvalla. When the results came we went to school to meet the teachers and get our certificates. Aleykutty Kochamma advised me to go only to Women's Christian College, Madras for my higher studies. Instead of giving me my caution deposit in cash, she bought me three books – "Oliver Twist", "Tom Brown's Schooldays" and "Pride and Prejudice". I loved them all my life, especially Jane Austen, which I always kept close to my heart.

I have friends even now from Nicholson School though. I studied there only for two years. For we were a close-knit community. We regarded our school as a home away from home and all as our sisters, older and younger.

We spent our holidays in Chathenkary and Thalavady. Sunny and Baben too came to Chathenkary from Keezhillam where they were in the boarding school. Kariyachayan, Lizyamama and Pappachayan too were in Chathenkary. Kariyachayan used to catch a lot of fish from the "meenkulam", attracting them there with food. Once the fish came in, the string would be pulled and the door of the pond closed. Then he would jump in and stir the water until it was very muddy. Then all the fish would come to the surface, floating, and would be caught in a net. Sometimes a big fish like "Vaala" would jump out of the pond and escape to the river. All of us would be around and enjoy it. At times we too have jumped in and tried a hand at catching fish.

We loved going and staying in Thalavady. Sometimes Valiappachen would walk all the way to fetch us, or come by "Valavara vallom" (Vallom which had a roof at one side.) We walked all the way to Thalavady, crossing the river at Muttar and Kaithathode. We took short-cuts across paddy-fields. In the monsoon when the rivers were in spate we walked to Neerattupuram and then Thalavady. It was all an exciting experience. As we approached the house it would be nearing dusk. We always came to the loud cacophony of hundreds of crows sitting on the jack-tree in front, crying their hearts out. As darkness descended they all became quiet. The singing would start only early morning but not so loud. May be there were early birds and lazy ones.

There were no clocks or watches in houses in those days. When I went to Peringara School with Kunjachayan and Kochumamachy, Kochumamachy would find the time by measuring the shadow with her foot. Then she knew whether it was time to go to school.

In Thalavady, everyone looked after us in such a way that we did not miss our parents. When Valiappachen went with the "thandan" to pluck coconuts, he took us with him and we ate "karikku" or tender coconut. When it was time for harvest there was great fun with labourers bringing in the sheaves and thrashing their sheaves till the paddy was ready. It was a hectic time. When all the paddy was ready, the chaff was separated from the grain with skill when there was enough wind. When the harvest begins the owner has to sleep in the field in a "maadam", a small structure to keep guard. All would be busy, sometimes giving refreshments to the workers.

In summer the mangoes would be ripe and fall down day and night. There were three big mango trees and we would compete with other children and the crows to pick mangoes. Houses were not divided by walls and there was no restriction for others to come and pick mangoes. Summer was only for eating and playing.

Valiappachen would dry paddy in a special way to use it as seed to sow next year. When it was time for sowing the paddy was sprouted at home and then sown in the fields that were already groomed for the next crop. At a certain height, the small plants were replanted to keep the field full. Every day the owner and the labourer in charge watched over the paddy fields with great care until harvest.

Rice did not come from shops. Boiling paddy in big vessels, drying them in the sun, and removing the husk and the bran was also a big job. There were enough people to do all this and we played around and enjoyed ourselves. We got milk from the cow and eggs from the chickens at home. Valiammachy would also hatch chickens from time to time and we would wait for them to come out of their shells. So we learned early how many days it would take for eggs to hatch. Sometimes an egg would

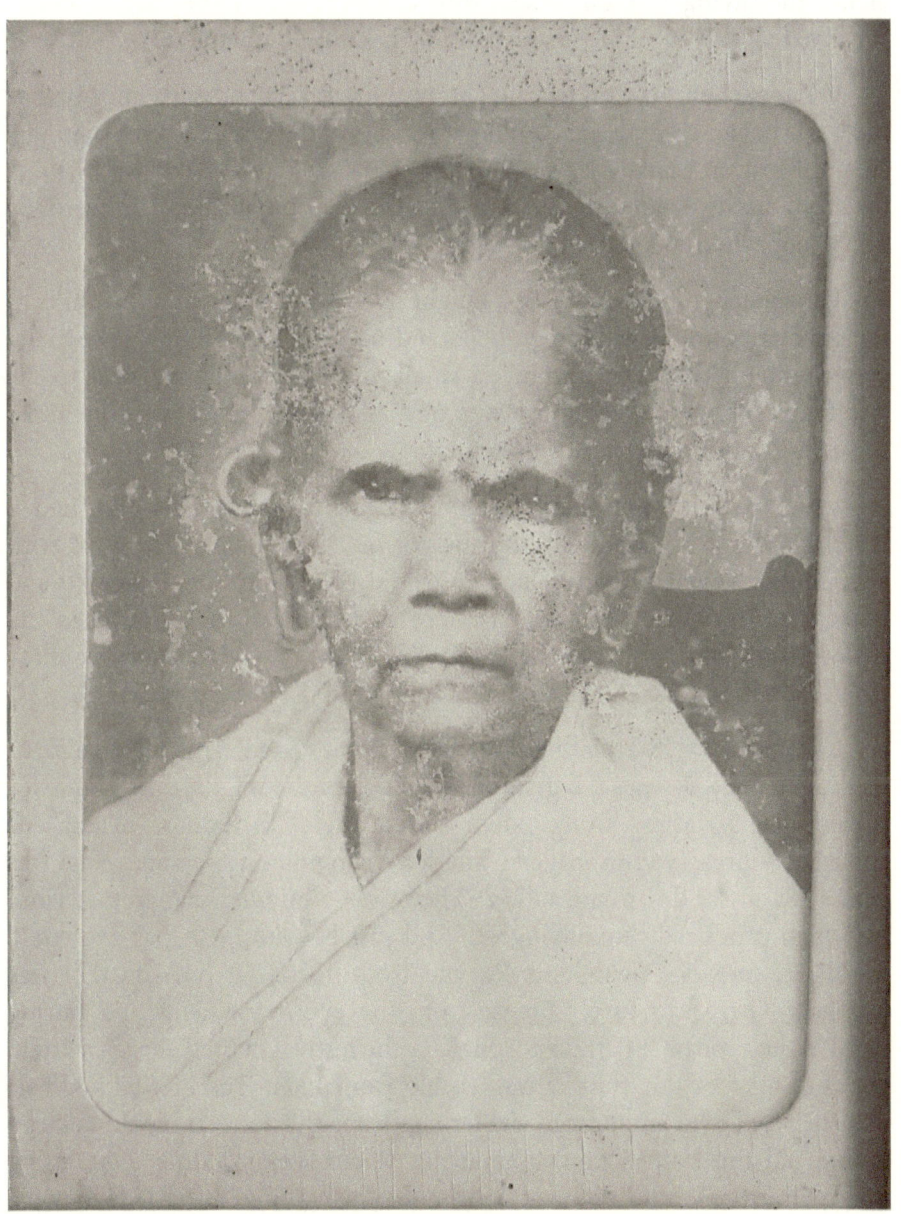

Chathenkary Valyammachi

not crack properly and Valiammachy would try to help the chicken come out. Finally we would count the chickens. A few eggs would turn bad. Hence the saying – "Don't count your chickens before they are hatched". We loved all this rural life growing up with nature, growing up in nature.

Valiappachen slept on the big cot on the veranda and early morning as the birds began singing, he would get up, sit on the cot and start singing a song for prayer. Usually it was "inneram priya deivame". That was the cue for all to rise up and come for prayers. The evening prayers too were led by Valiappachen.

Valiappachen played with us, taught us songs and took us for walks in the big compound. I still remember standing with him, enjoying the violet convolvulus in "thundiparambu", a small portion of our land next to the rice fields. These flowers still evoke nostalgic reminiscences in me and I travel back in time whenever I see them.

Valiappachen went regularly to Edathua to buy things. He had a "Kochu Vallom" (a tiny boat) and he got into it and rowed forward with a small oar. When he came back he would bring good beef, jaggery and other nice things. When bananas were ripe they would be hung in the eastern room and all ate to their hearts' content. There was a sweet smell when we entered the room.

Valiammachy had good things like "Uppumanga" and "chakkakuru" in the 'nilavara'. It was a big room which came under the "ara" built for storing paddy. Many things were stored there, including "nellika" or gooseberry preserved in jaggery. The long veranda on the south side was where we all sat down and talked. There was a budded mango tree close by which produced huge mangoes. And just beyond, as far as eye could see there were rice fields and coconut trees in the far horizon that was Edathua. There was lovely breeze from the open rice fields and during April at the time of "Edathua perunal", or the festival in St. George's church, the fireworks of the church was visible from here. The "Kadakkodikal" or fisher folk who came from the far south for this festival would later go around all the houses in neighbouring places seeking alms often using their palmistry skills. Edathua 'perunal' was also a time of trade for people would come from faraway villages to sell their merchandise here.

Upadeshis often stayed for a week or two in our home during summer. They prayed, took rest, and some taught us songs. When they left

Kochummammachi and Uncle

Valiappachen would always give them paddy to take home. Thankamama was always in Thalavady with her small children. She needed the support of her parents to bring up the children.

There were two people who had settled down in Thalavady from other places. One was called "Kodukulanji Thoma" and the other, "Mampuzhakari Keevareed". Thoma was married. Keevareed was a tall man who stayed alone in a small house and was available for all odd jobs. He was very gentle. People thought he was a little retarded and treated him like that. When Mama and we children were in Chathenkary, Valiappachen would send a big sack of "seemachakka" or breadfruit through Keevareed who would walk all the way to Chathenkary to give it. There was a very huge breadfruit tree (seema plavu) in Thalavady. Years later when this man died, his body had to be sent for post-mortem because he was discovered dead. The report confirmed that he had not eaten for days, and had died of starvation. In a place where rice was in abundance and all around were well off Christians, nobody cared about "the least of these His brethren" who had in his good days been useful to them.

We had a big "Cherumeen" in the well in Thalavady to keep the water clean. When the well was cleaned every year the fish would be kept in a big vessel with water until the cleaning was over.

All the houses were thatched with coconut leaves that had been matted earlier by women. It was the neighbours who helped thatch the roof. It was one day's ordeal and a good feast would be given to the workers. That was all. People helped one another. In the same way, after harvest the hay would be made into a big stack "thuru", again a skilled work, which was a celebration in the house. Sometimes a hen would lay eggs under this haystack and we would know about it only when she walked out with her chickens. When the Bible teaches us that "as the hen shelters her chickens under her wings so shall He cover you with His feathers and under His wings you shall trust," the concept is so real to us. It was an everyday experience when we grew up with the sudden swoop of the kite to snatch a chicken and the hen's warning alarm.

There were a few "pulaya" families staying in Arthissery, the border of Valiappachen's property. After bringing paddy from the fields after a day's work they would fry them, remove the husk and then make "kanji" for their meal. It would be almost midnight then. On seeing the lights, people would say it was the devil roaming about. They belonged to the lower class and hence they had to treat their landlords and employers with great respect. Even their language was different and they had no rights on the land until the E.M.S. government gave them rights on the land where they stayed. Even Christians who believe that God created men as equals, took advantage of what we call their "low birth". When later in Bishop Moore College I acted in a play as an old "Pulaya" woman, I had no problem speaking exactly as they do, for I was familiar with it.

At Easter Valiyammachy would make "Vellayappam" and beef "Ularthiyathu". Even as children, we would walk to the church with Valiappachen in the early hours of the morning, Valiappachen lighting a "chootukatta" to show the way. It was a torch made from dry coconut leaves and used when people had to travel by night.

Valiappachen, whose pet name was "Kunjachen" had only both of us as grandchildren then, and he loved us very much. I was very talkative, which he liked and he would say, "she will either become a professor or a lawyer."

Once when Leelamma and I were sent back by "vallom" to Chathenkary, he walked along with the "vallom" for a short distance. I felt very sad and said, "Valiappacha, we are alright. Please go back home". I never saw him after that, except when he became sick while I was studying in Union Christian College in the first year, immediately after school. I came with Babuchayan (George Idicula) by boat to Edathua and then to Thalavady. He had had a stroke, was conscious, but could not speak. Valiammachy's sisters Saramma Kochamma and Annama Kochamma came and stayed with her. They left only after Valiappachen's death and funeral. Valiappachen died within a few days. He was only 69. Kunjoochayan was then doing his P.G. in Economics in St. John's College, Agra. Mama could not see her beloved father as she was in Malaya. She was much loved by Valiappachen whom they all called "Achayan". All the children and grandchildren found security in this home according to their needs.

Mama knew about Valiappachen's death only by letter. I still remember the sad scene when Kunjoochayan came back for the first time after his death. There was such sadness in the house. Valiappachen had devoted himself to each one of us.

CHAPTER IV

TWO GREAT INSTITUTIONS

Though Aleykutty Kochamma insisted I should go to WCC, Kunjachayan who was working in Madras then told Papa that the women students of WCC went to the beach and strolled with boys and so I should be sent to Union Christian College, Alwaye, a very famous institution run only for the religious well-being and academic excellence of students. This was a college founded by K.C. Chacko, A.M. Varkey and V.M. Ittyerah, old students of Madras Christian college who prayerfully established it as an ecumenical institution under the Orthodox, Mar Thoma and CSI Churches, on a small hill in Alwaye. Their vision made it a great institution of excellence where students from Travancore's Christian homes came and stayed on the campus to study and find their vocation in life, through Christian training.

Valiamamachy bought me ten, lovely cotton sarees for a hundred rupees (a big amount in those days) from T.C. Mathew's shop in Tiruvalla. So on a day with heavy rains I travelled with Kunjoochayan of Inchanpura and reached Alwaye. We had to come to Kottayam and take a bus which passed through Muvattupuzha, Keezhillam and Perumbavoor. It was full of hair-pin curves and took more than three hours to reach Alwaye. I was admitted to second group but as I did not get admission in the college hostel, I was to stay in the YWCA in Thottakattukara just next to what they call "Paravur junction" now.

As both of us reached the YWCA all drenched, a senior student came and greeted me. This was P.C. Aleyamma, a beloved friend and older sister whom I have called Aleyamma Kochama all my life. Aleyamma Kochamma was nineteen then but already married. All the girls staying there remained close friends even years later. There was

Ammini, K.M. Chechamma, a senior student belonging to Kallupalam House, Chinnama who still lives in Piravom, Ruby and Lizy, the twin daughters of Mr. Simon, the chairman of Coffee Board and their sister Sophy our classmate, who really had their home in Thottumughom, near Mahilalayam, Leela who belonged to Kattumbhagam Edathua, and many whose faces I remember. We had a nice warden, and Varkey Chettan for all our errands. We lived as one family.

Every morning we walked to college. The place was serene and beautiful and we knew every house on the way and the people. We first passed the road leading to Mangalapuzha Seminary where "Achenkunjungal" as we called them (very young aspirants for priesthood), studied. During weekends when sometimes we took walks to Mangalapuzha Seminary we saw the cows, pigs and other animals they kept. Beautiful music from the organ would flow across the Periyar river, and into the quiet places around.

We often walked to the town for our shopping. We crossed the famous Marthanda Varma bridge on the left side of which was the Shivarathri "manalppuram". We went past Champion's studio which catered to the needs of photographs and took a shortcut to town going first to Baby Stores. When Shivarathri came the road in front of the YWCA would be teeming with crowds for it led to the "manalppuram". We would also go and buy small things and we enjoyed the whole crowd. The temple and flats that have now encroached the sacred river came up years later. Today when we enter the heavy traffic of Alwaye where there is not even a single parking space, it seems a ghost city, not deserted, but crowded with concrete structures and devilish traffic. It has lost all its goodness and beauty. The Periyar flowing close by where we would go and sit and sometimes bathe, was full of golden sand and one could walk to the middle of the river on clean sand while bathing. Today, the worst of creation, man, has drained out every grain of sand and Periyar has become a death-trap.

Our college had dedicated teachers who stayed on the campus or around it. Though the salary was very small they devoted their whole lives to teaching, and mentoring students, giving them a Christian training to help them find their vocation in life. The main student bodies were the College Union, Student Christian Fellowship (SCF) and Social Service League. There were men's hostels on the college campus and one women's hostel a furlong away from the college. Day scholars came from North Paravoor and remote places around Alwaye.

The college had a review system for evaluating students. The teachers would then sit in a circle and each student had to come for the review immediately after each terminal examination. We dreaded this. But it was a personal interest that the college showed about the academic and other achievements of the students.

On Sundays there were services for Orthodox, CSI and Mar Thoma congregations in the chapel. Then we attended Bible circles. The Orthodox, CSI and Mar Thoma associations too were very active. There was an annual get together, social, and photograph session for each of these associations.

The beautiful evening service on Sundays in the college chapel stand apart in our minds. It was an English service for all the denominations together. The college Prayer Book combined the services of each denomination and it was led by a senior member of the staff. That is how we learned all the English hymns. All students attended the service regularly.

The Social Service League and SCF conducted an annual entertainment programme which was a very grand function. The Social Service League staged a Malayalam play every year, and the function was attended by all the students and staff. These were events everyone looked forward to. The role of women were acted by boys whose voice and physique suited the role, and the plays maintained a very high standard.

I once took part in a shadow play presented by the students of YWCA for the Social Service League. It was the story of Sha Jehan and Mumtaz. I was Mumtaz with my thick long hair, rising from the Taj and dancing a few steps before presenting a rose to Sha Jehan who is plunged in grief. It was when Mumtaz presented it a third time that Sha Jehan saw her. But as he comes forward to clasp her, Mumtaz slowly descends into the Taj, looking at him. "She has gone forever. And, can thousand vaults, restore the loved one to her lover? "It was Ruby who read the beautiful introduction and then this last line. The shadow play was much appreciated. Later, someone wrote in my autograph – "When the lights are out, all women are fair".

Kunjachayan had insisted that I take Hindi as my second language because of its national importance. It was the most foolish decision I made. While Papa was very eager that I should go for Medicine, I failed in Hindi and lost one year. Later I went to Nampoothiri's tutorials in Tiruvalla to equip myself for the September examinations. In those days examinations were promptly held in March and September. There was no means of transport and I walked all the way to Tiruvalla and back everyday. I was joined by a friend from Kavumbhagom, who stayed with her grandfather in a big house by the side of the road. Distance was not a problem. Anyway I made it at the second attempt. After the examination I used to go regularly to the Chathenkary library in front of the Bhagavathy temple. M.N. Pillai uncle, who had been in Malaya for some time, and Papa's friend, encouraged me to read good books and then write down a summary of each book I read. I also stayed in Thalavady with Valiammachy. Leelamma was then studying in Women's College, Trivandrum.

During the next academic year I again applied to UC College for B.Sc Botany. Without informing anyone I took Malayalam as my second language. Though I had missed Malayalam education in the intermediate class, I stood far above many of my classmates in my second language. That is how I had the good fortune to study under Kuttippuzha Krishna Pillai sir, the famous literary critic who was our Malayalam Lecturer. The Malayalam classes were for all the B.A B.Sc students, and was held in the Assembly Hall. It was a large number and yet the teachers regularly took attendance calling out the names of each student, which was the regular order in UC College. We were so afraid of the boys that for general classes we went only after the teacher came out from the staff-room, and we huddled together in the front rows.

I was staying in the Women's Hostel, and life in the hostel was a rich experience. We had a resident warden who was one of our teachers and a non-resident warden who was Gracey Kochamma, Mrs T.B. Thomas.

Kunjamma Philip (Kunjochamma) was our matron. She was once in Malaya. But her husband died in the Second World war and she had to come back to India with two small children. She had a special love for me always because my parents were in Malaya. Kochama was a good manager of the mess. Good food with one "ethaka" everyday for breakfast, cost only seventeen, eighteen or nineteen rupees a month, never more than that.

Till the intermediate class, all of us walked bare-footed. Once I sent a picture to Malaya, me standing in the YWCA compound in a saree. One of Papa's friends noted I was bare-footed like the coolies in the estates in Malaya. So papa asked me to buy slippers. It was a long time after that, that students in general began wearing sandals. None of us had difficulty walking bare-footed, and since consumerism was unheard of, the land and rivers were clean and healthy.

All the girls in the hostel lived as one family. We still keep up that relationship and are in touch with our friends who are still alive. Leelama came for B.Sc Botany when I was in the final year. So her friends also called me "Ammama".

It was in this Botany class that Thirumeni became my classmate. There were only three boys – Oommen Koruthu, Thankappan and Xavier, but twenty-one girls. In the general classes we girls were dormant, but in the Botany and Chemistry classes we dominated. P.J. Mathew (Billy), Kuruvilla Mathew, and George Thomas (Thankachen) were in Chacko Hostel with Thirumeni (Oommen Koruthu). They were in the Physics main class but all of us came together for the language classes, English and Malayalam, and also for Scripture. Boys and girls did not mingle much. I taught Sunday School with Billy, Kuruvilla Mathew, Thankachen, T.M. Philip (our junior), Susan Samuel and Susan P. Abraham. So we were all close. They were the only boys I ever talked to in college.

Because of my command in the English language I had a special place in the hearts of C.T. Benjamin sir and K.C. Joseph achen. Aravamudam Iyengar sir was a great teacher of Shakespeare but he retired by the time I reached the degree class.

We had regular retreats in the college and also in the Fellowship house where M. Thommen sir was the secretary. We had regular visits from eminent speakers and a lot of extra-curricular activities in the college. The college annual sports was a memorable event attended by all. We had a good Physical Education director in the college, C.P. Andrews, Thampichayan's uncle. He was married to Bishop John's sister. Some of the students were eminent sportsmen and were State rank holders. So our annual sports maintained a very high standard under the efficient leadership of Andrews sir.

T.B. Thomas sir was our choir-master. Sometimes there were choir festivals in Ernakulam and we went there after good practice of chosen songs like "There is a balm in Gilead".

There were excursions and picnics. Malayattoor church was a favourite spot. During the final year, Botany students had to go to Ootty for herbarium collection. It was compulsory. But I was given exemption by T.C. Joseph sir and O.M. Mathen sir, our Botany Professors, because Papa and Mama were coming after six years. We hadn't seen them since we joined Nicholson School. We always had a jolly good time in the classes of Joseph sir and Mathen sir for they were very generous and never scolded us for our naughty tricks behind their backs. It was Sumitra, Kunjamma and others who collected plants for my herbarium. We had to press the plants in a press and create an album for plants belonging to all the plant families we had studied. It was a time consuming job and we had marks for the records.

Just before Christmas holidays Papa and Mama came to visit us in the college with Alice and James, for Thankamama was then staying in Alwaye. All our classmates were very eager to see them. Students having parents abroad were very rare. The only communication with our parents during this long absence was letters that took more than a week to arrive. Letters were the only means by which Papa and Mama knew about our studies and life in the hostel. Papa sent us money but he asked us to keep a regular account. We never spent money except for our essentials for we were very conscious that it was hard-earned money. I was always aware of my responsibility to my parents and never did anything that would ever hurt them.

During the final year I became a member of the hostel committee and was librarian. The hostel committee had the privilege of going to the men's hostels for socials. So too, the committee members of the men's hostels could come for the social at the women's hostel. It was a coveted privilege.

The college elections and the college union meetings were a big affair. There were unique events like mock-parliament, UN Assembly, mock-assembly and others. Once the students were persuaded by the union leaders to take part in a strike and it marred the discipline in the college. But the teachers handled it very wisely and very soon all the students who were arrested for picketing buses, were released. But that made the college authorities very cautious about selecting the right students to speak at the valedictory meeting of the final years. I was chosen as valedictorian for the whole B.A B.Sc class, and the function took place in front of the Assembly Hall. We also sang a farewell song "Proudly sweeps the raincloud over the hills" under the leadership of Santha John. I got the proficiency prize for English that year. The prize money was small but the college bought two books with it – "My Experiments with Truth" by Gandhi which was three rupees and "A book of Everlasting Things" which cost twelve rupees. Money was of great value then.

I have never spoken to Thirumeni when we were in college. He was gentle and friendly to everyone but too shy. He never entered our Botany class if for any reason, the other two boys were absent.

One significant characteristic of UC College was that we had a special bond with our teachers and they had a special bond with us. We called the Philosophy students "Vattu" (eccentric) and it was K. Jacob sir and the famous psychologist V.K. Alexander sir who taught them. We visited Jacob sir's house because Babukuttikochama liked students and she would always have goodies to give us.

Jacob sir with all his philosophy, was famously eccentric. So there were many stories about him. During his farewell he said, "I know there are many stories circulating about me. All are not true. But one thing I remember. Once I went to Muvattupuzha with Samkutty (who later became a famous doctor), a small boy then. I was making a little purchase and doing other things when I came to a small crowd. I too joined them wondering what it was all about. Then I saw a small boy in the middle of the crowd, crying. He was lost. Suddenly I realized that it was my son. Till then I was not aware that he was not with me!"

Baby Kochamma, Gracey Kochamma and Ammukochamma (Benjamin sir's wife) also welcomed us into their homes. They were all part of the students' lives. We knew the staff children also. They were young and some of them were studying in Mahilalayam where Babykochama and Graceykochama were teachers. Both had post graduate degrees in English and were very efficient teachers. Baby Kochama was a gold medallist. But UC College had the rule that staff-wives would not be allowed to teach in the college. Women would never be made permanent either. The rule changed years later. But Baby Kochamma and Gracey Kochamma taught for a few years when there was severe shortage of

English lecturers. So they became our teachers and they were excellent as teachers. Some rules can deprive us of excellence.

Friendship cultivated in the UC College has lasted all our lives. Such was the way we lived and grew up in UC College. The love, respect and bonding we had for our teachers and the concern they had about our lives, was something unparalleled. So the college has a unique place in the hearts of generations who have enlivened its campus.

During our final year before the examinations, there was a retreat when the staff tried to help us choose our career. I had always wanted to do postgraduate in English and become a lecturer like my teachers. K.C. Joseph Achen and Benjamin sir insisted that I do my postgraduate only in the famous Madras Christian College, Tambaram, where they themselves were students. When the results came I had second class in English, which was more than enough for a postgraduate admission. I could have gone for Malayalam or Botany if I desired. I missed a second class in Malayalam only by four marks. First classes were unheard of. The valuation was very strict but students got quality education.

We were either in Chathenkary or in Thalavady for our holidays. Both Benjamin sir and K.C. Joseph Achen gave me letters for Tambaram. I applied to Tambaram and Trivandrum and waited for the interview card. I prayed to God that I would first get admission in Tambaram. Fortunately, "Orana samaram" started under A.K. Antony's leadership. It was some strike about the boat fare. So all admissions in the state were delayed and I got the interview card from Tambaram.

T.B. Thomas sir's daughter Annu was doing her Honours degree in physics there and I sent her a telegram requesting her to meet me in Tambaram, not knowing that the one and only Cochin Express did not go via Tambaram. Anyway I reached Tambaram, attended the interview and came to Guindy where our hostel was situated by the side of the Race Course Road, in a rented building inside a big compound. It had once been a hospital. Guindy was twenty minutes by electric train from Tambaram, and then there was a long walk to the hostel.

V.M. Thomas Achen and Kochama were wardens of the hostel. There were students from other states and Ceylon, staying here. It was a very nice community. Maymi and Helen were already there, studying for B.A English. Our college which admitted ladies only to the postgraduate course had just begun taking students for B.A. Annu, Sumam, Sumana and Bharti from Mangalore, Betsy, Sarala, Prema and many whose faces I remember created the multi-cultural linguistic community. Our mess came from St. Thomas' Hall and George was in charge of bringing it.

MCC or Tambaram as the college was known, was a unique institution. It was a great privilege to be a student of this eminent institution. I am always grateful to Papa for sending me to the best institutions possible. The name of the college would tell what a product from it was worth. Rev. Dr. J.R. Macphail a Scot, was our principal then. He was a missionary who took up the reins from Dr. A.J. Boyd the famous principal whom I just missed. The rest of the teachers in the English Department were Indians. We had Mr. Bennet Albert, Mr. T.K. Thomas Mr. Subramaniam, Mr. Venkataremoni, Mr. Stanley and Mr. P.T. George.

Students came to Tambaram from other states and overseas, especially Ceylon, Malaya and Singapore. They stayed mainly in the Halls – St. Thomas', Selaiyur and Heber. Each Hall had a canteen and a good mess. The college buildings were situated in a huge campus with big trees and forest-like areas, for the campus stretched over a hundred acres. The campus itself had staff quarters and walkways and the whole atmosphere was a transforming experience.

Every morning just before classes there was a short prayer in Anderson Hall. It was the Principal who led the service. I can still hear Dr. Macphail announce in his Scottish guttural accent, "Hymn No: 6" which began "God who made the earth, the stars, the sky, the sea, who gave the light its birth, careth for me".

There were only ten of us in our English P.G. class, three girls, including me. The other two girls, Sarojini Packiamuthu who was on the staff of St. John's College, Palayamkottai, and Violet, were twelve years older than me. The boys too were older except one or two. It was when he was a student with us that Kunders had twin boys. Hrudayaraj, was big built and I was only the size of one of his legs! Shekhar was a brilliant student and Venkataremony was gentle and polite.

The classes were held in Selaiyur and we didn't have classes the whole day. The free hours were the students' library hours and we were expected to use these hours in the library. The syllabus was very vast and only the detailed texts would be taught in classes. We had to master all the non-detailed texts ourselves. The college founders wanted the students to develop originality in thinking and reasoning. It is originality that is given credit in Western Universities. We were expected to do it in Tambaram.

We had five of Shakespeare's plays for detailed study and all the rest for non-detailed study. There were commentaries and critical works and we could sit in the library and take down notes. Reference books were for reference only and limited number of books were available to take home. We also bought the essential critical works used by every student. One paper was the essay, also a three-hour paper and the topic would cover all the literary works prescribed. One of the topics given for our final M.A examination was – "The writer holds up a mirror to society".

We had Inter-collegiate classes in Presidency college once a week. Presidency college with its beautiful ancient building was situated by the side of Marina Beach in Chepauk. Stella Maris College had their first batch of P.G. students that year. So students from all three colleges attended inter-collegiate classes once a week in both Presidency College and Tambaram. I remember Mrs. Parthasarathy, wife of the Indian Ambassador to U.S., coming to class. She was strict and efficient and insisted that we bring the textbooks to the class. "If you don't bring Milton to class, Milton will see that you fail in your examination!" she would say. Dr. Macphail taught us two of Shakespeare's great tragedies in our final year; one was "King Lear" and the other "Hamlet." Another class which was doing the same text at that time, came with us.

Dr. Macphail asked three of us to study the songs in Twelfth Night and Hamlet and sing it in the class. I sang two songs from Hamlet and he was quite pleased. He said that when once 'Hamlet' was staged in MCC they had to choose a girl who had the right voice for Ophelia. Later in Bishop Moore College, I have surprised the students by singing these songs in class. They were enchanted by the songs from Twelfth Night, Hamlet and Tempest. It was in Tambaram I learned that Shakespeare's songs were meant to be sung, not read.

I worked very hard for my P.G. and left no stone unturned, for, a second class in those days was a hard, though coveted achievement. Brilliant students sometimes had to be satisfied with a third class because valuation was very strict. Second class was the qualification for a lecturer's job. That year we had only grades. There was a rumour during valuation that I might get a first class. So I trust I had very good marks, for I had worked hard and done my very best in the examinations.

The college authorities always feared having a Women's hostel on the campus. That is why we had to stay at a distance. On Sundays we went to different churches. Sometimes we attended a Tamil church nearby. At times I would go with Maymi to the Orthodox church in the city after which we went to Vallichayan's (N.P. Abraham of MRF) house and had lunch with them. Vallichayan was Maymi's uncle. Very rarely we had a Mar Thoma service in Heber Hall when after the service Kunjannama Kochama (Mrs. T.K. Thomas) gave us breakfast. Their son Prem was a toddler then and Pradeep just a baby. Mar Thoma students were very few.

The most important service we all attended and enjoyed was the evening service in Anderson Hall every Sunday. We caught the electric train from Guindy and reached Tambaram. It was a memorable experience. The vast Anderson Hall had no sound system and only students who read loudly and clearly were chosen to read the lesson. I read the lesson twice in Anderson Hall. Before choosing me, they made sure my voice carried to the back. When we came back from the service we would sing. "Father, Holy, grant us thy blessing" in parts and as a "round song" till we reached Guindy.

The train journey every day to college and back too was an exciting experience. There was a long walk to the station and a shorter walk to college, once we reached Tambaram. In case we were late we had to run to reach the college on time. Sometimes the local women would get into the ladies' compartment and they had a nasty smell. Water was scarce in Madras, rivers were dry, and the locals did not have the habit of cleanliness. Once for our Hostel Day, one of the brilliant shows was "From Guindy to Tambaram". The passengers sat on the stage, shaking their bodies to show that the train was moving. They stopped shaking when the train came to each station. As the train stopped at each station diverse people got in. The conversation was hilarious. At one station a local woman got in with a tiny, dirty, toddler. One passenger asked, "Enna Amma, intha kulanthai kanjupona manga kotta mathiri irrikithe?" (Why is this child looking like a dry mango seed?)

I learned to read Tamil on these journeys from the names of stations. Tamil is very similar to Malayalam.

The only holidays we would get in college was when it rained unexpectedly. Then it was difficult to walk on the fine sand that pulled our feet down. But rains occurred only once in a blue moon. So our joys were short-lived.

If any of the students had to do anything with the principal, he only had to meet his secretary. He handled everything. The fine for absence on the first day of any term was ten rupees which was a large amount considering that my fees for one term was fifteen rupees. The rates were a little lower on the second and third days. Life on the campus was very disciplined and enjoyable. We had enough freedom in the hostels. We were allowed to take "night out" "weekend out", and late permission. We had only to write it in a book. We never misused it.

In the first year I suffered from jaundice. Neither I nor the doctor who saw me, diagnosed it. The bathrooms were old and the toilets were yellow in colour. Hence even the colour of the urine never showed. I was vomiting all the time and could not retain even water in the stomach. I phoned Thomachayan who was my local guardian and Reji who was still in school, came with the car to take me to Thondiarpet. I still have their address in my memory – No.6, Balu Mudali Street, Rainy Hospital, Thondiarpet!

As soon as Kochama saw me she knew it was jaundice. She asked the village women who came to sell vegetables to bring "kizhukanelli" (Phyllanthus niruri, being the botanical name). It was ground, root stem and leaves in unboiled milk and taken early in the morning for three days. Avomin was given earlier to prevent vomiting. It worked like magic. The urine cleared and I recovered though I lost weight and looked lean. I stayed with them till I recovered fully. Joy and Laila were small then and Thomaskutty had not even started school. That is why I have a close bond with this family even today. Kochamma and Thomachayan helped many cousins who came to Madras to study and they all have a great regard for them.

Maymi was my room-mate in the second year. Kuttymon was born when we were in Tambaram. Maymi was very excited to have a brother. We travelled together during the holidays. Maymi would be standing excitedly in the train long before the Cochin Express reached Alwaye. Thommen sir would be in the station. He bought me oranges because he knew I was convalescing after jaundice. Thommen sir and Saramma

Kochamma were very close to us. When I was working in Alwaye we stayed in the Fellowship house when we came for remedial classes. Soma became my student later on. Rema was at that time convalescing from a rheumatic heart. Fr. Paul Varghese who later became Paulose Mar Gregorius Thirumeni, had a small house in Chacko Gardens and it was Kochamma who looked after his needs. Thommen sir was a great leader of retreats.

We did not have university exams in the first year and Papa allowed me to make a visit to Malaya during the summer holidays of 1960. I sailed with all the students in the various colleges in the city from Malaya and Singapore and it was very exciting. Lilly, K.T. Thomas uncle's daughter was travelling by the same ship. The ship has created in me a deep love for the ocean. Papa decided to meet me in Penang the first port in the north of the Malay Peninsula. I still experience the joy when we first saw the festal lights of Penang. Papa came to the harbour and took me to M.C. Chacko uncle's house. We had dinner there after which we took the night train to Kuala Lumpur. It was just an overnight journey. I recalled my childhood years in Sentul. Now Papa was living in a bigger quarters, close to P.G. Thomas uncle's house and not far from our earlier quarters. I had a lovely holiday with my parents and enjoyed the good food that Mama cooked. We still had ducks in a small pen inside the house.

Malaya is a beautiful country and the vegetation and the weather similar to Kerala. I went to see my old school which was not far from where we stayed. My health recovered. The holidays were over soon and I sailed back just before the college reopened. But in June the sea was rough and all of us had sea-sickness and were down in our cabins without being able to eat anything. Finally we landed in Madras.

We had two weeks' holidays in the middle of the second term and I decided to stay back and study. Our hostel would be closed but the university hostel in Chepauk would be open and they admitted students from other colleges. It was lovely staying there near the Marina beach and going to the Chepauk library to study. The university was close by. The then famous Madras University had two eminent Vice-chancellors, brothers, Ramaswamy Mudaliar and Lakshmana swamy Mudaliar. The present Vice-chancellor was Lakshmana Swamy Mudaliar.

Hall days and sports days were a grand affair in MCC. Students could invite anyone to the grand function arranged on Hall days. There would be a three course dinner. We too in the Women's Hostel tried to make it grand though our resources were limited and food had to come from St. Thomas'.

V.M. Thomas achen and Kochamma were a great help. Their children Rema, Reji – Revi who were twins and the children of the labourers on the campus were all part of our community. So were Kuppan and Patti. In our final year our chief guest was Rev. Dr. J.R. Macphail our principal for he was to retire the following year. Mr. and Mrs. Kibble retired during our final year. Mr. Kibble was in the Mathematics Department.

I will never forget the day just before our final examination when our Principal Dr. Macphail addressed all the Postgraduate final year students together. It was a tense moment for we were about to leave college. He advised us about very small things like having good pens that could write clearly, not to forget the ink and the hall ticket, and to be cool-headed. He then reminded us that by studying in this college we had entered into a rich heritage and that we should always remember one thing; the prayer for old students of the college would be prayed every day in the college during the morning service in Anderson Hall. And he read out the prayer.

"O God whose gift alone it cometh that thy faithful people do unto Thee true and manful service, we pray Thee to follow with Thy blessing on those students who have gone out from amongst us to serve in the wider arena of life outside these college walls. Strengthen them to meet victoriously all temptations; enable them for the faithful performance of their life-work; and may they ever without fear of man follow steadfastly, where duty, right and honour lead; through Jesus Christ our Lord. Amen".

It was a solemn moment.

Dr. Macphail retired the following year and Dr. Chandran Devanesan became the first Indian principal of Madras Christian College. We invited him to Alwaye where Benjamin sir, K.C. Joseph achen and a few others were old students. He was only 60, and we presented him with a walking stick. I had begun my teaching career in UC College and I remember him saying that I was then from the freshest batch for I had just passed out. He went back to Scotland but sadly, very soon he died of bone cancer at the age of sixty-three. By sheer accident I happened to meet Mrs. Martin, wife of Dr. G.C. Martin who eminently served the college, in Glasgow in 1971. She then told me about Dr. Macphail's last days. I thank God for the

2nd MA Class, Madras Christian College, Tambaram

sacrifice of great missionaries who came to establish eminent institutions of higher learning, to make us what we are.

There is a prayer that goes thus – "O, Thou who in days past didst put in the hearts of good men to found this college for the imparting of sound learning, the building of character and the spread of spiritual truth and knowledge of Thyself…"

It was only because of such good men, eminent institutions like Madras Christian College were established. As Rev. Dr. J.R. Macphail has put it – Our fathers were men like Abraham who in obedience to a call left all the comfort and security of their own country to set out on a voyage of faith.

Rev. John Anderson who came to Madras in April 1837 was rightly considered the pioneer of higher education in South India. He always wanted his students to develop originality in thinking and reasoning. Rev. John Anderson died an untimely death in 1855. At this critical juncture, a young Scot named William Miller aged 24, came in December 1863 and put things in place. Miller, the son of an accomplished ship company owner sold his property and his sister's property and came to India. He became the first principal of Madras Christian College and served the college till 1909. According to him the aim of the college was to send out men into the world with their whole being so developed, that when truth comes before them, they will love it; that when duty comes to them they will do it.

After his retirement William Skinner took over as principal. He and his wife used to invite students to their residence for home-meetings, and they enjoyed a good relationship with the students till his retirement in 1921. There is a hostel named after him in UC College.

The most enviable personality and lovable gentleman of all the principals, was Dr. Alexander John Boyd who was a giant among educationalists of his time. He had great gifts of administration.

William Hazlitt says that if he stopped being dumb and inarticulate, it was because he met S.T. Coleridge. It was the same effect that Dr. Boyd had on young men and women of Madras Christian College.

Abraham Lincoln said, "Character is like a tree and reputation like a shadow". Character which is a very important virtue in a person is built on the campus of these institutions.

It was Mrs. and Prof. Barnett who landscaped the campus by planting seeds and saplings all by themselves. The hundred acre campus in the college is like a great gift of nature.

R.S. MacNicol, G.C. Martin and J.R. Macphail (the last of the Scottish principals) are also amongst these people who helped our home, Madras Christian College to be built on a rock that will never be shaken.

"Remember your leaders, those who spoke to you the word of God; consider the outcome of their way of life and imitate their faith in Jesus, who is the same yesterday, today and forever". (Hebrews 13:7,8)

There is a multitude of students who attained greatness from the portals of this institution, men like Dr. S. Radhakrishnan, first Vice-President of India, Sri T.N. Seshan the great reformer of elections, and hosts of others renowned and not so renowned, who made a mark in the fields of their work; who had character and courage to stand for the Truth. There were also myriads of unknown warriors like me who did not leave an indelible mark but owed so much to this campus, our home.

The famous journalist and author T.J.S. George writes – "I missed out on a lot of things, a lot of opportunities, a lot of enriching friendships. I derived only a tiny fraction of the benefits I could have from the universe that Tambaram opened up for me. I am saying it because I don't want others to have the same sort of regret when their turn comes."

He continues – "What I know now is that college is the place and late teens and early twenties are the time, when one can find one's bearings, set the compass and embark on great voyages. When the college happens to be one with a great tradition and a great faculty, the opportunity is unmissable. Madras Christian College is among the rarest of opportunities."

I have written so much about this beloved institution to show what the great sacrifice of others did to benefit so many for so long. The coming generations should commemorate the works of these people so that these institutions will not be used for profiteering. They are hallowed places whose children would kiss the earth where their feet have trod, and even have a pinch of it thrown into their coffin when they are buried, as was done by one student from Union Christian College, Alwaye.

CHAPTER V

SETTLING DOWN

I came back from Madras and spent my holiday in Chathenkary and Thalavady. When colleges reopened in June 1961, there was great shortage of English teachers. Prof. T.B. Thomas, principal of UC College contacted me and asked me to join the faculty of UC College. I hesitated. I told him I did not want to join before my results came. But he insisted and thus I went to Alwaye to join the English Department of my own college. An eminent college's very name was enough in those days to get a job. It was a great privilege to teach with all my teachers, where I had been a student just two years ago. Benjamin sir was the head of the department of English for K.C. Joseph Achen had gone to teach in Ethiopia. There was no B.A English main in those days but just a one-year Pre-University course and a three-year B.A B.Sc undergraduate studies. But students of all streams gathered in the general classes for Part I English. The Degree students were grown-ups and some might have been a little older than me. One advice given to me by T.B. Thomas sir and P.M. Mathai sir on my maiden venture as lecturer was that I should put on a serious face in classes and be strict. I have done it throughout my career except in the years I was about to retire, when students never went out of control because of their respect.

I put up my hair and dressed neatly and respectably. The teacher had a raised platform so that all the students could be seen from a distance. Attendance was taken every hour, calling out each student by name. This had a great advantage, for the teacher knew the student by name, not his roll-number. We went to the general staff-room only to take the registers before leaving for classes. Otherwise we sat in the English Department. Once two goats came bleating into my degree general class and naturally the students created a stir. P.M. Mathai sir came that way and fortunately the goats went out. The ordinary Muslims around kept goats for their livelihood.

It was a great joy, honour and privilege to teach in my old Alma Mater. The results came only by the middle of August and I was appointed formally as lecturer in English with a salary of Rs.125/- per month. The salary for the previous months was given as honorarium. Private colleges paid their own salary until direct payment came years later after a big strike by teachers' unions. The salary varied in colleges according to the management and teachers got Rs. 95/- though they signed the receipt for Rs125/- in some colleges like BCM.

UC college had a Fellowship system where teachers were made permanent only with the consent of all the members of the Fellowship. Members of the Fellowship drew only less salary than the other teachers for they considered it a sacrifice. Kuttippuzha Krishna Pillai sir, T.R. Anantharaman sir (Chemistry), Venkitaraman sir (Mathematics), Aravamudam Iyengar sir (English) and Govindankutty Menon sir (Physics) were permanent teachers, very brilliant, and devoted to the college, but they were not qualified to join the fellowship because they were non-Christians. Joining the Fellowship was a coveted thing but extremely difficult. Ladies were not made permanent, in spite of their efficiency and never entertained once they got married. That was the rule.

I was resident warden of the Women's Hostel where I was an inmate two years ago. The college hostels had tiled roofs and the beams were made of cured coconut wood. My mess fees and room rent together came to twenty five rupees while students paid less. Nothing was run for profit but for the benefit of society.

Money had value though it was scarce. A blouse could be stitched for thirty paise and gold cost around seventy-five rupees. Many people around the college worked there as lab attenders, clerks and peons. Their salary was low but their loyalty and faithfulness was very high. They attended to the needs of the college day and night. Sometimes T.B. Thomas sir had to ask Annama the clerk who stayed nearby, to work at night. Then sir would be in the Principal's office. It was a normal routine. No one will forget the tall Abdu who always stood outside the principal's office for any service. He was the main peon in the college. He was illiterate but knew every single thing a visitor or student wanted to know about matters in the college. Years would go by, but Abdu remembered every student past and present by name, and all his details. Such was the selfless service even ordinary people rendered to this institution that was established in their vicinity for the well-being of society.

Kunjamma Kochama ran the mess very efficiently with loyal servants and helpers. She had a very close relationship with me and was very considerate. She was the one who taught me to put sugar in my Dosai chutney for I couldn't eat it otherwise. This habit has passed on to others in our home. Her daughter and son had grown up. The daughter went to England and settled down there while the son became a doctor, graduating from Vellore. After leaving Alwaye she was matron in many places including a hostel in Vellore and finally settled down near Toc-H School in Ernakulam. I saw her for the last time when I went there for Rajankunju's son Reuben's wedding reception. Her son had died a few months earlier and she was very sad. She died soon after that.

Gracey Kochama was the non-resident warden of our hostel. Susan George, my classmate, came to teach next year and she was co-warden. I would sleep early so Susy took care of things during their study-time. It was in my first year as lecturer and warden that Bessy joined the Pre-University class. She came with her father to the hostel – a tall, grave, retired headmaster who looked frightening then. Bessy had a warm relationship with me as teacher and that developed into a close friendship when we both became colleagues in Bishop Moore College. That precious relationship lasted till her untimely death in 2001 but goes on in Babu and the children.

In the meantime Leelama's wedding was to take place, on January 4th 1962. She had known Kunju since she was a student in Alwaye, after I left. He was lecturer there. It was I who wrote to Papa about it for we did not know how he would view it. Besides Kunju belonged to the newly formed Evangelical church which did not have much respect then, for they had split from the Mar Thoma church. One thing that helped was that Achen uncle had become one of the founders of this church.

Since the younger could not be married before the older, there was a frantic search for a bridegroom for me. It was then that Thampichayan, Aleyamma Kochama's husband, came with this proposal. Thampichayan's father, M.C. Chacko Achen had been vicar of Mavelikara Christ Church as well as Kodukulanji Christ Church. So he knew the family well. Achen uncle with Mathukuttychayan (T.B. Mathew Vakil) went first with the proposal. Though they had scant assets, Appachen was a greatly respected person and Achachen was then lecturer in Peet Memorial Training College. Earlier he had been teaching in the CMS Schools.

Anyway the matter was settled after the bridegroom saw the bride in Thankamama's house in Alwaye. Leelamma was to be given Rs.10,000|- as dowry and that package was to be given to her sister too. It was a huge sum in those days because land in Mavelikara town then cost less than forty rupees a cent. C.T. Benjamin sir's wife Ammukochama's home was very near to Achachen's and Ammukochama's mother exclaimed – "What! a girl with an MA Degree and ten thousand rupees as dowry! What do they have at home to deserve that! "

That was true. As soon as the wedding was over, Rs. 5000/- was gone! Achachen said it was used for wedding expenses and paying back old debts. Appachen and Ammachy had retired long back and Appachen didn't even have pension. Achachen was the youngest and they lived on his income. The others were all well-placed and independent.

When Mama saw her son-in-law's house for the first time she exclaimed – "There is not even a mango tree or jack-tree here for her to eat"! But I had to be married and so it was fixed. I did not have much worry because I knew nothing about such material consequences. I only had prayed that God would choose the right person. Achachen has told me ever since that when he repeated the solemn marriage vows, "I make you the rightful heir of all that I possess in this world"! he thought it was a false pledge for he knew he owned nothing. The family property was only forty cents of land for all the five brothers.

Anyway the wedding was to be fixed on 1st January when either five or seven (an odd number) older people would come for the engagement. It was to take place on 25th January 1962.

In those days weddings were conducted in the afternoon and a small number of relatives and friends attended the wedding. There was no beautician.The bride dressed up as usual in her wedding saree. Neighbours helped to prepare the feast that is served on the eve of the wedding. That is a customary celebration. After a wedding, "irachi ularthiyathu", fish curry and kachiyamor" would be given to neighbouring houses. Food was greatly valued and people helped not for money but out of love.

Only Mama could come for our wedding. Papa did not have leave and James and Alice had school. Besides Papa must have felt it would be too much of a financial burden. I remember receiving Mama at the Alwaye railway station as she arrived by train from Madras. I was singing softly the hymn, " How sweet the name of Jesus sounds". A nun standing close by was listening, and she said, " How beautiful the words are! Please sing it again."

The wedding took place in Christ Church and Bishop M.M. John led the service. Benjamin sir came from Alwaye to attend the wedding. The reception was grand with appam and chicken curry served in the pandal in the courtyard of the house. Two things stand out in my mind. When I invited Thommen sir and Kochamma, Saramma Kochamma said to me, "Molly, in a marriage you have to make a lot of adjustments to live happily. It will be the woman who will have to adjust more. Her advice is very true. Today no one can talk of "adjustments" for the modern generation abhors the word. Hence we see a lot of divorces which was unheard of in our days.

When we visited Thalavady, we visited Papa's cousin "Thadathil Appachen". Appachen lovingly said to Achachen, "She is our pearl", in appreciation. Achachen immediately retorted (but not to hurt). "Do not cast your pearls before swine!"

January 25th has always been a celebration in our home, a greater celebration after Thirumeni came into our lives. It was a day of feasting, for wherever he was, Thirumeni would come to have dinner with us. I would very carefully go through Mrs. B.F. Verghese's cookery books and prepare a grand three-course dinner. Children enjoyed the occasion very much because there would be plenty for a few more days. There would be new dishes every year and it was a festive occasion. Sadly, Achachen became sick after forty-one years of life together, and we could not celebrate our golden jubilee. One half of my life was cut off.

We began our life together with just Rs.5000|- as our capital, not a penny more. We used that money five years later, to build the house. Usually when a teacher gets married everyone waits to see the silk saree she receives as a present from her husband. We went to Chakolas and I bought a saree with the money I had, to save my face. I even had to give him money for his trips to Alwaye. The salary of Rs.150/- would be given every month to Appachen. Yet I did not say a word to Mama. I thought she would be pained. There were other financial difficulties all along for years. But I have never hinted it to my parents for I did not want to worry them.

We always had to be very careful with what we had. I have never bought a silk saree in my life for it was not possible. But we never borrowed any money from anyone. We always lived and spent within our means and tried to live contented lives.

Later, I have deeply felt hurt at the injustice of the Syrian Christian hereditary norms. It is a son's right to inherit everything even if he is born years later. And if on the husband's side there is nothing to inherit except eighteen cents of land (our whole wealth) the disparity is a chasm. Since I never complained of anything everyone thought that I was rich. This was the house where Leelama and family stayed during holidays. This was the home that Mama came to, often. This was also the home that helped Mama and Papa in all their needs, except finances, which was not necessary.

UC College had a strict rule that married lady teachers would not be allowed to continue further. Teachers in private colleges were at the mercy of the management. They did not have direct payment, maternity leave, security of service or any other gain. But they only thought of serving the college. Even after my wedding I was given extension for another year because they valued me very much as a teacher. It was very unusual. Years later, after direct payment came into aided colleges, all these rules changed, and women became permanent in UC College. I have always envied them, for though I taught for long years in Bishop Moore College, my heart is still in UC College where I studied for four years and taught for two. It is such a nostalgic memory and relationship embedded in the heart and I love visiting Alwaye whenever possible though the serene and resplendent Alwaye is now gone and it is now a jungle of concrete structures and never-ending traffic.

I taught in Bishop Moore College for twenty-nine years and the staff was close to one another and had a warm relationship with one another. But time has taught me that lasting bonds and relationships come only from Nicholson School and Union Christian College. For wherever there is one anywhere in the world from these institutions they still cherish an unbreakable bond of friendship that is vent only with death.

Today's generation and their parents do not give importance to building of character. They give importance only to consumerism. A man's worth consists in how much he possesses whether legally or illegally. When in UC College, the principal P.M. Mathai sir gave me an exemplary character and conduct certificate which in those days was very valuable. "A conscientious and loyal teacher, she was liked by the students and staff alike. She can handle large classes without any difficulty. She possesses agreeable manners and excellent character". What value does such a certificate have today where everything is measured by what a person owns and the money he can pay as bribe for appointments and admissions? People of worth are left out and people of political power and black money power have invaded church and society. The church is more desirous of political clout than with the teachings of Jesus Christ who is the true head of the Church. That is the root cause of rottenness in church and society today.

After leaving Alwaye in 1963, I came to Mavelikara and did not immediately look for a job. This turned out to be a disaster later on when direct payment came for it brought break of service and I suffered monetary loss. When I had almost finished my P. G. in Tambaram, Kunjachayan had asked me to write the IAS examination. Sarala Gopalan who joined the administrative service was my senior in Tambaram. So did Helen who was my junior. I should have written it as soon as I finished M.A. Achachen too had encouraged me to write it but I was satisfied with a lecturer's job, though I have regretted it in later years.

Since English lecturers were in great demand then, I got an appointment in BCM College, Kottayam. The salary was only Rs. 95/- for they paid less than the normal salary. The food in the hostel was horrible with worms peeping out of the cooked "uppumavu". But everyone endured it in silence. I worked there only for ten days because Oommen Mathew, later leader of the Kerala Congress, who was working in Catholicate College, Pathanamthitta, came here to invite me as lecturer there with an offer of Rs. 125/- So I went to Catholicate College and met the Principal, who was Dr. J. Alexander who was earlier principal of Wilson College, Bombay. He was actually Soman's grandmother's brother but Vinitha was not born then and Soman must have been an infant! Dr. Alexander was a very dignified person and he immediately appointed me. That was the great demand for English teachers. When junior colleges came into existence in 1964, many went to North Indian universities like Sagar to get a postgraduate degree in English, to be appointed as teachers in these junior colleges. The standard of these mushroom universities in North India was nothing remarkable whereas in our days the name of the institution was sufficient for an appointment.

I stayed in the YWCA in Pathanamthitta at the base of the small hill where the college was situated. Everyday it was a march up to the top of the hill. That was 1963. It was in November while I was working there that the sad news came of John F. Kennedy's assassination on November 22nd while he was President of the United States. He was a great world leader and became a hero during the Cuban crisis when the Soviet Union sent missiles to Cuba. Kennedy declared that he would sink the ship if it did not turn back. The whole world watched with bated breath for the world was on the brink of a nuclear war. The ship did turn back for Nikita Krushchev who ruled the Soviet Union turned out to be a leader who did not desire war. Thus a great crisis was averted.

The world lost a great and much loved leader and Lyndon Johnson became President. This was followed by the murder of Martin Luther King (Jr.) another great American leader, who said, "I have a dream" for America. That dream too was cut short. There is a speech that Robert Kennedy who was Secretary of State in his brother's Cabinet, makes to inform the people of Martin Luther's assassination. That shows the man. A great leader, worthy to take up the reins from his worthy brother, he stood for President in the next election. But he too was assassinated, and the world lost another charismatic leader who would have contributed so much to the world.

Catholicate College was under the management of the Orthodox church and Bishop Daniel Mar Philexinos the manager, stayed close by. There were many batches for the Pre-Degree course and the college had a large number of students and staff. I used to come to Mavelikara every weekend and so the Pathanamthitta – Pandalam – Mavelikara route became very familiar. Before the academic year was over, the Principal called me and said that I should continue in the college for I would be made permanent on the staff. But it was in early 1964 that the government decided to start junior colleges in Kerala just for the Pre-Degree course. The Orthodox management in Mavelikara, under the leadership of C.I. Ninan sir of Kunchattil was actively around to get sanction from the government to start a college in the church's property in Kunnom. He was Appachen's friend and Appachen hoped I would be able to get an appointment. At the same time the CSI Madhya Kerala Diocese under Bishop M.M. John was persuaded to apply for a college in Mavelikara and they were actively pursuing it. Rev. C.I. Abraham who was then vicar of Christ Church and Dr. P.M. Mathew who had helped start the Training College, and a close friend of Bishop John, encouraged the Diocese to take a leap in the dark. They chose the compound in Kallumala where there was a small church and a small house for the upadeshi. All the members of the parish belonged to the backward community but they were emancipated people. Their cemetery was in the compound and convincing them about the college and its future benefit to the community which made it necessary to move the cemetery to a convenient place was not easy. No one wanted to move or disturb the bones of their forefathers.

At last the Diocese was able to persuade them and that was the spot pointed out to the commission that came for inspection. Since the CSI had no other college they were able to influence the authorities. Rev. K.C. Mathew who was then working in CMS College, Kottayam was appointed as principal. The house in Kallumala called Chakkalayil was taken on rent as residence of the principal and college office. The college was to commence in June and appointments were being made. There was a rumour that women were not likely to be appointed because of problems with maternity leave in the middle of an academic year. Though there is none not born of woman, such an inconvenience was not acceptable. Besides I was pregnant and Vinitha was to be born in early June. I went for the interview in the parsonage. Thomas Ninan, my college mate in Alwaye and son of the Diocese's powerful advocate, Mr. K.T. Ninan was appointed seniormost in the English Department though he had less experience than me.

Later I got the appointment order and they asked me when I would be able to join. I replied that I would join on the day the classes began.

Vinitha was born on 8th June in Pushpagiri hospital, a small but very nice hospital then, and we chose that hospital for two reasons. First of all patients were taken good care of and there was no need of any help from home. Secondly, Koshy Chacko Achen, my colleague in Pathanamthitta who knew it well, said that there were very good doctors. Anyway, since my parents were not here this was a blessing. I came straight back from the hospital to Mavelikara.

Classes started on 6th July and I joined college when Vinitha was just twenty-eight days old. By that time, sheds had come up in the college and permission was given to start all three groups, first, second and third, with two divisions for each, one with Malayalam as the second language and the other, with Hindi. There were only 480 students in all with a small number of staff and a cool staff-room just under the huge jackfruit tree that stood like a giant at the entrance of the college.

Every morning started with prayer in the staff-room and the classes too began each day with the college prayer. As in UC College, the names of students were read out each period to mark attendance. So, we teachers learned the names of our students and that made a huge impact on discipline. Mavelikara and its suburbs were having a college for the first time and admissions and appointments were purely on merit. So we had brilliant students who came from schools around and there was perfect discipline in the college. K.C. Mathew achen had a bicycle, which was a luxury and the staff who helped him to go to the public for contributions for a building, had to take rented bicycles. The bachelors lived in a rented house close by. Since the community was small we were very close and loved one another and cared about one another. The early years were really great with warm co-operation from the staff, parents and public and K.C. Mathew achen was efficient in all these public relations. As wardens of a class, we tried to find out details of all the students in our charge and even visited their homes. Slowly the buildings came up and the college grew in stature. It was in 1972, after a year-long strike by the managements and Teachers' Associations that the private college teachers started getting direct payment.

In the early days, every function in the college was very grand. There were choir festivals, radio plays and later on two plays staged by the staff. The plays were very well received. I acted in the play "Akkaldama" as an old Pulaya woman in a rural setting who comes to a doctor for asthma, accompanied by her daughter. Dr. P.M. Mathew who saw such real patients everyday split with laughter. It was in this play that I hit Vattaparambil with an "ulakka" when I realized he had come to arrest my son Gopalan (Kovalan) whose role was performed by Rajan Verghese. During Prof. D.G. Isaac's time we also took part in a radio play where I acted the part of Lady Macbeth in the "sleep-walking" scene. I have loved acting and used to act out everything whenever I taught drama and Shakespeare in classes. I enjoyed it, and so did the students. A good teacher is always a good actor! The rare opportunities I got to act are hence imprinted in my heart.

By that time Papa and Mama came to settle down in Chathenkary. When we were in Malaya and very young, Papa once felt profuse sweating and weakness one evening and we went to call a dresser (a male nurse) who came and discovered that his sugar level had dropped. Alice was then three and James just six months old. At that time whenever Papa came for lunch he would tell Mama that he was getting insatiably thirsty. Then he was diagnosed with diabetes and every morning he used to test his urine in a test-tube, pour Mandel solution and heat it. The colour of the tested urine denoted the level of sugar. So Papa had diabetic onset very early in life. This later on affected his heart. He had a severe heart-attack in the sixties and doctors said he had only six months to live. That was how they decided to come back to India. Alice was then studying for Pre-University in Stella Maris College and James had one more year to finish school. So James stayed back with P.G. Thomas uncle and Mary Auntie and their children Roy and Prasad. Joji and Sunny were much older, and our age. Uncle and Auntie had a daughter Karuna who they loved very much but she died when she was five years old because of some congenital illness. She was always remembered in the family.

Papa first stayed in a rented house in Theepani, Tiruvalla. Leelama's younger son Kochumon was very small and he was baptized in that house so that Papa could be his godfather. Later on they shifted to Chathenkary.

Papa was getting better and he wanted to build a new house. There were enough Jack-trees for carpentry work and sand could easily be bought, the river being just in front. Cement had to be bought from Pulikkezhu. Both of us used to visit them often and I wanted to help him as much as I could. I remember going with Avutha by "Vallom" to buy cement. Once, on our way back before we entered the small canal ('thodu') a motor-boat passed, creating swift waves and the vallom started swaying violently. Avutha knew how to keep it from capsizing but I got the fright of my life, and Avutha who was my age, kept on laughing.

Vallimamachy was staying in the house and perhaps she did not want Papa to come here. She created a lot of trouble for Papa who was very straight-forward and did not know the crooked ways of this spinster sister and her accomplices around. She even made others steal the wood from the house. Mama knew nothing about worldly cunningness.

She just looked after Papa and was often tortured by this sister-in-law. Vallimamachy had a feeling that everything in this house had been managed by her, forgetting that all the money came from Papa. She created lots of worries for him overlooking the fact that he was her older brother who had looked after the whole family and was now sick. Her ways were mysterious because of spinsterhood's frustrations. In spite of all this Papa was able to build a fine house for he was good at management.

We visited Papa and Mama very often and as a responsible first-born I saw to it that none of his needs was left undone. Very soon Uncle and Kunjumamachy too settled down in Karipuzha. Years earlier Kunjumamachy had stayed in a rented house in Tiruvalla S.C. Junction when Sunny and Baben studied in S.C. School. Later they went to Keezhillam and because Baben was a bit backward in studies, he was later taken to Malaya. Sunny did Pre-University in Tambaram and joined Manipal for medicine.

Before Uncle retired, the government gave Uncle the big opportunity to go on a tour of Europe with his wife. Valsala was six or seven years old and she was left with Vallimamachy in Chathenkary. While they were on tour Valsala fell ill and the doctors suspected typhoid. She was admitted to Mission Hospital which was the sought-out refuge for all around Tiruvalla. Communication was only by letter or telegram. Finally, Vallimamachy sent a telegram, and they had to cut short their long-awaited tour and return to Kerala. Uncle was terribly disappointed at the loss of a golden opportunity.

When Sunny finished Medicine, Uncle wanted to send him to England for FRCS. Though he was very young, Uncle wanted him to get married lest he bring back an English wife. Panampunnayil Thomas Thirumeni was a great friend and it was Thirumeni who brought the proposal of Mariamma, Mr. and Mrs. B.F. Verghese's daughter and a close relative of Thirumeni. The wedding took place in Karippuzha and there was a huge pandal in front of the house. Thomas Thirumeni conducted the wedding and Valsala, though just completing school, stood behind the bride in a saree. The reception was grand with fine food for everyone. Both of them left for England very soon.

Uncle had an imported Mercedes-Benz and since Karippuzha was close by, we always had a close relationship with Kunjumamachy and uncle. We could hear the soft, but carrying sound of the Mercedes whenever Uncle passed this way.

Uncle would visit Papa often and he had great concern for Papa. When James came back after his studies, he did his Pre-University in Madras and his Pre-professional in Nagpur. Papa wanted to send him for medicine. In the meantime Alice had passed her Pre-University and she expressed her intense desire to go for medicine. Papa said, "I don't have money to send both of you for medicine. But if you get admission on merit, I shall educate you." She was a brilliant student and very hard-working and she got admission in CMC Vellore. I still remember getting her telegram from Vellore for I was in Chathenkary. It read "Selected, Elizabeth." Papa was very happy.

But when James' turn came for being admitted to a professional course, Papa asked him what course he would like to pursue. He just said, "As God decides." This was the only answer he gave whenever Papa asked him this question. So Papa was upset for he wanted to make sure his son was willing to join MBBS. When P.G. Thomas uncle came for leave, Papa sought his help. I was there when uncle came to Chathenkary. After lunch Uncle called him and asked, "What professional course would you like to choose?" He gave the same reply, "As God decides." Uncle repeated the question and he got the same answer. Finally Uncle got impatient and said, "Are you willing to go for medicine?" Then he said, "Yes" and Papa and Uncle were relieved. That was how Papa informed Karippuzha Uncle and he went to Manipal to secure his admission. I remember that the total amount including fees came to Rs.20,000/- Papa said, "Nothing should be extreme, even religion".

Anila was born on Sunday April 21st, 1968, early in the morning in Pushpagiri hospital where four years earlier Vinitha was born on a Monday morning at 10 o' clock. We came straight from the hospital to Chathenkary on the third day. Papa was delighted to see her. He said "Oh, she is a little dark and that is good." He thought the gene came from Chathenkary. Unfortunately, I developed an abscess after bathing with "Pinda thailam" which did not suit my body. I was also eating a "lehyam" which was carefully made by Manthrayil Vaidyan, a respected Ayurveda physician who was also Papa's friend. I had to be admitted to the hospital again and the baby had to be looked after by Mama. James was also there.

Appachen and Ammachy

The ordeal over, I returned to Chathenkary. Mama brought Valiamachy from Thalavady and there was also "Annakochu" to help us. Valiamachy was ever willing to be of help to Mama and she bathed the baby as an experienced grandmother for she loved little children. Her baptism was in St. Paul's church, Chathenkary and Mama was her godmother. When college reopened I went back to Mavelikara.

We were staying with Appachen and Ammachy. When Vinitha was a baby, Appachan used to rock her to sleep in the wooden crib that had been used for babies down from Achakuttichayan.

When Anila was just an infant, once, all of a sudden she felt suffocation. Immediately they took her to Dr. A.D.Verghese's hospital and Achachen came to call me urgently from college. By God's grace she became normal after the great Dr. A.D. Varghese gave her an injection. I remember "Angele" Achayan (K. Thomas sir) saying – "It is when children fall ill, we realize how much we love them."

Later Anila had "Theepollal karappan". Boils would form suddenly on her skin. She was only three or four months old then. A.P. John sir from Anand Bhawan came and he brought "chembaruthyathi keram" which he himself had made from coconut oil and chembaruthi. (Hibiscus rosa sinesis). He was a good Ayurveda physician and Appachen's friend.

All four of us had to sleep in the small side-room in our ancestral home and we wanted to build a room as an extension to the house. One day Panicker Kunju came to visit Appachen. He, being an engineer, advised us not to attempt it since the house was old and made with "vettukallu" and lime. So finally with fear and trembling Achachen requested Ammachy's permission to build a small house on the Western side, using the plan of the FACT quarters in which Amamma lived. Nothing could be done without Ammachy's permission and her moods were like changing tafetta. Anyway, she agreed and immediately Kuttan Asari, Kochaniyan's older brother was sent to Eloor to bring the plan and measurements of the quarters. Finally all arrangements were made and Kochukeevarchan, a well known contractor, and Elanjimootil Kunju's father was put in charge of the construction.

"Red Vettukallu" was brought everyday from Kallumala by bullock-carts. The wages of the mason and carpenter was seven rupees per day and that of "maikadu" was four rupees. Cement cost nine rupees per sack. Our salary was very low but money had value. A family could live with a man's wages of rupees four. We had just Rs 5000/- in the bank and we borrowed another five thousand from Papa. Housing loans were unheard of.

The foundation stone was laid by Appachen after prayer. Kochukeevarchen looked after everything well and Achachen paid him. It was Kuttan Asari and his brothers who did the carpentry work, and the masons came from Kallumala. Kochukeevarchen came on a bicycle, and Vinitha being very talkative used to shout with excitement "Cycle Appacha!" The house was small but normal for those days, and when it was completed with a well and a wall in front, the whole cost came to Rs. 20,000/- It was 1967. We had a small house-warming ceremony and the college teachers too were invited. K.C. Mathew Achen said that there should have been one more room. Our side-room with an open veranda then, was to have been built on the Western side with an entrance into the drawing room. Somehow that room became separate and independent, which turned out to be a blessing in later years when an attached toilet was added to it.

As soon as Georgekuttichayan heard that his brother was building a house on the plot, he turned heaven and earth and sent a telegram to Appachen that his job was at stake and asked Appachen to send him a large sum of money. Appachen borrowed the money and sent it to him. All this turned out to be a hoax. Appachen had retired when Achachen was in Form III and was now dependent on Achachen's salary. Only Ammachy had a small pension since she was in government service as sewing mistress. Appachen had to borrow whatever was needed, otherwise.

Then Georgekuttichayan himself came and wanted Appachen to divide the property and register it. He called K.P. John his friend who stayed close by and Georgekuttichayan decided upon everything while Appachen was forced to put his signature. That was how the nineteen cent plot and the house went to Georgekuttichayan, the "chira" and "Kunnu" to Mathukuttichayan, and the "kandam" (wetland) to be divided between Achakuttichayan and Kunjachayan. Achachen got eighteen cents on the west. That was all the property that Appachan had. Georgekuttichayan immediately cut down a few trees including the "elanji" on the eastern side, to prove his ownership.

CHAPTER VI

WINDOW TO THE WORLD

Achachen was always applying to different places for a better job – to places like Bankura in West Bengal and even Somalia! But nothing actualized. In the meantime, a friend told us about the Asia Christian College Scholarship to study in England. In those days the only amount you could take out of India was Rs.60/- which came to three British pounds. Achachen got the scholarship and also admission in King's College, Aberdeen for the Diploma in Higher Education for Teachers' Training which was a one year course, after which he could do Master's in Education in the same college. Aberdeen University was an ancient University and so was King's College that was affiliated to it. The building had a huge crown at the top to honour its name. The scholarship was just enough for his essential needs and he had to struggle a bit but the education was of a very high standard. The brothers had to support Appachen and Ammachy since Achachen was going away and Kunjuchayan and Achakuttychayan agreed to send some money to them. Meanwhile we had temporarily shifted to the new house and Karunan, a small boy related to Achakutty, was to look after Anila while I was away in college. Achachen left in early September 1969, and Anila was hardly one and a half years old.

Classes commenced and Achachen got accommodation with a nice family and for the first time he cooked his own food. His address was 12, Ashgrove Road, Aberdeen, and his land lady was Fiona. At first he was terribly homesick, especially that winter was drawing near, but no one encouraged him to come back. While he was there, he gradually contacted K.C. Joseph Achen our teacher in Alwaye, who was then Scholarships Secretary in World council of Churches.

God's ways are mysterious. Achachen asked Joseph Achen if I could get a scholarship to study in England. I had been a favourite student of Joseph Achen and immediately Achen sent me an application form with a copy of the letter he had written to Mathai Zachariah who was then Secretary of National Council of Churches in India (NCCI), requesting him to forward my application to Geneva though it was a late entry. I applied immediately and it was duly forwarded to Geneva. That is how I got a scholarship from the World Council of Churches to study in Westhill College, Selly Oak, Birmingham for the academic year 1970-71. It came with a scholarship including boarding and lodging together with travel and a small allowance of three pounds every week.

Vinitha was then studying in Std I in Bethany. Every day as soon as I came back from college, Anila would never allow me to step into the house without first carrying her. At home she usually piled up all the books on our shelf and then sat on top with one book open in her hand. Meanwhile she had "Karappan" on her face and ears and I gave her some Ayurvedam as advised by Leelamma. But it only worsened. So, as advised by the wife of Kochunnoonni sir the Compounder in the hospital, I took her to Dr. A.D. Varghese. "Karappan" according to those who knew about it should never be healed quickly because it would have serious side-effects. I expressed this fear to the doctor. He said, "We shall give her medicine to heal it from within and there will be no problem. Only don't bathe her for some days". Dr. A.D. Verghese was a greatly respected and trusted family doctor. He gave us medicines from capsules divided into small parts and packed in small pieces of paper. This treatment was very effective and to our great relief she was healed quickly.

When the children and I went to Chathenkary for the holidays in December, I requested Mama to look after her in Chathenkary. Mama had to look after Papa's needs and she herself had sudden bouts of asthma, yet she agreed. Mama fed her well and she became plump and sweet. Papa used to walk around with her sharing everything he ate including raw mangoes, saying, "Appachen can't carry you. So hold my hand." Papa enjoyed her very much.

For the Easter of 1970, Papa asked me to come on Saturday for they wanted to attend the early morning Easter Service after which Achen too was having breakfast with us. So I went with Vinitha. One thing stands out clearly in my mind. There was a big, bright comet in the sky in the early hours on Sunday. It seemed very close by with a long, bright tail. The sky was very clear. I haven't seen comets after that. It was in June that year that Papa died. So Shakespeare's lines from "Julius Caesar" always came to my mind after his death.

"When beggars die, there are no comets seen; But the heavens themselves blaze forth the death of Princes."

I got a letter from K.C. Joseph Achen that I was to join classes in early September, in England. When I told Papa about it he was overjoyed. He gave great value to education and regretted he didn't have the money to send any of his children to England for higher studies. With a face overflowing with joy but with a little regret, he said to me, " But it must be your husband's name you write on the enrolment form!" I said, "No, Papa. They haven't even asked about the husband. They have asked for only the father's name. So I will be enrolled as Anna Chacko." He was so proud that I could go and study in England as his daughter!

Once, some time that May I was in Chathenkary with them and Papa was standing in the dining-room near the net, applying "kuzhambu" on his legs and body as usual. As he stood there he asked me, "Edi, even if I am gone won't you look after them?" He meant Mama and the younger ones. I was shocked. I wanted to tell him there was no reason for such a thought and simply exclaimed, "What Papa!" But he asked me again, "Will you not look after them?"

Then I replied, "Surely. Will I do otherwise Papa?" And he held his peace. None of us knew death was very close· For though the doctors in Malaya had given him only six more months to live, he had lived for five years now, built the house and done many things. Alice was then studying in Vellore and James was to join Manipal that year. His financial condition was alright but he only wanted his eldest child to take the responsibility of the home, Mama and the future of the younger children who were still studying.

I have stuck to that promise all my life and Achachen has supported me all along. But because I wanted to be true to my word to Papa I regarded my siblings and their children later on, as my very own as if I was responsible for all of them in Papa's place. I also helped Mama in every decision she had to make, about their education, marriage etc. I did everything with their ultimate good in view, obeying Papa's wishes in letter and spirit.

Leelama and family were then in Thuruthicadu. She never visited Chathenkary as I did and Papa was somewhat anxious to see her. He would look to the south hoping to see her coming. One day he asked me, "What is this! Will I not be able even to see her!"

James was at home then. Some time during the first week of June, Papa felt uneasy and was taken to Mission Hospital by James. Mama didn't go because she always had breathing problems. As Papa was about to leave he turned back and kissed Anila who came to him. Then he went to the hospital.

I had been to Chathenkary during the previous weekend. When the school year began, Vinitha was admitted to Std II and placed in the boarding in Bethany for I would go to England in September. When Achen uncle heard that Papa was in the hospital he sent word to Leelamma asking her to go immediately and see him. It might have been on the 10th of June. On the 11th morning, Papa shaved as usual, had breakfast, and was reading the newspaper when he suddenly felt uneasy and breathed his last. It was 9.30 a.m. Only James was in the hospital. Leelamma got ready to go and see Papa that day, but by the time she reached the hospital Papa had died. I heard the news while in college. That morning I had entrusted someone in the office with Rs.500/- and immediately I got back the money, called Shivan who had a taxi and left for Chathenkary. Vinitha was later brought from the school by Sunny. Karippuzha uncle, both Appachens from Chengannoor were already there. I entrusted Uncle with the money to look after the needs of the funeral. I remember that when Uncle took matters into his hands and was paying for all necessities, Appachens thought that they too should share the expenses. That was a custom in those days. But Uncle said, "No, I am spending only the money that Mollykochu gave me this morning." Uncle always called me Mollykochu.

There was pouring rain from morning till evening on the 11th. The funeral was to take place on the 12th afternoon. Kunjachayan would arrive the next day with Alice. In those days, the Bishop Moore College staff was very close to one another and all of them came in the pouring rain, crossing the river by "vallom". It was a first experience for some of them.

The next day, the weather was fine. I was going to be thirty-two that month. None of us could bear Papa's loss. He was only sixty three. Mama must have been just 54 when she lost Papa. She had been a very loving, caring, faithful wife looking after his every need. We have never seen Mama disobeying, or saying a word back to Papa. She looked up to him for everything including all decision making. So she was really helpless. Only when I lost Achachen did I realize how Mama must have suffered at such a young age.

Valiammachy came and stayed with Mama after Papa's death. Valiammachy, who had good health was always a tower of strength for Mama. So Anila grew up with them both in Chathenkary. I remember how sad I was when I went to church in Chathenkary before I left for England. When Papa was laid in the tomb I was hesitant even to look. When I turned my head with great sorrow and hesitation this verse from the Bible came to me – "He is not here, he is risen." I remembered it during Easter when I was in Edinburgh, as the first flowers of spring, the crocuses were coming up as a symbol of the resurrection.

Meanwhile, my travel arrangements had to be made. After getting my passport I had to go to the British High Commission in Madras for the interview prior to getting a visa. I stayed with Kunjachayan and Kochama and also visited Thomachayan. There were just four or five people sitting outside the High Commissioner's room. My turn came. I was offered a seat and he asked me questions. What he particularly wanted to know was what guarantee there was that I would return to India. I told him I was leaving two small children behind. It was a warm conversation and he issued the visa. As I was leaving, he got up from his seat to open the door for me. I was surprised! What British politeness! I thanked him and came away happily. I then went to the Air-India office to book my tickets. I remember meeting one Ramaswamy there whom I later met at Orly airport, Paris.

Kunjachayan said to Kochamma – "Look at her. She does everything on her own and has some Ramaswamy or other to help her". Kochamma was always dependent on Kunjachayan.

During the days before I left, I always ate in Ammachy's house. I used to buy "Kayal meen" (from the lake) for her when the fishmonger came and she liked it very much. She used to make lovely fish curry with "Kanambu" and "Karinchi" and send it in an earthen vessel (chatti) through me to Papa. Papa enjoyed it very much though it was too hot to his taste.

It was two days before I travelled that I went to say farewell to Mama and Valiammachy. I came back in the morning to Mavelikara. But on the evening of the next day the "Karshakan" bus that plied from Tiruvalla to Thattarambalam overturned and fell into the canal from the narrow tricky bridge at Manipuzha. The morning newspapers the next day came with this news. Mama was shocked. I consoled her saying I had returned on the morning of the previous day and there was no reason to worry. There was no phone and the communication was only by letters. I think we used to write constantly so that no one would get worried. I travelled with that newspaper to England and when Achachen saw it he exclaimed," I always feared some bus would fall off the bridge into the water!"

Appachen was not well and Veluthakunju, Achakutty's father, a tall fair man, was appointed to look after Appachen during day-time. Vinitha was in the boarding in Bethany, and when I went to see her, Sister Dorothy and the Headmistress said she would cling to their robes all the time, and the sisters had to twist the cane around their dress, to keep her aloof, otherwise other children would follow suit. It was Karippuzha uncle who took me to the airport in Kochi, the old naval airport. It was my first flight and I was thrilled.

We took off from Bombay at 7.20 a.m. and reached Palam airport Delhi at 8.51 a.m. It was a 707 flight. From there we flew to Beirut. Delhi to Beirut is 2420 miles and it took five hours and forty minutes. By 1.15 p.m. we were passing over Teheran flying at 31,000 ft at 550 miles per hour. There was a change of crew at Beirut. I was thrilled to see the name "Lebanon" written in bold letters, for it brought memories of the references to Lebanon in the Bible. Beirut was a mountainous city by the sea. Just fifteen days ago, an American plane was destroyed by terrorists in Beirut. But Beirut seemed calm, and there was another four hours' flight to Geneva.

We flew over Cyprus at 35,000ft. As we crossed the Alps, the view was breathtaking for it was a very clear day and an awesome sight. All below, one could see the tops of the mountain ranges. The captain pointed out the highest peak of the Alps, Mont Blonc where an Air-India 707 flight had crashed in 1966 and India lost her great nuclear scientist Homi J. Bhabha in that crash. K.C. Joseph Achen had given me an open ticket, to fly to Geneva first, stay with them during the weekend, and then fly to London.

Travel has enchanted me always. Seeing new countries, new places, new people, has always been my joy. And here I was, in Geneva! I just followed the signs to the exit. Doors opened as you approached, and that was amazing! Finally I came to the exit and met Achen and Babykochamma. The first question Babykochamma asked me was, "Have you travelled before, Molly? Your face does not show any bewilderment of a maiden travel!"

I said, "Yes, Kochama, by ship, not by plane." I went with them to their flat. The only thing Babykochama wanted from India was "Uzhunnu" (urad dal) and "pappadom." She had also advised me to take as less luggage as possible, for then I would be able to bring back more things. She said, "No one will see if your blouse matches the saree for you will be covered up in a cardigan and overcoat." So I took only what was essential. Mariama gave me a very fine overcoat which she had used in England, and it kept me warm.

Babykochamma also asked me to buy a good pair of Hush-Puppies and an umbrella from Mark and Spencer, for the goods there were very reliable. Woolworth was just fancy and not durable.

I still remember Babykochama sitting in their little kitchen and making "poori" for dinner. She told me, first we should add a little oil and press the flour with it and then we could straight away fry it after mixing it with water. That evening her Japanese neighbour came with her little daughter. Babykochama said she was teaching her English and she in turn, helped Kochama with Japanese. Kochama gave us home-made cake. The little girl ate a piece and wanted more. When her mother offered her a part of her cake, Kochama asked her not to do that. She could have another piece. She should learn that mothers too have a right to their own portion!

The next morning Achen and Kochama took me around the city to see the WHO, UN European headquarters, formerly League of Nations, ILO and other important organisations. At noon we had lunch in a park and Kochama said, "Achen will sit on the bench and take a nap for ten minutes which is his habit wherever he is." Then we drove around, Babykochamma pointing out to me the famous Swiss Brown cows. Kochamma explained that the Swiss were famous for creating landscapes. Wherever there was a mound of soil they would immediately plant grass around it and make it look beautiful like a small hill. Achen stopped by the row of poplars on the way. I was thrilled to look at them for all three of us knew the poem by William Cowper, beginning:-

"The poplars are felled,

Farewell to the shade

and the whispering sound

of the cool colonnade.

The winds play no longer

Or sing in the breeze

Nor Ouse on her bosom

Their image receives."

We saw the river Ouse on our way back. As we went to the wide Geneva Lake, we saw the world's tallest fountain and had a view of Mont Blonc.

The Communist Government of Kerala had just lost in the elections after the famous "Vimochana Samaram". The previous day's papers contained the exciting report. Babykochama wanted to know all about it but unfortunately I didn't know we could take away the newspapers supplied on the flight. Very recently, a man who runs a small shop near Mont Blonc came across newspapers and other items on the mountain, where snow had melted. It was from the Air India plane crash of 1966. Then reporters wondered how the newspapers were there. In this lap-top electronic age, they cannot imagine passengers reading news papers on the plane!

Babykochama told me that I should watch the landscape and buildings whenever the plane descended at any airport. Each city would be different.

Next morning I took the flight to London. It was forty minutes to Paris and another forty-five minutes to Heathrow, London. We landed in clear weather at Orly airport, Paris. We just got down for an hour or so. I met Ramaswamy whom I had met in Madras and he pointed out to me the Jumbo Jet, Boeing 747, that was at the airport. It had just been manufactured and not yet used for regular flight. So it was a sensation. There were about seventy planes at the airport and that itself was exciting.

After forty-five minutes' flight we reached Heathrow. The Secretary of Asia Christian Colleges Association, Mr. Angus and his wife came to the airport according to Achachen's request. Miss. Dunning of the British Council of Churches was also there. She first took me to the YWCA where I was to spend the night. Then we had tea with Mrs. Chaplin, the secretary of the British Council of Churches. Later Mr. Angus took me to their home for tea and dinner. They were a very nice couple and they had ice-cream and other good things for me. But my stomach was a bit upset. So they gave me medicines and a hot water bag. After dinner they took me to the hostel.

I remember going to the post-office next day to buy postage to send letters to India. It is in England we learn the value of "please" and "thank you". When you request postage you say "please": The lady tells you how much to pay, again with a "please". When you give the amount, you say "thank you". But when the postage and change are given she says "thank you" again while the customer receives it with another "thank you." We Indians stop saying it the moment we reach India. As A.G. Gardiner says, "please" and "thank you" are little everyday civilities that radiate goodness around us.

As I looked around I exclaimed, "This is London!" I couldn't believe it. It was a city I had read of, dreamed of! But to be right there was like a dream come true in a fairy tale. I remember with what excitement I wrote "London" on the right-hand side of the letter. That day I wrote letters to Ammachy, Mama, and Achachen. Achayan (K. Thomas Sir) later told me they used to read my letters like an article in Malayala Manorama, with all the detailed travel experiences. In fact I got the art of letter-writing from Mama who used to write long letters in beautiful hand-writing, describing every detail using every inch of space.

The next day I had to catch a train to Euston and from there go to the Euston coach station to take a coach to Selly Oak, Birmingham. After coming out of Euston Railway station, I asked one or two passers-by the way to the coach station. I knew it was very near, but they had no clue about it, however much they tried to help me. "Could you please tell me the way to the coach-station?" – this was my question. With my good accent, I wondered what went wrong. Finally one person said, "Oh, the coach station!" and she gave me the correct direction. What had happened was I had pronounced "coach" as coach with an "ou" sound, and by the time I reached England "ou" had become "əu" which brought the difference! Daniel Jones' English Pronunciation Dictionary had not yet recorded that!

I reached Selly Oak, a very serene place and came to the YWCA hostel just close by. This hostel actually belonged to Westhill college. Miss. Bottoms, a nice elderly lady was the warden. I was allotted a single room and I took some rest. We had to cross the road and go to the college dining hall for every meal.

Mr. Cliff was in charge of our classes. It was a small class consisting of students from many countries and we had to learn many subjects including Christian Education, Sociology, Educational psychology, Child Psychology and a few other subjects. We also had to visit various churches on Sundays. It was a certificate course in Christian Education. There was also a regular Teacher training course in Westhill college and these students too stayed in the hostel. In our class there was the blonde Minne from Hamburg, Chris, Peter, Pakdee from Nigeria, Cameroon and Thailand, and Andre, and others from Congo, Kenya and Sierra Leone. There were two from Scotland also.

In India, I used to have severe cold and allergic problems during the monsoon when the climate was wet. But I did not have any such problem in England. The air was clean, healthy and dry. Clothes would dry quickly even in winter. We always kept the window a little open to let in fresh air. The food was plain English food, but healthy.

There were many colleges in Selly Oak and students from fifty-three countries had studied there, the previous year. During the combined morning worship in George Cadbury Hall, I once read the prayers. Mr. Cliff and many others were impressed by the clarity.

Mrs. Cliff helped us with shopping in Selly Oak and I bought an umbrella, raincoat and a few other things. Mr. Cliff gave me a pair of snow – boots that was essential in winter.

Mr. Cliff took us to visit different places. We first went to Stratford-upon-Avon to the birthplace of William Shakespeare. On our way we saw Anne Hathaway's cottage. (Shakespeare's wife to whom he bequeathed his bedstead). Stratford is situated upon the river Avon. It is still preserved as it was and is a great tourist attraction. There is the Royal Shakespeare Theatre as well as a huge statue of Shakespeare surrounded by four characters from his plays – Lady Macbeth (washing her hands), Hamlet (looking at the skull in the grave diggers' yard), Falstaff (Tell me a story) and Prince Hal (putting on his father's gown). There is another statue of

Shakespeare in the Town Hall which was presented by David Garrick, the great actor. Inscribed on it are the words – "You'll never see the like of him again."

You can enter the house where Shakespeare was born, with a little garden, a cradle made of wood, the fireplace, cauldron and other memorabilia.

Shakespeare was baptized in the Holy Trinity Church, Stratford and the great bard is buried as well inside this church. These lines are etched on the tomb inside the church.

"Good friend, for Jesus' sake forbear

To dig the dust enclosed here.

Blest be he that spares these stones

And curst be he that moves my bones."

There is a similar house where the American flag flies. Katherine, mother of John Howard, founder of Harvard University was born and brought up there. Later the house was bought by Edward Morris a millionaire and presented to the Harvard University. It was there I first saw the 'weeping willow' by the side of the river. Mrs. Cliff told us, her sister in the U.S. always said the grass is greener in England than anywhere else in the world. It is very true.

Meanwhile Miss. Elliott who was living in the Little House, Brownshill, Cheltenham had invited us a few Indian students to stay with her during the weekend. She had a great love for Indian students ever since she taught in CMS College, Kottayam. It was one and a quarter hour's bus journey to Cheltenham. Miss. Elliott came with Christine to meet me. On our way we had lunch with a Malayalee family and the lady who hosted us turned out to be Mrs. Annie Itty's mother's sister. In the evening we cooked rice, egg curry with vegetables and pappadam. There were two boys also. Miss. Elliott made them do the washing-up since we had cooked. Miss. Elliott took us around the famous Cotswold region which in Autumn is amazing with its colours.

On our way back we visited Painswick, a beautiful village with a little church and a cemetery that has ninety-nine yew trees. The legend goes that every hundreth tree withers and dies. We also visited Gloucester

Cathedral. Some parts of Gloucester Cathedral date back to the time of William the Conqueror. The tomb of Edward II that reminded me of Marlowe's play "Edward II" is there, as well as those of many who lived in the 14th and 15th centuries. There is a statue of Edward Jenner who invented "vaccination".

On November 12th we watched De Gaulle's memorial service in Notre Dame Cathedral attended by world leaders including Mrs. Indira Gandhi. The choir was singing "O sacred Head sore wounded." Prince Charles represented Edward Heath, the British Prime Minister.

I visited the famous Coventry Cathedral with Minne my German friend and the German minister. The old Cathedral was bombed in 1940 but it stands beside the new structure that was built in 1962. The altar has a "charred cross" made from the charred beams of the old Cathedral, and also the "nail cross" made from nails taken from the beams. Behind the altar is written the words, "Father, forgive." The Cathedral also has the chapel of reconciliation. In East Germany people have decided not to build any more churches. They want to gather in some place and pray, and thus make the church alive and not be bound within four walls.

Apartheid was blazing in South Africa then, and a smuggled film on television showed the desperate condition of the Blacks. Many young white people in England showed their protest by not eating South African oranges. Miss. Elliott was dead against apartheid.

During Christmas holidays, arrangements were made for me to see Oxford and London. First I was to visit Miss. Elliott who would take me to Oxford where I would be hosted by Miss. Evelyn and Miss Rosemary Maddock. Miss. Maddock was gardener in one of the colleges in Oxford. I went with Miss. Elliott to the Reperetory Theatre to see Shakespeare's "A Midsummer Night's Dream." We also went to the little brown church in the village for communion service and then drove to Oxford. The drive through the Cotswold countryside was marvellous through hills and dales with the little stone houses and miles and miles of countryside stretched beyond. We saw "Bagley wood" and the "festal lights of Christ Church Hall " as we drove through Matthew Arnold's countryside and neared Oxford. I read "The Scholar Gypsy" again to revive Matthew Arnold's memory of Oxford and came to the Maddocks' house. Next day we visited the old Bodleian library. Huge buildings with beautiful emblems are typical of Oxford. The library preserves originals of Chaucer, Nelson,

Duke of Wellington, Queen Elizabeth I, Saxton, George V and also Shakespeare's Folios, the first English translation of the Bible, original of Shelley's "Ode to the West Wind", Jane Austen's letters, and even locks of hair that belonged to Shelley and Mary Wollstonecraft.

There is a Science Museum that keeps all the ancient watches, microscopes, kaleidoscopes, Mariner's compass and other things. We also visited the ancient but famous colleges in Oxford – like New College, St John's College, Balliol College, Christ Church and Trinity. They are huge, silent, scholarly and stately with quiet surroundings. In one of the colleges we saw the wooden gates that stood where Latimer and Ridley were martyred.

Great men like Swinburne, Cardinal Manning, Cardinal Newman, William Temple, Matthew Arnold, Lord Peele, Robert Southey, Toynbee and others walked the portals of these great institutions. When we come to the entrance of these colleges, there is only a low opening to enter the courtyard of these majestic structures. A student has to stoop to enter. For it is written there – "They that seek the goddess of Wisdom must go down on their knees."

Next day we went for the morning service to Christ Church. Alice's shop – the sheep shop – in Lewis Caroll is close by. Lewis Caroll wrote these stories for the children of a Don in Oxford. We visited Avesbury with its stones from the Neolithic period, and the view from the hills was enchanting. I then went to Lady Margaret Hall Settlement where my stay was arranged. It was a horribly dirty place and my bed was in a big hall with a little electric heater, in the cold winter. I had a row with Miss. Dunning, an old spinster who was secretary to Mrs. Chaplin. I wanted to be in London for Christmas in order to walk around with a road map and an underground railway map, to see historical places and landmarks. But the hall where I arrived was disenchanting.

Anyway I was very successful with the maps and never lost my way or made a mistake. A worker at the Hall told me to be very careful with my hand-bag. It was easy walking around at will, sightseeing. All the landmarks in London are etched in the mind of a student of English Literature. So it was with great fascination and joy that I walked around making these discoveries. First I went to the Tower of London, saw the Traitor's Gate and the Scaffold. Anne Bolyn was the first to be executed at the Scaffold followed by Mary Queen of Scots and others. The Tower is so full of bloody history. Sir Walter Raleigh, the two innocent princes Edward and Arthur, Earl of Essex are just a few of those who were imprisoned in the Tower and later executed. Anne Bolyn's House there, was presented by Henry VIII and later St. Peter's chapel became the place where the bones of all those executed were interred at the order of Queen Victoria. There is an old legend which says that when the ravens are extinct the British Empire will be destroyed. So there is a special place in the Tower where the ravens are carefully kept and looked after.

The White Tower exhibits all the ancient armour and swords of all the kings. The crown Jewels, including the Kohinoor in the crown made for Queen Mary, and that of Queen Victoria, Queen Elizabeth II, with goblets, gold plates and precious stones are kept in the Jewel House. The Tower Bridge with the drawbridge, is a magnificent site from there.

The Planetarium holds anyone's breath for it is just like looking up at the sky and studying the stars, moon, planets and the Milky Way.

Next, I went to the famous Madame Tussaud's. Here one can see a realistic presentation of the French Revolution with the fall of the Bastille. Many of those depicted there were Madame Tussaud's friends for she herself was put into the Bastille prison and only narrowly escaped execution. One can see the Chamber of Horrors, the key of the Bastille, the guillotine and models of murderers of various periods including Oswald and Adolf Eichmann.

The Great Hall shows leaders of past and present, kings of yesterday and heroes of today. Henry VIII is presented with all his wives around him. There is a tableau of the execution of Mary Queen of Scots and Napoleon's death in St. Helena.

The British Museum is a treasure-house of discovery. I bought a few picture post-cards after seeing the literary section. I shall mention just a few.

There is a letter in Latin from Elizabeth to King Edward VI written about 1550 when Elizabeth was seventeen.

We can see John Milton's, agreement for the sale of **Paradise Lost** to Samuel Symmons, printer, for five pounds, on 27th April 1667. As Milton was then totally blind, the signature was written for him and certified by the impress of his finger on the seal.

A fair copy of Thomas Gray's "Elegy written in a country churchyard" enclosed in a letter to his friend Thomas Warton, Cambridge on 18th December 1750 is kept here. The poem was not published till February 1st 1751.

There are parts of the poem **Kubla Khan** by S.T. Coleridge, with the poet's own account of its composition. This, and a good deal more was composed in a sort of reverie brought on by two grains of opium taken to check a dysentery at a Farm House in the Fall of the year 1797. When someone called him from below, he woke from the reverie and the poem remained incomplete.

Nelson's last letter written to Lady Hamilton on board the "Victory" dated October 19, 1805, is of historical importance.

Alice's adventures underground is an interesting piece. The original autograph written and illustrated by Lewis Caroll between July 1862 and February 1865 for Alice Liddal, daughter of the Dean of Christ Church, Oxford, and subsequently developed and published in 1865 under the title "Alice's Adventures in Wonderland" is exhibited here.

A letter written by John Keats the poet, to his sister Fanny at the beginning of his last illness, telling her of his proposal to go to Italy – 14th August 1820.

Also of interest is the letter from Oliver Cromwell to William Lenthall, Speaker of the House of Commons on the day of the battle of Naseby, 14th June 1645.

These are only a few examples of the mountainous materials one can see in the British Museum. From the British Museum I walked back in the rain to Trafalgar Square with Nelson's column, the fountains and hundreds of pigeons fed by tourists. Walking past Big Ben and the Houses of Parliament, I stood in front of No.10 Downing Street. It looked so simple like any other house on a street with the number that made it famous, for it is the British Prime Minister's official residence.

With wide-eyed wonder I went past the Queen's guards, the Imperial Arch, leading to the Buckingham Palace, the Cenotaph and Westminister Abbey.

Westminister Abbey is a marvellous, magnificent building with all the various chapels and the tombs of ancient kings, from Edward the

Confessor who built it and was interred here in 1066. Seventeen monarchs lie buried here including Edward I, Richard I, II, and III, Elizabeth I, Queen Anne and Mary Queen of Scots. So buried here are Cromwell, Lady Jane Seymour, the two princes and kings, queens and nobility. The Poets' Corner has tombs or Memorials of Macaulay, Southey, Robert Burns, T.S. Eliot, Stevenson, Wordsworth, Ben Jonson, Samuel Johnson, David Garrick, a statue of Shakespeare, tombs of Dickens, Campbell, Thomas Hardy and a number of others.

One cannot enter Westminister Abbey without paying respects to the tomb of the Unknown Warrior at the entrance. Hundreds of British Soldiers laid down their lives in different battle fields in Europe during the first World War. Their bodies could not possibly be brought to Britain to be buried in their homeland. So the bodies of four unknown British soldiers were brought from four battle-fields and out of the four, one unknown body was chosen to be buried with kings in Westminister Abbey. It was on November 11, 1920. There is a beautiful passage written by Sir Winston Churchill about the unknown warrior.

The British throne, a simple wooden structure on which all British monarchs are crowned, is kept in Westminister Abbey, with the Stone of Scone under the seat which came when England and Scotland were united under King James I who became heir to both England and Scotland. There is also a wooden double throne made for William and Mary because they had equal rights to the throne.

On Christmas eve I went to Jan and Ian James' home which the CMS arranged for me for Christmas. They were a lovely young couple with their mother and two children Rachel and David, Rachel being Vinitha's age and David younger. I spent a happy Christmas with them. It was there I experienced what Christmas is like in an English home. The Christmas tree was decorated and surrounded by presents from family and friends, which are opened only on Christmas morning. I received Mrs. Angus' present and also a present from the family. There was snow all around on Christmas morning and we went to see Morris Dancing outside the pub. Ian took part in the dancing.

After coming back to Lady Margaret Hall, I visited St. James' Park, Buckingham Palace and Victoria monument the next day. The National Gallery is one of the best in the world. In the afternoon I visited St. Paul's Cathedral. It stands on the site of former Saxon and Norman churches.

The latter was destroyed in the Great Fire, and the present Cathedral completed in 1710 is the work of the eminent architect Christopher Wren. It is the largest Protestant church in England and its dome is a prominent landmark. As you walk around you will see these lines written under the name of the Sculptor – "Reader, if you seek a monument, look around you".

Nelson and the Duke of Wellington, both war heroes, are buried here. The famous painting, "Light of the World" where Jesus knocks at the door of our heart, is found in St. Paul's Cathedral. The Duke of York monument, Marlborough House and Lancaster House are close by.

When I came to Hyde Park it was very foggy. In one place was the Speaker's Corner where anyone is free to stand and speak his ideas. It is a huge park with Children's playground, Elfin Oak, fountains and acres of trees and bushes. From there I walked along the famous Oxford Street teeming with people doing shopping at the Christmas sales. I went for service to a congregational church and then to the Royal Foundation of St. Catherine. One of the priests told me how he once met a priest from South India and asked, "Were you converted after you grew up or were your parents Christians?" Then he said, "My father's family was converted in the first century and my mother's, in the second." Nobody knew of how Christianity came to Kerala in the first century when Thomas the disciple of Jesus came by sea, and there was close interaction with the Christian Church in Antioch. The Royal Foundation of St. Catherine was established in the 12th century and is part of the High Church. So even now they pray for the souls of the King and Queen who lived in that century.

On 6th January I went to see the famous musical "Fiddler on the Roof", the story of Jews in 1905 in Russia. Great works of art have eternal value and are everlasting and so is the "Fiddler on the Roof." A seventy-foot Christmas tree in Trafalgar Square was also a fabulous sight.

Next day I came to visit Annu and Brian. Philip was a little boy then. Together we went to Windsor Castle and Windsor Safari Park. We drove among lions, zebras, and baboons which jumped on to the cars. There were many other animals and birds. The tricks of the Dolphins and the baby "Killer whale" jumping, singing and catching fish, were all new to me.

After returning to Birmingham on the 10th, I went to Aberdeen on the 21st. In fact after I arrived in Selly Oak, Achachen had come for a weekend and it was a happy reunion after one year. Later, after settling down in Selly Oak, I had visited Aberdeen during a short break. I was then thrilled to enter Scotland. Aberdeen is further north of Glasgow and the people are so different from the tight lipped English. Achachen's landlady, a very friendly woman asked with guttural "r" "Do all the gir.ls have cur.ly hair in India?" The Scots are simple people, very straight-forward. We went to an old-age home to visit his former landlady, who was a lovely lady: We took her some flowers, as is the custom and she was overjoyed. She presented me with a brooch and much later I discovered it was a precious stone. We went around King's College which was established in the 12th century and set in beautiful surroundings. Achachen's guide for Master's, later went to Hebrides to teach in the Primary School, saying good education should start in the primary classes.

This time I went by night-train via Edinburgh. The city is built of granite and when the sun shines it glitters. Hence sailors called it "the silver city". I returned after a week via Monrose, Dundee, Carstairs, Glasgow, Stafford and Wolverhampton. The Scottish countryside with its rivers, hills and fields look very enchanting and would be more so in spring and summer. The river Dee and Don celebrated in poetry, flow through Aberdeen.

There was a film in the college on "Four Religions" – Hinduism, Budhism, Islam and Christianity. During the discussion Bishop Sadiq said how Christ's suffering and death had appealed so much to Gandhiji. He had visited Sevagram one week after Gandhiji's assassination. There was only one picture on the wall of the little hut in which Gandhiji lived – that of Christ. And underneath was written the verse from Ephesians, "He is our Peace." This picture was removed from there and replaced five or six years later.

We celebrated Chinese New Year with Pakdee, a nice young man from Thailand and then watched Apollo 14 take off, and docking about sixty miles above the moon. Minne and I regulary went to Miss. Bottoms' room to watch the BBC serial "The six wives of Henry VIII." We always had a lovely evening with her and enjoyed a hot cup of cocoa.

Winter was very cold in Birmingham but fortunately there was central heating in the hostel. In the classroom we had a gas-heater. By the end of March, the first flowers of spring, the snow-drops, bravely peeped out of the ground. We were all happy for Mr. Cliff said it was the harbinger of spring after a long, long winter. He said the snow drops would be followed by the crocuses and then the daffodils. In spring, all the ground is literally carpeted by the flowers.

At the beginning of Easter, on 25th March I went to Aberdeen. The journey was pleasant and we cooked lots of rice and curry. I walked around the town and bought a number of things for the children. I gave Achachen twenty-five pounds out of my savings from the pocket money, for his travel back. We were able to meet many people this time and I had a longing to go to Inverness, far north in remembrance of **Macbeth**. Sometimes it was difficult to understand the broad Aberdonian accent.

On the 10th of April I came by coach to Edinburgh. There was one hour's stop at Dundee for lunch. The countryside looked glorious in the sun and one could see whole fields stretching with daffodils. Mrs. Lauden came to meet me at the coach station. Her daughter Felicity took me for a ride around Edinburgh. We saw the famous Holy Rood Palace and Abbey. The story goes that James VI saw a cross when he was alone hunting in the forest, and he built an Abbey there. The weather was supreme and Edinburgh was filled with crowds. All were enjoying summer, wearing their summer dresses. We attended Easter service in the morning and evening in Grayfriars church. The church was filled with daffodils, a very appropriate symbol of Easter and the Resurrection. The seeds that lay beneath the winter snow for months, sprout at the arrival of spring and sunshine and cover the earth with flowers. I remembered Papa for it was the first Easter after his death, and Christ's Resurrection became all the more meaningful for me on seeing the earth too resurrected with beauty after the long winter months. The Edinburgh Castle built on a steep rock can be seen from almost any spot in the city. We had lunch with a lady whose grandfather had been Professor of English in Madras in the 19th century. The Laudens were very friendly and hospitable.

Next day I came to Dunblane by coach. We passed through Linlithgow, Bannockburn, Fulkirk and Sterling. There is a castle in Linlithgow where Mary, Queen of Scots lived and Sterling has a Wallace monument. The Scots take great pride in Robert Bruce and Wallace and their own history and culture. Dunblane is a lovely place and we went to the fields to see the larks celebrated in literature. They build their tiny nests on the ground in the midst of the long grain and as you come closer they fly off from their nests so that man will not discover them and destroy them.

Together with the missionary girls working in Zambia, Malawi and Aden we visited Loch Katrina and two other Lochs (lakes). The Scottish Highlands are marvellous. There was a Tinker Scottish Highlander with his wife and their little daughter playing the bagpipes, for money. They are very rare now. The Highland cattle were grazing around. Words can never describe the beauty of the Highlands. One cannot but adore God as we adore the beauty of His creation.

The Cathedral in Dunblane dates back to the 12th century. Bonnie Prince Charlie passed this way when he was chased by the Duke of Cumberland. The Scottish Church House is opposite to the Cathedral. Yuhannon Mar Thoma came here to unveil the plaque, for the house is established by various churches and is a small step towards unity among the churches.

It was here that I accidentally met Mrs. Martin. Mr. G.C. Martin and Mrs. Martin worked for long years in Madras Christian College, Tambaram. I recalled that the piano in the college had been a present by Mr. Martin in memory of his mother. She told me about the last days of Dr. J.R. Macphail who died soon after he retired and came to live in Glasgow. Mrs. Martin died recently at the age of 95. In Scotland I met a few people who know Kerala well, because all our missionaries were from Scotland. But in England they are ignorant of such places. I remember how once Mrs. Cliff was surprised to hear that Christianity had come to Kerala in the first century. I then remembered Miranda's lines in "The Tempest" O brave new world with such people in it! and Prospero's response – "Tis new to thee!"

The next halt was Scargill. I remember that when I entered the coach in Dunblane the conductor told me that there were no coaches at that time to my destination. But he took me to Morecambe and then to Lancaster and put me on the right coach to Skipton and then Yorkshire. He was so helpful to me.

In Scargill I enjoyed the beauty of Cumberland and Westmoreland. There was a tiny church and a churchyard all filled with a host of "golden daffodils". The hills and dales stretch for miles and miles spotted with sheep-farms. Spring is the lambing season. I was surprised to find that nobody looks after the sheep-farm. They are left to graze and give birth and the shepherd comes with his dog once in a way to tend to the sheep.

Two days later we came to the Roman Catholic and Anglican Cathedrals in Liverpool. They are comparatively new and very huge. Someone had scrawled on the walls outside – "Christ was homeless as many in Britain". Two thirds of the people of Liverpool were then homeless.

I returned to Birmingham by coach via Leeds, Mansfield and Nottingham. Nottingham reminded me of Robin Hood and Sherwood forest.

It was May, and the time drew near for me to plan my travel back.

K.C. Joseph Achen wrote to me that he would provide me with an open ticket to go back to India, which meant I could visit places en route. He asked me to plan my stopovers and then write to the respective WCC offices in those countries to provide me with food and accommodation. I had a great longing to visit as many places as possible using this once in a life-time opportunity, and so I did as Achen guided me. Summer was drawing near and nights were becoming shorter day by day. Dusk came only after 9 p.m. and by 3 a.m. it was dawn.

Two of the favourite places that I wanted to visit was Tintern Abbey made famous by Wordsworth's poem, and the Lake District itself where Wordsworth lived. On 9th June, Sophie, John, Hans and myself went to the ruins of Tintern Abbey with Mr. Cliff. I had fallen in love with the poem ever since I studied it in Union Christian College, Alwaye and I knew most of it by heart. I had enjoyed teaching it too. These are lines written a few miles above Tintern Abbey on revisiting the banks of the River Wye on July 13, 1798. It begins,

"Five years have past, five summers

with the length of five long winters.

And again I hear these waters

rolling from their mountain springs.

with a soft inland murmur..."

Wordsworth continues to tell the reader what the place had meant to him during these five years of loneliness and distress and what immense wealth he owed to it. He goes on to write that these beauteous forms have not been to him "as is a landscape to a blind man's eye." He owed to them feelings that have had no trivial influence.

"On that best portion of a good man's life,

His little, nameless, unremembered acts

Of kindness and of love."

It is poetry recollected in tranquility. The Wye Valley stretches for miles and is very beautiful. It was nature's beauty that influenced the Romantic Poets.

On our way back we visited Stratford again. Many roses had come out there, it being summer.

The next day we went to Lake District with Mr. Smith. We had fine weather and first came to Windermere lake and then to Rydal water and Grasmere lake. Wordsworth's later home was Rydal water, but his home in the prime of his fruitful poetic years was Dove Cottage, a little house near Grasmere lake. It is a very small cottage with a little garden where he stayed with his sister Dorothy who was a great companion. They used to go for long walks together. The house has many relics, paintings and pictures of Wordsworth, Mary, Dorothy, Coleridge and even Matthew Arnold. Many, including Dr. Thomas Arnold, Matthew Arnold, De Quincey, Coleridge and others of the Romantic period often came to stay with Wordsworth. Manuscripts of "Sohrab and Rustom", Wordsworth's own poems, diary of Dorothy, the family Bible and Prayer book with recordings of births and baptisms in Mary's own hand, are preserved there. There are also records like the certificate announcing him as Poet Laureate, an autograph written in a book just before his death, for Susan Arnold, Matthew Arnold's daughter, Coleridge's manuscripts and numerous other relics like Mary's brooch, plates and tray.

There is a copy of the letter written by Dora's husband about how during her last days she very much adored the hymn "Just as I am without one plea" which was sent to them by the author Charlotte Elliott soon after the hymn was written. She was a friend of the family. The sculpture of a lamb on her tomb alludes to the reference in the line "lamb of God I come". Dora, Wordsworth's beloved daughter died when she was only seventeen. Hence, though Wordsworth loved the hymn, he could not bear to hear it sung or read in his presence.

The little Grasmere church is close by. We entered the church hearing the clock strike three. Eight of the yew trees in the churchyard were planted by Wordsworth. Under the shadow of one of them, beside the river is his grave with the simple inscription "William Wordsworth 1850. Mary Wordsworth 1854". The next is that of their daughter Dora and the next one that of Dorothy. West of her grave lie the two children Catherine and Thomas. Wordsworth's son William and his wife Fanny too are buried there. Wordsworth died on 23rd April 1850.

The beauty of the Lake District, the blue water, the blue hills, spotted with the sheep and cattle is indescribable. No wonder Wordsworth and the Romantics became one with nature. It was really a pilgrimage for me.

It was time for Achachen to return to India after successfully completing his Masters in Education. He first came to Birmingham and then to London to Annu's place and took the flight next day. I had bought Ladybird books and other things with my pocket money and he took back what he could while the rest of the books were sent by sea mail. I bought a two-burner electric stove which was quite light. Gas connection was unheard of in Kerala and even electric stoves were very rare. I had a great wish to bring a Philips tape recorder which was the ultimate in gadgets in those days and I bought one from Netherlands.

My travel was finalised. In the meantime I had written to the WCC offices in Athens, Cairo and Beirut and they were kind enough to find sponsors who would take care of my stay in each place. Sophie a very efficient church-leader from Papua New Guinea and our friend, had her brothers in Amsterdam. It was my lifelong wish to travel to Berlin which was then divided into East Berlin and West Berlin after the Second world war. The war had also divided Germany into two – East Germany and West Germany. East Germany and East Berlin were occupied by the Russians while West Germany and West Berlin were free. The Soviet Union also occupied other countries like Czechoslovakia, Poland, Austria, Hungary and others which were known as the East European countries under the iron grip of Soviet Union. Berlin had suffered during the years 1933-1945 under Hitler. Even when the war came to an end, the situation did not change, for East Berlin then came under the Communist Government of Soviet Union. Every day there would be reports about violence in Berlin where people tried to escape from the East to the West. There was total repression, and barbed wire walls were guarded by

Russian soldiers. East Berlin, thus notorious for its oppression and the wall, was always in the news and ever since then I longed to visit Berlin.

Sophie decided that after staying with her brothers for one week we could catch a train to Berlin, stay there for three days and then travel by train again to Rome. After spending three days in Rome our ways would part and she would fly to Papua New Guinea while I would fly to Athens, Cairo, Beirut and then Bombay.

Achachen reached India by then and he wrote a desperate letter saying Europe was very unsafe for women. It was Mama who gave him the fright. I ignored it for it was a lifetime opportunity to fulfill my dreams.

Before I left England I first came to London to be with Annu and Brian. Then on 25th June I boarded the train from Liverpool Street Station for Hook of Holland. That was goodbye to England for ever. As the boat cut across the English channel, England faded in the distance. We reached Hook of Holland in the morning. The landscape looked very flat and in marked contrast to England. We went with Cori, Sophie's sister, to one of the islands where the Dutch still wear wooden shoes and old fashioned black dress and bonnet. There were windmills everywhere.

Papua New Guinea was under Dutch rule and it was the Dutch church which converted these man-eaters, said Sophie. They were a very tough people before they became Christians. Sophie herself was a very efficient leader in her physique as well as her personality. The Indonesians as a community, get on very well with the Dutch. Next day we came to Sophie's brother's place and went for an Indonesian service in the church. Sophie's sister made a very special cake for my birthday.

Amsterdam is on the mouth of the river Amstel. Both Amsterdam and Rotterdam are ports as well as industrial cities. A round-trip on the canal and harbour was nice. When we came back from the trip our pictures were ready to be bought. We also had a glimpse of the countryside with its endless stretches of red and yellow tulips. The Dutch are famous for building dykes. I remember reading the story of a boy closing an opening on the dyke with his finger, spending the whole night doing it and saving his land. They are still building dykes to keep off the sea and use more land.

After a week we boarded the train to Berlin. We found our seats and sat comfortably. After a long time a ticket examiner came to check our tickets. He told us we were on the train going to Paris! But he told us we could get down at the next station and catch the same train to West Berlin. The train stopped only after one and a half hours when we got down and caught the right train to Berlin.

At the border between Holland and Germany, both the Dutch and German immigration authorities came to check our passport. The German landscape was a contrast to the flat Dutch landscape. From Hannover we reached Helmstedt by 4 pm. Then they changed into an old-fashioned steam engine for we were going to get into East Germany. Within ten minutes we reached the East German border and immigration officials came in. While we filled a form and gave five marks for the visa, Police with dog squads were checking our luggage. Any books or literature would be confiscated. It was a frightening experience.

When we reached Griebuitzee we were on the border again and checking of passports with soldiers and dogs began afresh. A man entered with a torch and ladder to check the toilet, wash room and other corners to make sure that no one escapes from the East. We saw very few people except a few farmers going back from work on Community farms. At last to our great relief we reached West Berlin and free air.

We stayed in a hostel close to the border. There, a lady was crying. She had come to see her son and family and she was waiting for permission. Tourists were allowed a visa for a day to visit East Berlin. We decided to go the next day.

We reached Check point Charlie by 9.30 am and waited there for visa. When our numbers were called we collected our passports and went to the train. The train passed over the border and we reached the East. Guards were everywhere. There was checking at three points and we stepped into East Berlin.

The main parts meant for tourists are well-kept with shops and big buildings. The East German soldiers stand guard at the War Memorial and they change guard every hour. The Alexander Plaza was a beautiful place but no one spoke. Many were staring at me and some tourists took my photograph. I seemed to be from another planet.

An East Berliner, may be from the Secret Police, walked with us for some time as we went around the University and the Maxim Gorgi theatre. He knew English. While crossing the road on the way to

Marienkirch he asked me, "Burma?". I said, "No, India". Then he asked something more. I understood the word "stat" which means "state". I said, "Kerala." His eyes lit up. "Kerala?" "Communist! Good! " he exclaimed.

We talked to two soldiers by way of asking the way to the museum. They touched their hats to greet. They were just boys! Good food was kept in shops open for tourists but cheap food for others. I felt pity looking at the faces of the people. They looked cheerless, and none talked to a stranger.

We returned by quarter past three. But Sophy had some extra money and so we had to go back to spend it for you cannot take money to the West. We then passed through three check-points. At one place he asked, "Do you have any German money?" I put on a straight face and said, "No..." In fact I had thirty pennies with me!

At the check-point I saw a man kissing his family profusely. They had just come from the West, perhaps for a visit. All of them were crying. A young soldier stood watching. He must have been touched too. After all, he is a human being under his uniform.

Next morning at breakfast, we had a conversation with the German minister and his wife and also the lady who was born in East Berlin and had her sons and daughter in the East. She had just come back from a visit to her children. Her face lighted up when she talked of her children and three grandchildren. Her husband had been in jail for six years in the East. So he couldn't bear to go to the East even to visit his children. Her son was a doctor who had once wanted to work in Africa as a missionary. But now they were working hard for the state and the state paid just enough for their living. Her face trembled as she spoke. The mother had come two years ago to the West when she was sixty years, for the German regime allows old people who cannot work to go into the West. The minister said that when parents died, children could not come. An old man's daughter was in the East and when he died she went to the police and said that she was leaving her husband and children behind and begged to go just for a day. But the police said, "No." Another lady wanted to see her dying mother, and the police said, "Your mother dies alone".

Even the previous day a soldier had escaped to the West. He was shot many times but he made it. Soldiers were not allowed to guard alone, for fear they would escape. Propaganda and brain-washing were their tools. Someone had written on a postcard – "There is no peace without freedom".

We went on a tour of West Berlin for ten marks. West Berlin had been re-constructed and looked huge and new. But still there were bombed buildings which had to be pulled down. We saw the ruins of a beautiful Cathedral that had been re-built. There was a big statue of Christ that had lost its arms in the bombing. So they put it up in the church with these words written underneath – "Christ has no hands except ours!"

We visited the wonderful West Berlin Zoo which kept all animals in their natural habitat. They even had a baby elephant Shanti which was a present from Pandit Jawaharlal Nehru to the children of Berlin. The Polar bears lived as if they were in the Arctic! It was an unforgettable experience.

We saw Check-Point Charlie, Brandenburg Gate and the Wall beyond. We peered into the East over the Wall, standing on a platform. There are houses in the West which are very close to the Wall but it is simply impossible for people from the East to get there, with two layers of the Wall, a death-trap and another wall next to the old one.

Sophie and I visited Plotzensee, the place where thousands were "hanged" or "guillotined" by Hitler's "People's government". A monument is there, the Plotzensee Memorial for these victims of Hitler from 1933-1945. Nineteen resistance fighters stand for the countless men and women who stood for human rights and wanted to save Germany from the evil Fuhrer and his National Socialist tyranny. The irony is that East Berlin was part of Deutschen Demokratischen Republik where there was no democracy, while West Germany was called the German Federal Republic.

Last year, when speaking to the graduates of Harvard, Angela Merkel, first woman Chancellor of Germany, said how her house stood near the Berlin Wall, and every day as a student and later when she got a job, she saw it. On the other side of the Wall was hope and freedom but she could not go there. But in December 1989, people from both sides of Germany, finally tore down the Wall with their own bare hands and sledge hammers. Thus a door was opened. Victors and the defeated reconciled and a peaceful order based on democracy and human rights took the place of oppression. Germany that was divided, became one again.

The line separating freedom and oppression is very thin though very stark, we realized, as we stood in Berlin that was divided among the

Amsterdam

British, French, Americans and Russians as spoils of the war. It should ever teach us the value of freedom and democracy that a nation should always protect with earnestness and vigilance.

On the 10th of July we boarded the train for Italy. Within half an hour we were again in East Germany. The police came to check and stamp passes. This was a different route and we were crossing the whole of East Germany. At 5.30 p.m. we came to their border again. Intense checking started with dogs and ladder. First a man came and stamped our passports. Then two others came in and lifted the boxes. One man opened my blue bag and asked me if I spoke German. I sat like an idiot. The train left and crossed the border and we came to Breba, the West German border station. There, West German immigration controls came in for checking. That went quickly through. What a contrast between a free country and one in which the State is Almighty and most powerful. It was an overnight journey and as the glimmering light of dawn broke out, I understood that we were going right across Europe with the Alps on either side. When we reached Roma I gasped in wonder. For the first time I realized that "Roma" and not "Rome" is the real name. I was happy we had the correct name in our Malayalam Bible. We went to the YWCA. where we would be lodged for "bed and breakfast".

I went in the morning to the U.A.R. Embassy for the visa to Cairo. An Italian lady very kindly took me right up to the Embassy. First they said I would get the visa only the next day, but when I told them I had to fly the next day, they gave it in five minutes. We did not speak Italian, nor did the Italians know a word of English! But we managed to find the way by saying one word that they and we could understand; for example, just the word "bus" and the number of the bus!

I have never felt as hungry in my life as I did in Rome. The breakfast was just a cup of coffee and three thin slices of plain bread. We had to dip it in the precious coffee and eat it.

The sculpture in Rome is very different from that of Greece. Roman sculpture is super-size while in Greece, everything is life-size.

The river Tiber flows across Rome. We visited the Forum where Julius Caesar was assassinated, the Colosseum, a super monument preserved as it is though partly ruined. It can be seen from anywhere in Rome. It is known for the cruel persecution of early Christians by throwing them before hungry lions, which the Roman elite considered as an entertainment. All the Basilicas are huge and of great religious significance. Of these the Basilica of St. John in Lateran is considered very holy. On one side is the Holy stairs which according to legend was the staircase in Pilate's house, which Jesus climbed on the day of His passion. It was brought to Rome by St. Helena and covered with wood in order to preserve the stones. The faithful go up the steps only on their knees, saying prayers as they climb each step.

The next day we went to St. Peter's Square, Vatican, to see the Pope. The Sistine chapel, the great work of Michael Angelo, was closed for the day. La Pieta, his famous sculpture is in St. Peter's Square. The Pope was to give a public audience the day we visited Vatican. So Sophie and I waited with the crowd in St. Peter's Square. Pope Paul VI, a very benevolent man, came to bless the people. He was carried by sixteen pall-bearers, with three in front. The Pope spoke in Italian, French, English, German and Spanish. Then the Creed was chanted, hymns in all these languages sung and prayers said. While the Pope was carried back I was standing in front and saw him close. As he passed, he looked at me, so conspicuous in my bright blue saree and he stretched out his arm with a smile and blessing. Everyone around was looking at me happily, saying I got a very special blessing from him that day.

We also visited the Catacombs or the underground church at the time of persecution and bought tiny vessels containing the earth from the Catacombs. The Pantheon which was built by Agrippa in 27 B.C. is one of the most majestic and best preserved monuments of the Roman civilisation. It was dedicated to the patron gods Mars and Venus who were considered to be the ancestors of the Caesars. A fire destroyed it, but Emperor Hadrian re-built it in 130 A.D. The artistic and cultural magnificence of Rome cannot be described in words.

In the evening, I went with Sophie to the station. Sophie was on her way to Papua New Guinea and I was to fly to Athens the next day.

I got up in the morning and walked with Frances to the station and caught an early bus to the airport. The plane took off at 11a.m. It was an Olympic Airline flight and took an hour and forty minutes to reach Athens. We flew at 580 miles an hour at 30,000ft. The first glimpse of Greece, was of the deep blue of the Aegean sea and ships and hills. Maria's

Westhill College in 1970

sister and her friend came to meet me. On our way we saw the Acropolis which stood elevated. We went home and had lunch. The mother and the girls were very nice and I felt very much at home.

In the evening I went with them and saw the Old Theatre, Parthenon and the Temple of Artemis. St. Paul must have spoken to the people of Athens from here. The city looked beautiful at night. The hill was lit and looked like a huge bowl of ice-cream. Greeks had only limited freedom at that time. The Greeks who always had great thinkers and philosophers who taught the people to think, were then restricted from reading books by foreign publishers. They were hungry for books. I sent them a few books including Tagore's "Gitanjali" but I do not know whether it reached them.

In Ian and Jan's home – Christmas in London, 1970

Leaving my very kind hosts Maria, her mother and her sister, I caught the flight to Cairo which took one hour and thirty minutes. Mufeed, Atef and two others were at the airport. They welcomed me enthusiastically. As we travelled from the airport he showed me how the river Nile divided Cairo into four parts and so whenever we went out of Cairo we would cross the Nile.

In the morning we went to visit various Cathedrals, churches, Roman fortress of Babylon and suspended church. In one church they had the bones of three saints. We visited the tomb of St. Mark. Since Coptic Church is Orthodox people pray to all the saints, and there are two altars in every church.

The Copts are the native Christians of Egypt, and the direct descendants of the ancient Egyptians. They are one of the people with the longest of recorded histories. The land has always had two names "Misr" and "Egypt", of which we find a glimpse in the Bible: "Mizraim" and "Caphtorum", the first running through the Semitic languages and the second through the European. The Coptic language is a development of the ancient Egyptian language spoken since the early days of the Pharoahs and originally written in picture form called hieroglyphics.

"Out of Egypt have I called my son" (Matthew 2:15). The Copts believe that a special blessing was conferred on Egypt when our Lord spent his early childhood in this land. It was St. Mark who established the first Christian church in Alexandria in A.D. 42. He was born in a Jewish family of Cyrene in Libya, which had migrated to Palestine a short time before the birth of Jesus. He was a nephew of Barnabas and a relative of St. Peter whose house in Jerusalem was a resting place for our Lord and His disciples. St. Mark was martyred, and to mark the passage of 1900 years of his martyrdom, arrangements were made to bring the body of the saint which rested in Italy, to bury it with the head that remained in Alexandria, in the New Coptic Cathedral.

In the evening we went to Cairo tower and had a marvellous view of Cairo. Then we went for the light and sound show at the pyramids and the Sphinx. The programme was superb. It was Heroditus the Father of History and a Greek traveller, who gave the Sphinx its name. The first pyramid was constructed 4500 years ago by Titen Khamen. The second one, that of his son was built a bit smaller.

On the 17th of July we went to the Museum and got a glimpse of the ancient Egyptian civilisation that existed in Egypt thousands of years ago when in Europe they were still in the Stone Age, living in caves and walking about naked. Most famous of all is the tomb of the boy-king Tutenkhamen. The Egyptians believed in a life after death. So when the King was buried they provided everything from grains to provisions, chariots, chairs and all royal things necessary in the next life. Three thousand years later, we are still studying the mystery of their skills.

The innermost coffin containing the mummy of Tutenkhamen is made of solid gold and weighs two hundred and forty-three pounds. It is inlaid with semi-precious stones. This coffin is laid in two other outer coffins. There are two life-size statues that face one another on either side of the entrance to the funerary chamber. They are the guardians of the tomb. The golden throne of state of the Pharoahs is made of carved wood and inlaid with silver and semi-precious stones. The mummies, or bodies that gave up life four thousand years ago are still preserved intact. One woman had her hair plaited in a hundred small plaits.

In the afternoon I took leave of my warm hosts and flew by Middle East Airways to Beirut, Lebanon – the Lebanon I gaped at in wide-eyed wonder as I flew from Bombay to Geneva. The man at the airport checked my hand-luggage that was heavy with books. He weighed it and looked as if he would charge me extra. I was really frightened and finally he heard my plea. Miss. Adele Manzi was at the airport and I stayed at the University Christian students' centre. Beirut was a rich and prosperous city then, with handsome, hard-working Lebanese people. Miss. Adele told me that before the ties with Israel weakend, we could easily go and visit Israel during a week-end. As I expressed my wish to see Israel, she said they would not allow it since I had come from Cairo! The Middle East is where the Prince of Peace Jesus Christ was born. But very sadly, it is the most turbulent place on earth.

She took me to the beautiful mountains to see the "Cedars of Lebanon". We could literally smell the sweetness of the fresh air of the mountains. She introduced me to a friend who had married an Egyptian. It was interesting that he had green eyes that showed his birth. The people of Middle East are very handsome but unfortunately they do not like the word "Peace" and go on killing one another in the name of God and religion.

On our way back we went to Sidon, sat in the rest house and ate ice-cream. We came back to the Syrian family and went out for a Lebanese dinner. There were so many dishes made with sea-food. The restaurant was jutting out into the Mediterranean Sea. It was a beauteous evening calm and free.

One thing has always ripped my heart. The Beirut I saw was very rich, peaceful and prosperous. In later years it became a cauldron of disaster and ruin all because of political feuds. Recently, what remained of the city near the sea was again destroyed by terrorists. But the Beirut from which I flew to Bombay was still rich and radiant, with dew falling on Mount Hermon!

At last I reached Bombay. I was praying throughout that the only dutiable item I had, the tape-recorder, would not be charged. When the customs officer opened my box I told him it would be helpful for my teaching. He closed my box and said in Malayalam – "I would not even have opened the box if you had not come from Beirut", a place from which gold is smuggled. Thus I happily came through the customs to Mathukuttichayan's house and caught the domestic flight to Cochin. Achachen was at the airport to meet me and very soon I was home.

CHAPTER VII

BACK IN MAVELIKARA

Anila was then with Mama and she had turned three while Vinitha was at home. When I reached Chathenkary, Anila of course did not recognize me but when Mama said, "Don't you know? It's Mummy", she immediately came into my lap. For, Mama always used to tell her about me and so she knew her mother would come one day. But Achachen had been absent for two years and she was just getting to know him. We brought her back with us. But when it was time to go to bed she wanted Mama and I tried to make her understand. But she started crying and Achachen got irritated. There was no point in being irritated because it was natural for a little child to miss her mother-substitute. She had to get used to us anew.

Gradually we settled down and both of us joined college. After studying child psychology we were convinced that the mother-tongue is the best medium of instruction for children. So we admitted Vinitha in the primary school next to the church. Bethany convent was not eager to relieve her. Mother tongue is in fact the best medium for education but we discovered to our dismay that the classes were not handled by the best of teachers and so she slowly lost all her innate and acquired smartness. The problem was not the mother-tongue but the way these schools were neglected. So the following year we got her re-admitted in Bethany Convent, Nangiarkulangara.

Appachen was always a well-known popular figure in Mavelikara. He had been a great teacher and much loved by all his pupils. The love of his pupils resonated long years after his death and I have heard each one say, "Chandy sir loved me the most!" He held various positions in church and society after retirement and was in Taluk Office governing body, and even held a post as magistrate for some time. He was church warden for years and "Upadeshi" in Kallumala St. Paul's church.

Appachen was known as "chirikkunna Chandy sir" (smiling Chandy sir) while there was another Chandy sir (A.J. Chandy) who was known as "Karayunna Chandy sir" (crying Chandy sir). Both were from Kodukulanji. That name stuck to Appachen as a hall-mark. He was always smiling and talking and making people happy except at home where Ammachy's fickle temper ruled the roost. He had to adopt skilful ways to please Ammachy. When I came for week-ends while working in Pathanamthitta, Appachen would say, "The house seems full of people when Molly comes!" When Vinitha was born and Achachen announced it was a girl, Appachen told him, "girls are better."

Every evening Appachen would dress up immaculately in a "mundu" and "Juba" and get out of the house to meet people. He would come back only after dusk. Achachen too cultivated this habit. While Ammachy did not have more than two or three friends, Appachen knew "every stick that grew on a fence and would talk to it on his way", as Ammachy would say. Sometimes when Appachen was too late she would send Mathukuttichayan and Achayan to find him. They loved it. They would find Appachen, laugh and talk with him all the way to the house, till they reached the gate. Then all would enter in total silence dreading what was coming next! Appachen wrote his diary in English with a beautiful hand-writing. His sermons too were written in it with important points. Once when we took Prashant to Dr. A.D. Verghese's hospital, he looked at him and said, " He looks just like Chandy sir. Sometimes the genes combine in such a way that the resemblance is total".

We also had Raman Pillai, called Pillachen who was an inseparable member of the house who did all odd things. He helped Ammachy with the cow and cultivated what land we had with vegetables and varieties of root tubers. Relatives and friends often came to see Appachen and Ammachy, and Ammachy would give them "chakkara kappi". She didn't like anyone coming from Kodukulanji.

Appachen stopped going out when once or twice he fell on the road. That made him weak and disabled and finally he became bed-ridden. In fact Appachen's brothers too were bed-ridden in their sun-set days and the trend ran in the family. Appachen's inheritance in Kodukulanji was just a little portion of the family plot which he gave to Kochunnoonni Uppappen who stayed in the ancestral home. All his brothers loved and respected him though they feared Ammachy's moods.

By the time we came back from England, Appachen was bed-ridden and we had Veluthakunju chovan to look after him. His daughter-in-law, Thankama, Achakutty's wife was her help in the house.

Prashant was born on Tuesday, May 9th 1972 in the Mission hospital, Tiruvalla for there was no gynaecologist in Pushpagiri. I remember the day we were discharged from the hospital. We came to Chathenkary "kadavu" by car. But we had to sit in Oommachen's tailoring shop from three o'clock for there was roaring thunder and lightning and heavy rain for hours. Finally we reached the house when the rain subsided a little. As soon as Anila saw the baby she snatched his hands with a smile.

I was in Chathenkary with Mama, Valiammachy and the children. Bathing new-born babies is supposed to be a skilful art. It was Valiammachy who bathed Prashant as well. She loved it. She told me, "You don't have to wipe the head too dry. A little water will help him resist catching colds quickly". Valiammachy had the privilege of bathing her great-grandchildren! Mama would always ask me to sit on the floor when feeding the baby at night. I was famous for my sleep and the baby could easily fall off from my hands. Mama, with her asthma, could not help at night.

After forty days we came back to Mavelikara. Appachen would sometimes sleep for days together. So one day when he was awake and sitting in a chair in the drawing room, Ammachy put the baby in his lap and said to Appachen, "See who this is." Appachen opened his eyes, looked at him and exclaimed, "Why, it is Chandy sir!" All of us laughed. Achayan (K. Thomas) who was standing near with Kochama said, "Chittappan's eyes opened when he saw his grandson!" For, Appachen usually proclaimed that he could not see anything.

Prashant was baptized in Christ Church and we had specially invited godfathers, T.V. Thomas achen, and James. Kochamma, Mrs. George Chandy, who was already here, became his godmother. Years later though we informed all three of them about his confirmation, surprisingly, no one responded.

After returning from England I paid a visit to Kamalalayam Sri.N.P. Chellappan Nair's house. My friendship with this home started since Kalyanikutty began teaching in Bishop Moore College. Her sister Indu B. Nair was editor of "Vanitha" for long years and brother C.P. Nair became

Chief Secretary. Kalyanikutty's mother (Kamalamma) whom I always affectionately called "Amma" inherited this property from her father Parameswaran Pillai Vakil. Her sister Chechyamma stayed on the opposite side of the road in "Madhom" by the side of the Achenkovil river. All were respected, prosperous families and they had great respect for Appachen who was their teacher.

Kalyanikutty's father Sri. N.P. Chellappan Nair was a great litterateur and wrote satirical plays. A good speaker and debater, he once held a high job in Government service. Writers and people of social standing were constant visitors to Kamalalayam.

Kalyanikutty and I walked together to college every day and because of that friendship I visited Kamalalayam, and Amma became like a mother and friend to me. We bought milk from Kamalalayam and Amma sometimes sent us "payasam" through Thankappan Pillai. It was from Amma I learned to make good payasam. The family was a part of our life just as it was a landmark as well as an esteemed "tharavadu" of Mavelikara. When later, Kalyanikutty was to be married, Atchen laid down this condition "undu marannavanum, kandu marannavanum" – only their alliance should be considered. What Atchen meant was, they should not be upstarts; they should not have greed for food or money.

When I went with Amma to Atchen's room where he sat in the midst of books, Atchen said, "miduki, miduki (clever), you went alone to England and have now come back and you have been able to see the older people you left behind, safe and sound". What he meant was it was all by the grace of God.

Later Kalyanikutty got married to Dr. Gopan who was an only son. Kalyanikutty stayed in Kamalalayam with her children and Prashant used to go to Kamalalayam to play with Kannan, and Ayyappan, both doctors now. But sadly, years later Amma fell sick and I was able to visit her when she was admitted in Trivandrum and Kottayam Medical Colleges. When we lost her we lost everything that represented nobility, goodness and love. Later when Gopan sold the house for money, it was greatly lamented by all who knew Kamalalayam, Atchen, Amma, Indhechi and Kalyanikutty. The landmark that was a refuge for so many is now no more and the beautiful house and surroundings full of mango trees has now become a nameless petrol pump. Thoughtlessness and greed can wipe out traditions and heritage that were valued by others.

Appachen died on September 20, 1972. He was eighty. Achachen was about to go for Gideon's meeting when I said that Appachen had not been cleaned or fed since Veluthakunju chovan was sick and in hospital. So he stayed back. He gave food to Appachen, lifted him on to a chair and cleaned the cot. Then he carried Appachen back to lie down on the cot. Immediately Appachen's breathing changed and he breathed his last. Prashant was only four months old then. The funeral was held the next day and Bishop John led the service. Ammachy continued to live next door to us.

Vinitha had studied in Thazhakara Mar Thoma Nursery school but we decided to send Anila to Infant Jesus school close by. She went there for a month. One day when I came back from college, Achachen said that he had taken her to Thazhakara Mar Thoma nursery school and admitted her there. It was for a small reason. The Infant Jesus school had asked him to pay the fees of the previous month as he walked to the Training College. Achachen was not used to such demanding behaviour in the other two schools. So the next day he walked with Anila across the paddy-fields near our home, to Thazhakara. On the way, they both fell in the mud. But Achachen bravely cleaned himself and Anila and reached Mar Thoma Nursery school with a triumphant look! Thus ended our relationship with the Infant Jesus school.

One day an Achen belonging to the Mar Thoma Church came to our house. He was the Vicar of Thazhakara Mar Thoma church and just wanted to pay a friendly visit to a CSI home where the children were studying in a Mar Thoma school. He was Rev. M.I. Alexander who later became very close to Thirumeni, and his Secretary.

The year Prashant was born, there were two all-Kerala strikes in the college for three months each – one by teachers for direct payment and the other by the managements, against it. So I had a holiday of six months to look after him. Finally when college re-opened we could not find a suitable help. So we employed Veluthakunju chovan to look after him when we were away. We adjusted his stomach to a four-hour interval diet so that Achachen could come and feed him when he came to have lunch. All this I learned from Dr. Spock's "Baby and Child Care" that I was using every day. It worked out smoothly.

While in England in Glasgow I happened to find a very interesting book in the library – "How to create a more intelligent child". Not only did

I read it, but I wrote everything down because I was so fascinated by it. It described in detail the attention you should pay a child from the moment of his or her birth. They are all very simple things, but intelligently and wisely applied, it creates a sea of difference. I did try out all this for the children as soon as I came back from England, and for Prashant from the moment of his birth. I also bought a copy of Dr. Spock's "Baby and child care" which was the Bible of parents for decades in the West. Achachen too was fascinated by child psychology which he taught in the Training College. The book much talked about in England was that of Piaget. I bought a copy but Achachen borrowed it from me and I never saw that precious book again.

I used to rock Vinitha and Anila in my lap, tell them stories and we acted out the stories on our front veranda. As a three-year old, Anila used to imitate Appachen and Veluthakunju perfectly. Nursery rhymes too were acted out. So many story books were available, and Achachen and I read out the books to them. Time was precious but Achachen and I took turns and gave our very best. I remember talking to Prashant from day one, as is instructed in child psychology for learning experience. Every day I took them to the junction to make him watch the bullock-cart and teach him words as carts and animals passed by. It was all a discovery and a joy for me, as all study should be. It was a very intelligent way of bringing up children with acquired skills and knowledge of child psychology, and we left no stone unturned.

But when our children grew up and had their own children, they went back to the age-old lazy ways when bringing up their own little ones. Only Vinitha made a real attempt with Sourabh in the beginning but she was handicapped and hardly had time or help. Child psychology and Adolescent psychology are extremely useful and interesting. If for a profession you need a basic qualification, you cannot walk into marriage and parenthood following your instinct. For bringing up children in the right way you need wisdom and knowledge. Nobody is born a wizard. So much authentic knowledge is now at our finger's ends. In our days we took pains to read and study and put things into practice. My colleague staying near us in those days, J. Alex used to say – "Teacher you never go anywhere once you get back from college". I told him – "The children come back tired from school and they sometimes sleep early. So I have to be there to give them food and make them secure". I considered it a duty rather than a sacrifice.

My blue book in which I wrote down "How to create a more intelligent child", is with Prashant. Though he did not use it, I hope some day, someone will have the common sense to make a valuable use of such research.

I have felt later on, that unless your children recognise and appreciate all the efforts and sacrifice parents have put in for their upbringing, it is no use. Sometimes parents who do not do all this are loved more than children who got much better. That makes you wonder if it was worth wasting so much time on them which you could have used for yourself!

Aleya chedathi came every day to our house with fish for Ammachy. Her sister's daughter Kunjumole came as a part-time help for me. Their mother had died, and the youngest child Saji was only two years old. All the three girls in the family, Kunjumol, Rajamma and Molly came intermittently to help us. We treated them lovingly since they did not even have a mother. Molly, a small girl then, was engaged to look after Prashant and Rajamma helped in the kitchen. When Prashant was two years old I caught chicken-pox. Though Rajamma insisted she would come, we could not put her at risk. It was a very difficult period. I didn't have many boils and I would cook the rice in the morning. Breakfast was always bread. Ammachy would bring whatever she cooked. One day Anila came back from school with a cold and slight temperature. I declared it was chicken-pox and made her sleep on my bed. In spite of all this no one else caught chicken-pox, including Ammachy, for whom it would have been very risky. It was purely God's grace. Meanwhile, Ammachy was growing weaker. She had Thankamma to help her, yet, without eating properly she became so weak that Achachen carried her in his arms and brought her to our house. With good food and care, she slowly recovered and became her same old self again. Her neck and shoulder had bent to one side because of weakness. But now she walked straight. Achayan (K. Thomas sir) exclaimed, "Oh Kochamma's bent has straightened!"

But on becoming stronger, Ammachy went back to the other house with Thankamma. A few months later she became weak again and Kunjachayan, Georgekuttichayan and Mathukuttichayan came with their families. One day Kattikulathil Kunjoochayan's wife and Roy's mother called "West Ammachy" came to visit her. I happened to enter the house when they were there. Then one of them said, "Chittamma, say who this is." They probably expected Ammachy to say something rude about a daughter-in-law. But Ammachy said, "This is Molly, my Molly. Give me a kiss." I bent and kissed her gratefully for those loving words.

Kunjachayan thought that Ammachy was dying and walked to and fro on the veranda in a tense mood. Ammachy's feet were getting cold. But when I walked in with some sweet lime juice and made her drink it, she recovered her senses. What happened was, as all of them were merrily enjoying one another's company, they happened to ignore Ammachy. Soon everyone left and life continued as before.

When finally Ammachy felt weaker and was in bed, it was time for colleges to re-open. Thankamma was helping and so was Puthenmadothil Ammai. But a full-time presence was essential. So Achachen went to Ottappalam and Achakuttichayan immediately sent Kochamma with him. I cannot describe what a great help it was. Kochamma took charge of everything and Ammachy was looked after very well though her condition was slowly deteriorating due to old-age ailments. We were getting help from Dr. A.D. Varghese but towards the end she had breathing problems and outwardly she seemed unconscious. We were alarmed. Achachen brought home the very caring Dr. A.D. Varghese. He said there was nothing to worry for though we felt distress when we saw her straining for breath, she felt nothing for she was unconscious. Slowly her kidneys collapsed. Many came to see Ammachy for the last time. Her condition was deteriorating and we all kept vigil by her side on the night of July 3rd. There was visible difference in her breathing and it was the first time I saw how the breathing seems to stop, and then starts again. The intervals become longer, and finally the breathing stops. Ammama came on the 3rd evening. Early morning on July 4th, Kochamma gave Ammachy a few drops of her beloved chakkara kappi. We had spent the whole night there and were walking to our house when Kochamma called frantically. We all stood by as she gently breathed her last. It was 6.30. a.m. on the morning of 4th July 1976, four years after Appachen's death. The funeral took place the next morning. All the family reached by then. Kochama left with Achakuttichayan and family. She was indeed a great help to us in our time of need.

I have only fond memories of Ammachy. She was older than my grandmother and had a very bad fickle temper which Appachen and all her children and daughters-in-law dreaded. In Ammachy's days, there was a lot of poverty around and the women who came to help, took the extra food that Ammachy gave, to feed their children and send them to school. But now their children have gone to the Gulf and they all live in palatial houses. Neelandan chovan was one of Kuttichovathi's husbands and was ill-treated in his house. He was here for everything. Ammachy gave him food but he had to eat it with her taunts showered upon him. There would be loud quarrels rising from houses around, houses of daily labourers. It was all because of poverty. The Ezhavas have swiftly soared in wealth with their hard work and Gulf enterprises.

I too have tasted Ammachy's temper. Things changed only when Achachen went to England. I always tried to live up to the Christian principles I learned, to be kind, caring and loving as far as is possible. Besides I loved elderly people. Both of us also prayed about these difficulties. Ever since Achachen left for England she became very close to me. Even after we returned we were staying separate but were always kind, caring and loving. Never did Ammachy ever behave in an unkind way. It is a great lesson. Even Ammama her only daughter, always said, "Amma loves Molly more than anyone else."

I have told my children that their blessings come also from the way we could look after Appachen and Ammachy. One thing has puzzled me. It was Achachen who, as the youngest, looked after his parents ever since he became employed. I thought that as a result he would not have to suffer when he advanced in years. But he had to suffer long, though undeserved as seems to us, and even today we do not know why. We submit to the eternal wisdom of God who loves us all.

When Prashant was three years old, the Bishop Moore College decided to start a lower kindergarten school meant especially for the children of the staff. Prof. George M. Cherian took the leadership and went boldly forward, deciding on a temporary building in the compound of the Women's Hostel. Anglo-Indian staff who spoke good English were appointed and the school was inaugurated in June 1975. Somehow Prashant was not very happy with the school. As months passed by and we did not know why, we were disturbed. As Ammachy too was not well those days; we did not have time to make him adjust. He would simply lie down on the floor when it was time to go to school. So we decided to send him to our Malayalam nursery school in Thazhakara where Ammini teacher, Baby teacher, and Ammini teacher's family took good care of them till we came to pick them up in the evening. He learned in the usual way until the next academic year. He started writing the alphabet only when he was four. It was spontaneous learning. Nothing was forced.

During the next academic year I took him for a test for admission to Std I in Nangiarkulangara Bethany Convent School which admitted boys till Std IV. Vinitha and Anila were already studying there and they went by the bus "Blue Star" from the bus-stop, near our house. He got admission and he did very well academically, winning a gold medal set up by a Private School Teacher's Association. But in std V we had to shift him to Bishop Hodges High School where students took the SSLC Examination and not the ICSE as in Vidyapith, Kallumala. He had very good teachers in B.H. School and Achachen worked close by.

One great factor that benefited the children in their studies was being able to join Sreedharan Pillai sir's Mathematics and English tuition classes from Std VIII. Sreedharan Pillai sir was a great "guru", a genius in Mathematics and coached only selected pupils. He also loved teaching them English. His own children were brilliant students and one of them Hariprasad was my student in Bishop Moore College. Sir and his wife were very kind to the students. He never scolded them or frightened them but taught Mathematics in such an interesting way that all who studied under him scored almost hundred percent. He used to tell his students that if a student had any doubt in an examination hall, he only had to meditate on his "guru" and the answer would come to him! He is one of the greatest teachers I have ever seen, with his knowledge, skill, love and infinite ability for communication. All who passed through his portals were blessed. Vinitha had contact with all her teachers wherever she was. Their loneliness was lessened in their old age because of her love. Years later when Sreedharan Pillai sir died, Anila and I were here and we went to pay our respects. Even after that we were in touch with his dear wife. But she too passed away a few years later.

Sister Dorothy who worked in the office of Bethany convent was another person very dear to our hearts. She died just a couple of months ago in a convent in Pathanamthitta. Till her death, Vinitha was in close touch with her. That is a great quality to emulate and I am grateful to God that we have loved our teachers always.

Vinitha passed SSLC with very good marks and we wanted to send her to Assumption College. But K.C. Mathew Achen gave me a piece of good advice. He said that the Pre-Degree or Higher Secondary stage was when even brilliant students could lose focus if they were left to themselves in a hostel. So he advised me to admit her in Bishop Moore College. She had good friends in Bishop Moore College and joined the Mathematics group with Malayalam as her second language. She used to wander all around the veranda with her tall friend Anitha, the two being such a contrast, but scored the highest marks any student had scored till then. That record was not broken for a long time to come.

This was the year when the Kerala government decided to conduct entrance examinations for admission to professional courses. Till then, admissions took place on the basis of marks. By some luck they decided not to have entrance for engineering that year. So with her high marks she got admitted to the B.Tech Electronics and Communications batch in the Regional Engineering College, Calicut (now NIT). Her friends in the Second Group who had very high marks and were sure to be admitted to the Medical College were compelled to write the entrance examination with which they were not at all familiar. Unfortunately, they missed a medical career by sheer bad luck.

Anila was very hard-working and she too had high marks in the SSLC examination. She had a great desire to do medicine and hence chose Second group with Mathematics as optional. Medical seats were few and hence Mathematics would give better options. Anila too scored very high marks in the Pre-Degree examination, in Biology as well as in Maths. She was sent to a coaching centre in Trivandrum after which she took the entrance examination. She got admission in Allahabad Agricultural College, Government Engineering College Trichur, and REC Calicut for Architectural Engineering, a new four-year-course introduced by their principal Unnikrishna Pillai who had just returned from Canada. It was a combination of Architecture and Civil. Anila benefited from it for she easily handled construction and drawing when she set up her own office. In fact she had also got a veterinary seat on merit which she declined.

Prashant was a brilliant student. He did very well in the SSLC Examination but due to faulty valuation he got less marks than average students in his class for English and two other subjects in which he excelled. It was a great disappointment. He went to Thiruvananthapuram on his own to meet the Secretary of Education K.L.N. Rao, an IAS Officer. He understood that he genuinely deserved it but sent him back encouraging him but telling him of the difficulties in setting things right. He did not get justice but it was an encouraging attempt.

When he passed SSLC, Bishop Moore College was not as disciplined as it was earlier, for various reasons. Achen himself told me it would be better to send him somewhere else. His friend Pallathu Sabu constantly urged him to go to SB College with him and get at least an application form. Prashant just did not want to go to Bishop Moore College to study with the same students again. The moment he saw SB College he fell for it and decided he would not join any other institution. But I had Achen's earlier warning in mind about hostels. Besides our close friend M.I. Itty sir told me that his uncle's son, a brilliant student ruined his career in SB where he was staying in a hostel. All this baffled us and finally we told him that he could join as a day-scholar and not as a hosteler. It was more than one hour's journey by bus to Changanacherry. He used to come back dead-tired. This went on for some time. Soon he and Nirmal decided they would go by train and come back by the shuttle train which reached Mavelikara late in the evening. That helped restore his energy. He also had tuition at Sam Mohan's, K. Kurien's and Mammen Varkey's houses for Chemistry, Physics and Mathematics, just like Vinitha and Anila.

He simply adored SB College, the teachers, students, the discipline and extra-curricular activities. The Vice-principal Madathiparambil Achen was the one in charge of the students and discipline. He was a great teacher and encouraged the students in every way. When Prashant got the highest marks in first year Pre-Degree, he told us he could be admitted in a good hostel so that he would not have to waste time on travel. But we ruled that out. Since the students had a lot of time after classes and before the arrival of the train, the college gave them permission to sit in the library and make good use of their time. The college did everything possible to advise, encourage and help the students.

Prashant also formed a music troupe with others and they got a prize for Western music.

Both Achachen and I were very vigilant about the education of our children. We wanted to give them the best possible from what we ourselves learned. We did not follow the normal pattern but took decisions after intelligent assessment. That is how we chose Bethany School for them. I remember Achayan (K. Thomas) wondering why we should send a child so far. But we refused to be like the father and son who carried the donkey! Later on, they copied everything we did, after putting forth objections when we did things differently.

Achachen and I used to read well even though we had little time. We used our thinking, knowledge and prayerful life to make the best decisions for our children. We had our own different strengths. I always tried to provide balanced diet for them which I learned very early from my school-days in Nicholson. So eggs and green gram were a common dish in their tiffin for it balanced carbohydrate and protein. Protein is essential for the development of the brain. We also bought good milk from wherever possible for Papa always insisted that we drink good milk for Calcium intake. Good fish sometimes came from Kallumala market, which I carried all the way home. We shared our burdens and never interfered in each other's work. Achachen always encouraged me to write, speak and develop my talents. In spite of having a demanding teaching career I did everything possible to help Achachen and the children. I was always vigilant and my eyes were like the eagle's, hovering over its young ones.

A child's security comes from love. There was a long stick on top of the door in the early days but it was never used. Anila, when she was small, used to walk around the house as a teacher, beating children and talking to them. We put up a temporary room for Prashant on one end of our veranda when Prashant reached high school. He used to write letters from there. Once, in the midst of his SSLC examination, an envoy from the Soviet Embassy came here to meet him in response to a letter he had written to Raisa Gorbachev, about peace. The SSLC examination had a tough schedule with two subjects every day and just a short lunch interval. The envoy came home during the lunch recess. That made him famous at that time for it was flashed in the papers. Gorbachev became famous for his two principles "glasnost" and "perestroika" which meant openness or transparency and re-building. He was the one who paved the way for the fall of the Berlin Wall later on, but it led to the fall of the U.S.S.R. also which though not his intention, gave the U.S. freedom to make totalitarian decisions later on.

A problem arose when Prashant's University examinations came. He could not go everyday from Mavelikara to write the examination. So I requested Rajan George my colleague to arrange a lodging for him. But Rajan insisted that he stay in their house. Ammachy was staying in the family home and Rajan and Leela with their two children Arun and Anand, stayed next door. I agreed but I said he would eat from outside. Again Rajan objected. It was a great help and I always regard Rajan as my brother for he cared so much for us. Leela was very generous in such things. The family is always so precious to us. Rajan and Leela looked after him with great care during his examns.

It is not enough you write a University Examination; it is also important that good teachers should value the papers. Anyway, Achachen took him to Thiruvananthapuram to admit him in one of the famous coaching centres there. But they refused, saying it was too late. So Kunjachayan who was staying at Kuravanconam then, said he could stay with them and study on his own. While he was there, the Pre-Degree results came and he secured the second rank in the Mahatma Gandhi University for Pre-Degree that year. Immediately the press interviewed him and he became famous. The tutorials who did not admit him earlier, regretted it for it would have been a great publicity for them. All of us were happy that the rank he missed for the SSLC came at the right time for the Pre-Degree.

He missed the first rank only by two marks, and that too in Physics. He was sure he had answered all questions correctly. So the college asked him to apply for re-valuation and he promptly got the full marks he deserved. So he became the first rank holder, together with the girl from Kothamangalam who was the topper.

He also got good rank in the Entrance Examination and was called for interview to REC, Calicut. Anila was in the final year then, though Vinitha had passed out. He wanted to join Computer Science which was in great demand at that time.

Achachen had some very important engagement in college and so could not go with him to Calicut. That was how for the first time I went to Calicut. As instructed by Vinitha we discussed the branch and other details with Paul sir and another teacher. They both insisted that he join Electronics and Communication which would give him a good foundation for Computer Science which could be mastered at any time. Besides, they said a seat in Electronics in Calicut would be much better than a seat in Warrangal which had very hot climate.

Prashant had a chance to get the last seat in Calicut for Electronics and Communication under Travancore-Cochin Merit. So we gladly accepted it. Anila and Achachen were surprised.

Prashant participated actively in academic and extra curricular activities while in Calicut. All three of them were able to study with very good students who came on merit and also students from other states since they had quota in every REC. So the REC was a distinguished institution which represented a slice of India. That gave them good exposure to the vivacity of India by way of language, culture, dress etc. Since RECs were under the Central Government, teacher-parents could afford the fees. Prof. Y. Venkata Ramani (YV for short), Paul Sir and other Professors who taught them are still very dear to their hearts. We visited YV recently when we went to Pondicherry.

Vinitha had more than 90% marks in her Engineering final but she was very unfortunate with regard to a job. She got a job in Uptron, in U.P. but I became so distressed about sending her to North India. Then it was a struggle. She went to Bangalore and Bombay and finally got a Central Government job in Bombay. Anila practised Architecture at Koshy's in Trivandrum. The pay was very low but what counted was the experience. She finally came to Mavelikara and started an office of her own in Mitchell Junction which was inaugurated by Thirumeni.

During Prashant's last semester, many students got good jobs through campus selection. Prashant got a job in the prestigious C-DOT started by Sam Pitroda who was invited by Rajeev Gandhi to India to create a revolution in telecommunications. But unfortunately, with some problem in the Palakkad Engineering College which also came under the Calicut University, the examinations were threatened to be postponed. That would mean loss of jobs for all the students in REC. It was a heart-breaking situation, and I, like all parents, spent hours, praying. Students met the Higher Education authorities and after an intense struggle they finally decided to conduct the examination for REC. It was a great relief for the parents and students.

Thus Prashant was able to join C-DOT. The pay was not high but it was a privilege working in C-DOT. His mentor was Sreedhar and he enjoyed his job very much. All these wonderful institutions were later killed by subsequent governments for vested interests.

When Prashant got his first salary I asked him to send some money to buy a saree for Mama. He sent me four hundred rupees and I remember buying a pink saree and taking it to Mama who was then in Thiruvananthapuram. Mama was not very well then and looked lean and weak. But when I gave her the saree saying it was from Prashant's first salary, she was so overjoyed and held it close to her heart.

CHAPTER VIII

A NEW CHAPTER IN LIFE

After I studied with Thirumeni in UC College, all of us took our separate paths in life. I went to Tambaram and Thirumeni, it seems, taught in Settlement School, Alwaye, a school run for the backward class children. When I came to teach in UC College after two years, Thirumeni had left, and after finishing B. Ed in Titus Training College, Thirumeni began teaching in Ashram School, Perumbavoor.

After parting in 1959, I knew nothing about Thirumeni's whereabouts. But in 1978 November we went for Alice's daughter Manju's baptism in St. Thomas Church, Kozhencherry. Then Achachen told me it was Oommen Koruthu who was the vicar. I was totally taken aback. After the baptism service Achachen insisted we meet him. He was wearing the old type of cassock and had long hair and bushy beard, but the smile was just the same. The reception was to be in Sabu's father Prof. K.V. Varghese's house and Thirumeni (as Achen) asked us to wait for him for he would be a little late. So we waited for him, met him and talked to him after so many years. He learned that we were staying in Mavelikara. He had been in the U.S. for many years and had completed his doctorate from Princeton. Much water had flowed under the bridge since the year we parted in Alwaye. Later I used to notice that he was a popular speaker and there were reports of his programme in different places. Very soon he was elected to be the Episcopa of the Mar Thoma Church. So I wrote a letter congratulating him, for to be the classmate of a future Bishop was a great honour. The great humility with which he wrote us a reply was embossed in his character throughout, in spite of all the heights to which he soared as a Bishop. He wrote – "Have we ever thought that such a shy and shut-in person would become useful in some way! How great is our Lord! I am a wonder to me. What a big change God can make in people! I am going to witness Him who has made me so far. I need your continued prayer and advice."

The consecration was to be on the first of May 1980, and Thirumeni sent us a letter inviting all of us to be at the service. We were elated. Achachen bought tickets for seats and both of us, Anila and Prashant went to Tiruvalla early morning. Vinitha was at home studying for her Pre-Degree Examination which was about to take place. Prashant was to be eight years old that May and Anila had just turned twelve.

I still remember the service officiated by Alexander Mar Thoma, Chrysostom Thirumeni, Thomas Thirumeni and others. Thirumeni was kneeling as Achen, in a white cassock. When he read the pledge his voice broke with emotion. His hair was cut in the shape of the cross and Alexander Mar Thoma Metropolitan announced his new name as they robed him in the cassock of a bishop and covered his head with a "masnapsa". Oommen Koruthu became Zacharias Mar Theophilus Episcopa.

After the service, people were pouring out of the "pandal" and we waited for the rush to subside. Then I happened to notice that on the left there were steps leading to the church and very few people were going that way. I was relieved and told Achachen we would take the steps. The steps led to the place where all the former bishops were buried, beginning from Theethus II. As we passed it we saw people inside the church. Then I realized that they had come there to receive Thirumeni's first "kaimuthu" (blessing). We saw Thirumeni standing inside the church and blessing all those who came to him one by one. We gladly entered and received his blessings. He said he had received the book we sent as a present and was reading it. He saw the children for the first time. He told us later that many of our classmates had come for the consecration but we were the only ones who met him in the church for the first "kaimuthu". I still believe it was God's plan for that was the beginning of our great friendship with Thirumeni.

Later he told us that he was assigned to be the Episcopa of Adoor-Mavelikara diocese. Thus we were literally in his diocese though we belonged to a different church. I can never forget the day Thirumeni first came to our house for dinner. It was on November 9, 1980. Mama and Valiammachy were with us. As we sat for the family prayer just before dinner, Achachen read from the Bible and I read the notes. We were then using the "Upper Room" and the Bible portion was psalm 133. The reading was written by Caroline S. Wilde. It was about a family re-union that took place after thirty years. But they shared a life-time of experience in a few hours and became close to one another again. "God's love for us had reached across time and brought us together again. It had truly been a re-union". A sentence that stood out in that meditation was the "Thought for the day", which read – "True friendship lasts forever". It was as if God had intervened in our lives and brought us together to nurture and cultivate a friendship that would survive all barriers of time.

We loved him, cared for him, visited him, phoned him and wrote letters to him. Thirumeni, in turn, loved us deeply, visited us, took great care of each one of us and was always concerned about us – the growing up of the children, their education, marriage, everything, wherever he was. He became part and parcel of us and we loved him more than we loved ourselves.

On many occasions Thirumeni used to have all his extended family in Chennankery, his sister's place, for re-unions. We were a part of every family get-together. That is how Appachen and Ammachy became a part of our life. Ammachy was love incarnate and always called him only by his pet name "Sunnykunju" even after he became bishop. Thirumeni's bond to his parents especially Ammachy was something deep and inseparable. Thirumeni thus taught us to love his parents, brother and sisters and their families as if we were one of them.

Ammachy's death on November 7, 1989 was a great vacuum in Thirumeni's life and we filled that vacuum with love. In later years Appachen wrote regular letters to us about his family, especially his grand father, and all the visions he had in life. He wrote to us also the history of the Venparambil family and his letters came to us as a blessing as long as he could write. We were not only gifted with Thirumeni's love but also with the love of Appachen and Ammachy, and so much love made our lives rich.

As a small boy Prashant stayed more than once with Thirumeni. Achachen and I celebrated every wedding anniversary with Thirumeni when I prepared a three-course dinner very carefully. It was an annual event and the children loved it for everything was very special that day. There were many occasions like this when Thirumeni came to be with us. Our house was small and we built conveniences for him to stay with us whenever it was possible. When every January 25th comes I feel a great sense of loss, remembering all the good times.

On Thirumeni's first visit to the parishes in Australia he was driving with Kuruvilla Mathew, Valsa and the children, when they met with a terrible accident. Thirumeni was sitting in front, on the right. Luckily, Thirumeni was able to get out of the car. Kuruvilla Mathew and Valsa were in hospital for months and Valsa's condition was very serious. The children too suffered injuries but Thirumeni had just a small cut on his leg below the knee. It was a miraculous escape because of God's great protection. We did not know about the accident until Thirumeni came home and told us about it. He informed only Rajankunju fearing that Appachen and Ammachy might learn about it. He wrote later – "God has given my life back to me like a plundered treasure." (Jeremiah 45:5).

Thirumeni gave me a unique opportunity to attend the women's session of the Haggai Institute in Singapore in 1984. It gave me a wealth of experience to be with so many leaders from other countries to be

Haggai Institute, Singapore

trained as a church leader. Miss Power taught us how to be effective speakers. She told us that the speaker should be visible to the audience and not hidden behind a rostrum. There must be a smile on the face which creates a bond with the audience. It was there I learned to use Thesaurus. A Philippino church leader who taught us told me that I must get help in the home and use my talents to read, write and speak and not to waste them in household work. The whole place was air-conditioned so that we could work long hours without getting tired. I was elected Valedictorian by secret ballot and had the privilege of delivering the short valedictory address at the Convocation dinner in the Mandarin Hotel.

After the session I went to Kuala Lumpur where Thampichayan (Dr. P.O. Thomas who held the top job of Malaysian Rubber Board) hosted me. We knew Thampichayan from the day he came as a young man from Karthigappally to Sentul. He had been our first Sunday School teacher. Thampichayan took me to meet all whom I knew when I lived with Papa and Mama in Sentul. I saw the house in which we lived, my school, the church and so many memorable places. I met Mary auntie and Zachariah uncle who were age-old friends of our family. Thampichayan was an

Haggai Institute, Singapore

extremely friendly, generous and caring person and so was Babyammama who was the daughter of Papa's friend, C.T. Varghese uncle.

I had another chance to visit Kuala Lumpur years later with Vinod, Anila and the children when they went on a guided tour of Malaysia and Singapore. Then, Joji, P.G. Thomas uncle's son, and his wife Dooney both doctors, took me out to see friends who were still alive. Zachariah Uncle was then very old and weak and staying with his son. Aunty had died earlier. In the evening Joji took us all out for a grand Chinese dinner!

When I was at Haggai it was Anila who helped manage the house. Thirumeni was very anxious about them for he was responsible for sending me to Singapore! So he wrote to them and visited them twice, bringing cake and "karimeen".

Thirumeni was ever concerned about the growing-up, education, career, weddings and family lives of all three children. We were always in his thoughts and prayers just as he was in ours. Achachen often made visits to take good things to him. Thirumeni constantly suffered from migraine and his travels along the roads of Kerala worsened it. Then I went to K. George Achen in Changanacherry, a trusted homeo doctor and told him about it. He gave me medicine to take to Thirumeni. Thirumeni used this medicine regularly. The treatment continued and God cured Thirumeni completely. Later he wrote a letter to Achen thanking him.

Thirumeni caught diabetes early. Whenever he was tense with the burden of the church and could not take rest, the sugar level increased.

Sri. E.K. Nayanar was Chief Minister of Kerala then and his "Uluva" (Fenugreek) therapy was very famous. I wrote a letter to Sharada teacher and she gave me a prompt reply about how it was dried powdered and used. She was the wife of the Chief Minister, yet with very adorable character! So I made "Uluva" powder and sent it regularly to Thirumeni through Achachen. He did use it for a long time.

When Vinitha passed B. Tech and finally got a job, we wanted her to settle down in life. But a marriage was not easy and I was very worried when people asked me about it. So Thirumeni fasted and prayed about it. In fact I worried a great deal and many told me that I must go to fasting prayer conducted by religious leaders and put my pleas there. "To go, or not to go", that became a question. One day as I was walking back from

Thirumeni's first visit home

college as usual, I was thinking only about this. Finally when I entered our lane, I came to a decision. I said, – " I shall never go to others. I shall pray myself. Surely God will hear my prayers".

But the problem did not end there. I went on praying for four long years! I would get up at midnight, sit in our drawing room, reading the Bible and praying. I spent sleepless nights. Achachen was not so worried. It was a continuing struggle between me and God. At times he would strengthen me in my faith giving me promises from His Word. One such verse was Isaiah 41: 13, 14 – "For I the Lord your God hold your right hand saying unto you, "Fear not, I will help you; fear not you worm Jacob, I will help you".

Night and day I would cling to the promise with faith. Yet nothing happened and prayers continued. Then this promise came. II Cori: 1: 9,10. "We believe now that we had this experience of coming to the end of our tether that we might learn to trust, not in ourselves, but in God who can raise the dead".

Indeed I had come to the end of my tether. It was four long years! Finally the wedding with Soman was fixed! We wanted a boy from the

Mar Thoma or C.S.I. church but this was God's choice and we gladly accepted it. Soman was working in Bombay and his house was very close to ours, in Kallimel. He was from Thekkeveedu and his father P.K. George had been a devout Christian and his grand-father P.K. Koruth had worked in mission fields together with his daughter whom the children affectionately called "Kochammachy." His mother was Lilly George. The wedding took place in Kallimel Orthodox Church on February 4, 1991. Though Thirumeni could not attend the wedding in an Orthodox church, he was very concerned like a father about everything. Before the wedding we took Soman and Vinitha to Bethel Aramana, Manganam to receive Thirumeni's blessings. We had dinner with Thirumeni and he prayed for them and blessed them. Both of them always kept a close relationship with Thirumeni.

Since I had prayed four years in desperation for Vinitha, everyone said Anila's wedding would take place without delay. But I had to pray another four years for her. Thirumeni's Appachen too was then praying for us and Appachen predicted that it would take place soon. At that time I was working as Principal of IHRDE B.Sc Computer Science and Electronics College, Polytechnic, and Technical Higher Secondary School in Puthuppally, Kottayam. Every day I would catch Venad Express from Mavelikara, reach Kottayam and from there go by bus to Puthuppally. As the train neared Kottayam it crossed Kodoor river, and in the wetlands on either side there were beautiful red water-lilies. It was a glorious sight. This reminded me of Mathew 6:25-34 "… consider the lilies of the field how they grow, they toil not, neither do they spin. And yet I say unto you, that even Solomon in all his glory was not arrayed like one of these…" I learned all the ten verses by heart and prayed them every day on reaching that spot to reassure myself of God's great providence.

Four years later Anila, got married to Vinod who happened to be a student of mine, son of C.V. George and Saramma George, Cheppanalil, Venmony. The wedding was happily solemnized by Thirumeni in Varambur Mar Thoma Church, just next to their house. It was a very small church then. The wedding took place on September 10, 1994 and Thirumeni was delighted to see Sumithra, Susan and Molly (Ranni) all of whom were our classmates in UC College. As I was then working in IHRDE, Dr. M.P. Nair, Director of IHRDE, and Deputy Director Dr. Sukulal, Principal, Model Engineering College, Thrikkakara, and others attended.

Once Thirumeni wrote to us – "I have started praying for the right partner for Prashant also. Don't you want a proper person to come to your home?" So we too started praying. Prashant was only 23 then and we prayed for him for five years together with Thirumeni. I asked Prashant too to start praying. Finally, after five years his wedding with Megha was fixed and Georgie, Megha's father who belonged to Alummootil, Puthencavu, turned out to be my student in UC College. Her mother was Eaby.

Rev. Oommen George was then Vicar of Christ Church. The day he came he made it known, especially to his women flock that he had great powers of prayer and they should all come for the Friday prayers. At first he used to organize visits to the Poojappura Central Jail and I have been there many times with his father, a benevolent person. Those trips were a blessing. I have spoken many times to the prisoners about the Lord and they would crowd around me.

T.A. George, Clement and Suresh Kumar wrote regular letters to me. Clement had a talent for drawing and sent me pictures. George later became an evangelist in his place and invited me to speak at their convention.

It was a couple of years later that this priest got the idea of building a new church here after demolishing the beautiful heritage structure built by Rev. Joseph Peet the great missionary 175 years ago. His brain became the devil's workshop and all the women and those in the committee became adoring followers. The members of the church allowed the priest to do what he liked to a heritage structure that belonged to them and their fore-fathers. Only people who have tradition do value tradition. Just a week ago, I heard Caroline Kennedy speak about her father John F. Kennedy whose birth centenary falls on May 31st 2021. She and her brother were tiny children when President Kennedy was shot dead in Texas in 1963. Yet she and her two daughters and son speak about the great heritage through Kennedy and his brothers. The grandchildren knew of him only from history yet they studied the great traditions they had inherited and they were very proud of it. It was the mother who handed over this tradition to them. That is why it is written in Exodus about the Lord saying to the Israelites that when your children and their children ask you why you celebrate this Passover, tell them how God saved his people. Tell them.

Those who do not have traditions and those who do not value traditions cannot tell anything. That is what happened in Christ Church.

Achachen, as a committee member and as a loyal member of Christ Church, was dead against it. But the surprising fact is that there were few people to openly support him. All were after the robed man who moved them from the pulpit with songs and exhortations aimed at exhibiting his spiritual powers. Finally, after a great struggle, Achachen managed to prevent him from pulling down the church. But then the vicar decided to 'renovate' the church. He pulled out the ancient wooden window shutters built by Rev. Joseph Peet to guard the church from sun and rain even during the services and placed weakly built glass windows there that can neither prevent the sun or rain, nor can provide security. The contractor was allowed to take away the windows. The front door was also taken apart and the whole church was a mess of poles and dust and dirt.

Pappachen made Achachen understand that it would be impossible to conduct the service in the midst of this construction. So they got permission from the Bishop to conduct it in St. Paul's church, Kallumala next to the Bishop Moore College. Mammen Varkey sir, who was principal then, had already set apart the auditorium for the wedding reception. Appachen had once been "Upadesi" in this church and the community was happy to have his grandson's wedding here. Rev. K.J. Chacko, a very nice priest was vicar.

Prashant came ten days early. Every morning for family prayers we used to sing my favourite hymn "Fierce raged the tempest o'er the deep". We looked up to God and God alone. Bishop Sam Mathew and Thirumeni were to conduct the wedding.

It was the midst of monsoon but the wedding day came without any rain. Everything went off well. Bishop Sam Mathew was already there. Thirumeni told us that he would be away and would reach Chengannur only that morning. I can still see Thirumeni walking towards the church from the gate. Everyone else was in the vestry. I was standing outside. It was almost time for the service. I looked around for Achachen but couldn't see him. So I quickly walked towards Thirumeni and was the first to greet him and receive his blessing. The church was full and it was the Bangalore friends who formed an instant choir in the absence of the Christ Church choir. They sang serenely and ended with a seven-fold "Amen". There were more guests than expected. But the caterer, a new but dignified young man, managed everything, and we lacked nothing.

Everyone said that the wedding and reception was grand. I remembered the wedding at Cana. In fact it was Jesus' presence that made the ordinary seem extra-ordinary. Even the monsoon rains had kept away and there was peace, stillness and sunshine around. Our hearts were filled with immense gratitude.

When Rev. Oommen George found he had to give up the church construction, he decided to build an auditorium. He announced that the names of those who contributed Rs. 25,000 and more would be written in the auditorium, but threatened that those who did not contribute would have to spend the amount in a hospital. He used the same threat years later when he collected money to buy a plot in Manganam for a new building for the Ascension Church in Kanjikuzhy.

When he finished the auditorium he put his portrait in front and walked away with a large amount of money as parting gift from church. Then he flew to the U.S. where his brother was a priest. A few years later he returned to Kerala with a doctorate procured from the U.S. market and made a huge effort to become Bishop of Madhya Kerala diocese. People alleged that all his degrees were fake and the only genuine document

With Thirumeni's Appachen and Ammachi

was that he studied in an ITI. Yet he did not give up his determination to become a bishop. He competed six times in the various dioceses of the CSI, and at the sixth attempt became bishop of Kottarakara diocese which was conveniently manipulated for his benefit by the then Moderator, Bishop Thomas K. Oommen. This is how the institutionalized church works. As Fr. O. Thomas, Principal of the Orthodox Seminary wrote – "The church's values and Christ's values are as far apart as the North Pole is from the South Pole."

Sourabh was born on 6ᵗʰ December 1991. It was Prashant and I who sat outside the labour room in Pushpagiri Hospital and received him into our arms. Vinitha had a yearning that he be baptized by Thirumeni. Thirumeni had half a mind to do it but it was not possible. When Thirumeni came to see him, she put him in Thirumeni's lap. Thirumeni not used to such an audacious act looked happy but a little shy. Sourabh was baptized in Kallimel Orthodox Church and Sam became his god-father.

Santwana was born on 30ᵗʰ March 1996, on the day Achachen retired. We went with Anila to the hospital at night, and little Sourabh who was with us willingly went to sleep in Molly's house. Bela too came with us. Santwana was born in the morning and Achachen went back in the afternoon to hand over charge to the new principal. Sourabh used to enjoy helping me bathe her. Santwana was baptized in Christ church with Vinod's father and mother and Alice as god-parents.

Sruthika was born on April 9ᵗʰ 1999, again in the Mission Hospital. It was the time of VBS and Achachen had a tough time with Santwana because there was no help in the house. Anyway after coming back we got a part-time help. Sruthika was baptized in St. Thomas Mar Thoma Church, Varambur by Thirumeni himself and I became her god-mother since she inherited my name.

The day Sourabh was four years old he came to stay with us, for Vinitha found it very difficult looking after him together with her job. Unni brought him up to Ernakulam and Achachen went to meet him at the station. He had no memory of his grandfather. Yet when Unni told him it was Appachen, Sourabh happily responded, "My mummy showed me your photograph!" With what child-like trust did he come home with him! The two and a half years we spent with him was sheer joy. He was such an affectionate, smiling and sweet-natured child.

Once he had fever and it shot up at night. He told me he saw things moving around. I didn't understand it was delirium due to high temperature. I sat and prayed while he slept gradually. By three o'clock the fever subsided and the temperature became absolutely normal. He did not have fever after that. Only later did I understand the cause. So when once Santwana showed the same symptoms while she was here during day-time, I quickly reduced the temperature, wiping her with a wet cloth.

Namith was born on August 15, 2002 in Chennai where Megha's parents were. We went to see him as a tiny baby. Later he was baptized by Thirumeni in Chetpet Mar Thoma church. Achachen proudly became his god-father and he was named Verghis. Achachen adored all his grand-children and was their greatest friend and play mate. He was proud that Namith inherited his name. All of them, born and unborn, suffered a great loss when Achachen died.

Shobhith was born on August 13, 2008, five months after Achachen left us. He never saw Achachen or heard about him but as soon as he started walking and saying a few words, he one day, brought a framed picture of both of us to me and said "Appacha", pointing to him. Shobhith looked exactly like Prashant who when born looked exactly

Thirumeni's visit home after the book release of 'Where is Thy Sting'

like Appachen. Shobhith was baptized in Christ Church by Bishop Sam Mathew and since he was baptized in the CSI church, he too had three god-parents like Santwana, Vinod, Georgie and me.

That same evening Thirumeni came to our home to join our happiness. All of us were here except Achachen. Prashant placed Shobhith in Thirumeni's lap and that moment was caught on camera by Sourabh whom Vinitha had entrusted with a camera. It is a unique picture of Thirumeni, full of happiness, his eyes glistening with joy. It portrays Thirumeni's child-like heart. Shobhith's baptism was the day my second book, "Where is thy sting?" was released. I presented Thirumeni with a copy. Thirumeni enjoys making fun of me in front of the children and he did the same thing that day. We had a very happy time, all of us together with him, full of love, laughter and joy and Sourabh has caught it all on camera. Great moments, imprinted in our hearts!

CHAPTER IX

A LIFE MUCH TREASURED

Thirumeni was a great ecumenical leader. He told us that when he was a student in New York, he regularly celebrated both the Mar Thoma and CSI Services. His view of Christ's church was very wide. When Thirumeni attended the World Council of Churches General Assembly in Canberra in 1991, he was elected first to the Central Committee and then to the Executive Committee of WCC. He wrote, "The Central Committee today elected me to the fifteen member executive committee as the representative from Asia. What a great honour it is! God's blessings are infinite! The highest post the shy lad in UC College can ever reach! All because of the prayers of Appachen and Ammachy (when she was here) and all of you. Continue to pray for me."

"During my last visit to Australia, the accident was unexpected. During this visit executive committee was unexpected. Let us praise God for everything".

Thirumeni served WCC on the Executive Committee for a period of fifteen years. The wide exposure to the world and churches all over the world, enhanced his vision, competence and horizons. He was accepted as a world leader and a friend. This helped the Mar Thoma church in the U.S. to become part of the National Council of churches in America. They needed Bishop Zacharias and so they needed his church. That is why one fellow American church leader said, "Mar Thoma church is a small church but with wonderful bishops!" Thirumeni was an ambassador for Christ wherever he was. When Thirumeni got a share of his family property in Niranom he wanted to make good use of it as an old-age home. Later he felt it should be in a place where travel was easy, and so with great sadness he sold the home in Niranom and bought a plot in Edathala close to

Alwaye and named it Santhigiri. He himself drew the plan when he was in Denmark. He was always eloquent about it for it was his great dream.

"I want to make it a meditation centre." With this intention he visited many such meditation centres including the Taize community in France. He wanted to use it also as an international and national conference centre and as a blessing to the community around. Just as when he air-conditioned his car he had to face thoughtless opposition from so-called selfish lay leaders, when Santhigiri came up as a beautiful structure he had to face great pain from leaders who were well-known to him. They told Alexander Mar Thoma Metropolitan that he was going to keep it as a family property!

The dedication of "Anugraha", the first unit of the Santhigiri project took place on Sunday 5th December 1993 and Geevarghese Mar Athnasius Thirumeni came for the dedication. Thirumeni had asked a few architects to present a plan. Anila had just finished her B.Tech. and Thirumeni asked her also to make an attempt. Finally, Thirumeni chose her plan, for he liked it very much. So Anila has the privilege of designing the first unit of Thirumeni's dream-project Santhigiri, its motto being "Peace and Harmony". All of us attended the function. Santhigiri was supported by many friends. Thirumeni had no difficulty in collecting funds for he was very honest. We too gave our mite, and when the children got jobs they too contributed generously. In fact though we never had a big salary, we always gave Thirumeni what we could, to use for his work in the church.

Thirumeni was appointed as bishop of the North American diocese and he became a pioneer there, shifting the headquarters to New York, for which he had to collect a million dollars within six months. He had a multi-faceted ability to achieve all that he planned.

Maramon Convention became an integral part of our lives ever since 1980. We never left without meeting Thirumeni. February 17 was Achachen's birthday and we were always at Maramon. Achachen regularly made a contribution to the Home for the destitute, Kumbanad and he received Thirumeni's blessings and prayers. Thirumeni valued our assessment whenever he spoke at the Maramon Convention or when he began writing the column "Yuvakkalodu" (to the youth) in 1980 in "Yuvadeepam" and later "Spandanangal" (Heart-throbs) in Sabha Tharaka under the pseudonym "Theo". We did this faithfully till his last discourse in February 2015.

Thirumeni was a great success when he became President of the Evangelistic Association and in charge of the convention. He had unique qualities of leadership and his very presence was enough to put everything in order. "Please pray that I never miss the image of Christ," he once wrote to us.

His letters were a great treasure. " I thank God for giving me you both to pray, love and care for me. I am grateful to God for all blessings I receive from you and family. Well, it is a precious gift of God to me in my present tough task. I need your prayers, care, love, advice, and corrections. I will look forward to all these things from you both, in the coming years."

"I am touched by the sincere affection and care of you all. You all make my life a blessed one giving an additional dimension to it."

Saramma kochamma and Thommen Sir of Alwaye Fellowship House had given me a small book as a wedding present. It was a book of meditation, but full of good quotations. I gave it to Thirumeni for he would have wonderful ideas for talks when he read each quotation. He then wrote to me – "Most precious gift is the little devotional book which helps me to grow in my Christian life. It has become my constant companion. Reminds me of the greater love that Christ spoke." He valued little things because he was so humble.

We bought a sandalwood chain with a sandalwood cross which Thirumeni called the Anglican cross from the prestigious government handicraft showroom in Trivandrum. They took some weeks to make it after both of us went to Trivandrum and placed the order. The cross was of fine sandal wood with a small ivory cross in the middle. He valued it very much. In fact Thirumeni wears that cross in the only official photograph taken some time in Chengannur before he left us forever.

We met Thirumeni in person for his birthday whenever possible. Thirumeni's consecration anniversary and August twenty-nine, his birthday, were very important milestones in our life. Thirumeni's birthday was celebrated as a day of Peace and Harmony in Santhigiri, he, inviting eminent speakers to the function, until it was disrupted by the Metropolitan after his sad demise.

In 2005 when Thirumeni took charge of the Chengannur – Mavelikara diocese we were again in his diocese. One day when I phoned to wish him on his birthday he told me, "Today I will be in Aarattupuzha –

Rajankunju, Leelamma, all will be there. You must come."It happened to be "Thiruvonam" that day and there were no buses. But I have never refused what Thirumeni has asked me to do. So I called Gopi who was always a great help and went by his autorickshaw to Aarattupuzha. There was Communion service and other bishops were there, for Thirumeni was going to lay the foundation-stone for Tharangam and other projects he planned there. It was another of his dreams. As someone said, "Dream is not what you see in sleep; dreams are what do not make you sleep." When Thirumeni bought that beautiful spot by the river Pamba, we all thought it was very expensive. But from there began about forty projects of the diocese for people of various needs. It was for Tharangam that he made the last hectic trip to Gulf countries beginning with Muscat, as he was venomously transferred to Kottayam. But God stood by him and gave him a gracious successor in Thomas Mar Thimotheus Thirumeni who lovingly continues fulfilling those dreams in Thirumeni's name. It was a huge project, for his dreams were always on a higher plane.

I stayed there for the ceremony after the communion service, but not for breakfast for I had promised Vinod and Anila to be there with them. Many Achens were driving back in their magnificent cars as I stood there desperately for a bus. Finally a Sabarimala Fast Passenger returning to Chengannur arrived, and I got into it. There was no bus from Chengannur and I had to catch an auto driven by a drunkard because he was the only one available.

Thirumeni survived many critical moments he had to face in life. In 2010 after an operation for prostate in Lake Shore hospital his oxygen level dropped suddenly and he had to be put on ventilator. After coming back to Santhigiri for rest he phoned me. It was a shock but he said he would see me after coming to Chengannur. It was then, while he was taking rest that he wrote his beautiful autobiography – "Oormakalude idanazhiyiloode" later translated into English as "Down Memory lane". Thirumeni never got time to use his talents for writing. He could write with such ease and beauty in both Malayalam and English but never had leisure for anything. All his ideas, speeches and written works were unique and very interesting.

In earlier days he would always take an hour's rest in the afternoon. But he was so obliging, friendly and saintly that people pestered him with little things and did not allow him any rest. They needed a bishop

With Thirumeni

for everything to exhibit their own prestige and Thirumeni in his good-heartedness, never said, "No." When Achachen became sick Thirumeni found the root cause – "Baby never says "No" to all the engagements that come his way!" It was true. Achachen used to accept one programme after another without ever saying, "No." Later Thirumeni had the same problem. That snatched him away from us. There was no one to put a break to his breakneck programmes.

I went to Maramon to listen to his speech in February 2015, not knowing that it would be the last speech he would deliver in Maramon. I met him as he crossed the bridge and came to get into the car to reach the retreat centre. He gave me a blessing and asked me to come there. But the driver Raju said that he had programmes immediately after lunch. On his birthday that year when I phoned him I said, "I feared Thirumeni would be in the midst of a communion service." Then Thirumeni said, "I do not normally take a communion service on my birthday. I like to spend my birthday quietly, away from celebrations. So I am now in Santhigiri." It was Thirumeni's 77th birthday.

The first time Thirumeni came for dinner to our house on November 9, 1980, I showed him my autograph from our final year in UC College. When Papa and Mama came from Malaya they had given me a nice autograph and it is still in good condition with notes from classmates and friends. Thirumeni has written on the last page of the autograph – "Let my Lord Jesus Christ be with you always." Sunny.

This was written in February 1959. I told him, "Thirumeni has written like a bishop even then." All the thirty five years beginning with 1980 and ending on 27th December 2015, the love, prayers and blessings we received from Thirumeni through letters and visits if mounted up, are as high as the Himalayas. Thirumeni's letters were addressed only as "My beloved Baby and Molly" while he was "Our beloved Thirumeni". They always ended with love, prayers and blessings. We live on that prayers, love and blessings still and our generations that follow can live on that which God planned for us. Though Thirumeni and I were the same age, I would not normally have studied with him. When I came back from Malaya, I was admitted to a lower class for fear I would have difficulty with Malayalam. Then for Intermediate I failed in Hindi and lost another year. Hence I became his classmate in the Botany class in 1957 only because of the loss of two years. If it was not God's plan, what was it! Someone wrote – "The moment of gratification in a person's life comes at the moment a person understands what God's purpose for his life had been".

I believe that it was God's purpose for my life that we as a family be part of Thirumeni's life all these thirty-five years for God in his Omniscience knew what the church would do to this Saint the moment his breath ceased; how he would be insulted and trampled upon. But the Almighty God, the loving Father that He is, did not let go. When the whole of the Mar Thoma Church who had adored Zacharias Thirumeni till that moment, discovered that the very name "Zacharias", would arouse the wrath of the Metropolitan and stood numb and still, God gave me the courage and determination to take the initiative to publish a book on Thirumeni with the help of Rev. Vinod Victor, Thirumeni's dear brother Rajankunju, and Prashant. If God is our strength, who should we fear? It is an immortal book because it is a collection of the immortal memories of a hundred people. I like the Sufi saying that I have quoted in my article in that book "Such a man did live." "Seek not our sepulchres here on earth; seek them in the hearts of men."

When Chrysostom Thirumeni was interviewed by Rajankunju for an article about Thirumeni for the book, Chrysostom Thirumeni said "If ever the Mar Thoma Church canonizes a saint, it will be none other than

Zacharias Thirumeni." I remember once reading about Babu Paul IAS who had a chair at home which he kept as a treasure, for Mother Teresa had sat in that chair when once she visited him. Our small home then, is a treasure in itself.

Elizabeth Kubler Ross, Austrian psychologist, has summed up life like this – "The true measure of your life lies in how much you have loved, and how much service you have rendered." The tiny glow of light from within, that perennially made Thirumeni's face radiant, proclaimed, how much he loved and how much he served.

CHAPTER X

VALLEY OF SUFFERING

Achachen's illness for five years is an episode on its own. He had retired at sixty and yet was very active with Scripture Union, the editorship of "Our Magazine", role in the church and leadership in innumerable activities. He had no time for rest and did not feel the need for it. He would not say "No" to any programme, and took up responsibility of solving a problem in the CSSM and also Christ Church. I was then editor of "Kudumba Priyavadini" (Family friend) and enjoyed the work. I was also on the committee of "Njananikshepam" (Treasury of Knowledge), the official organ of the Madhya Kerala Diocese. It was at the time of Bishop Sam Mathew, which was a golden period in the history of the Diocese. Kochamma (Kunjamma Sam) as Chief Editor of "Family friend" was a gem of a person to work with. I came to know many ladies of great repute including, Moniekochamma (Kallupalam) sister of Sr. Susy Oommen and Bishop T.B. Benjamin's wife, Gracekochamma; Gracekochamma, a great woman herself and Rajan Ittycheria CMS Press Manager and person in charge of "Treasury of Knowledge". The bond that started then remained till the end of their lives, and Rajan continues to be a rock of support. Rajan always gave me topics to write on, and these articles were published regularly in the "Treasury of Knowledge". Besides, Rajan gave me the privilege of writing the monthly meditations twice in the "Treasury of Knowledge". It was a serene and happy period of our retired life in Mavelikara when we attended the Maramon Conventions and Diocesan Conventions regularly. It was during this period that Achachen represented Scripture Union for a conference in England. It was after he landed in Thiruvananthapuram that he learned about the 9/11 disaster in New York when terrorists hijacked planes to attack the World Trade Centre in 2001.

He would sit late into the night writing the editorial of "Our Magazine" and had great stress trying to solve a problem in Scripture

Union. Besides, every morning he would go to college for IGNOU classes, enjoying every bit of his interaction with students and teachers. Lack of rest took a toll upon his body but he would not say a word about it. Disaster struck on the morning of April 12, 2003. After preparing "Puttu" and "Kadala" for breakfast, I called Achachen for family prayers. But I heard only a small sound. That was typical of him and I ignored it. But when he didn't turn up after a few minutes, I called again. I heard him respond. So I wondered where he was. I looked in the room but he was not there. The response came every time I called him. Finally I discovered him in the bed-room, lying down by the side of the bed. I called him but he was unconscious. I sprinkled some water on his face but there was no response. Then I called Kunju, our neighbour. Immediately he took him to Philip's hospital. I made two quick calls to Anila and Prashant. Anila came immediately to the hospital. The doctor discovered that it was a neuro problem and sent us in an ambulance to Century Hospital which had a neuro physician. That was the beginning of five years of disaster, turmoil and questions in our life. He had had a stroke that paralysed him for the next five years. I realized that a stroke was not like any other disease from which you could recover after a certain period. It was an endless disaster. When Achachen was discharged from hospital and we came home, a great truth dawned on me, we are all living in rented homes. When the owner of the house asks us we have to leave everything behind. He was able to come back alive to the home only because the Master allowed it. Life's uncertainty, its short-lived temporal nature, was what stood out in my mind. It was not high blood pressure that created the stroke, but high stress, stress from all the responsibilities he had taken upon himself, especially Scripture Union and Christ Church. A subjective outlook had made him overstressed.

For me, the sky had fallen down. I said to myself – "All my life I learned to trust God and tried to do His will alone. Why did this happen to us? "It was as if God had suddenly left us helpless on life's way. The confusion, the chaos, the mental distress can only be imagined. We went to stay with Prashant in Bangalore for it was impossible to manage things without support. I remember we couldn't even pray. It was Sushma and Georgie who came to lead the family prayers every evening.

I thought to myself – "Perhaps I should pray, clinging on to God's promises." One day I thought of this promise – "Put all your cares on Him for He careth for you!" I said to God desperately, "I put all my cares on you; if you do care for us, let us see it!" Still, nothing happened. One day as I was sitting bleak in the drawing room, this verse suddenly flashed into my mind – "My God, my God, why hast Thou forsaken me?" It was Christ's words from the Cross. Suddenly it dawned on me that when Christ was on the Cross, at least for one moment, He experienced a total eclipse in His relationship with the Father. That was the moment He cried out, "My God, my God, why hast Thou forsaken me?" Then I said to myself, "I am experiencing the same thing. I have lost total contact with God. And just because Jesus suffered the same on the Cross for me, I was able to establish a small relationship with Christ. That was how I gradually came back to God.

K.C. Abraham Achen and Kochamma, a medical doctor herself, stayed just next door to our flat. Whenever we were with Prashant they were a great help. K.C. Abraham Achen would sometimes conduct a short Communion Service. Kochamma could guess our needs before we even thought about it and was always present with food, acupuncture and all means of human care. That love envelopes us even today wherever we are. We took Achachen to Vellore for treatment. But just before that I had a fall as I was standing with my lunch at the door of the kitchen. I fell on to the floor outside and broke two of my toes. That was another disaster. The leg was plastered, and together with the stroke patient I sat in a corner of the drawing room with my leg elevated on a low table. I remember my dear friends Chechamma Kochamma, Leela Kochamma, Ammootty Kochamma, sisters in Bethel Ashram, coming to visit us then. I looked calm and just responded, "It may be God's will." I could say nothing else. I still remember their loving faces, now gone beyond the veil, trying to comfort me. I cannot describe what they were to us through all these years of suffering. They phoned me, comforted me, prayed for us, and the whole community of Bethel prayed for Achachen's full recovery, every morning, and evening. I was unable to attend Bethel Day, Associates' Retreat or anything. But later on, in the midst of all this, Chechamma Kochamma said, "We'll invite Molly to give us the main talk on "Human relationships" for the retreat". I could not refuse for they had decided on it, out of great love. I still remember having someone to care for Achachen, and going to Bethel. I made a very simple speech. Chechamma Kochamma turned to me – "As it is, you are a good speaker, Molly. But when this came out of your present experiences it was so tremendously appealing". Kunjamma Sam Kochama's sister told me later – "Everyone was saying that they had never heard a talk like that." I wondered what had happened. I had spoken in simple words. But the experience that came out of suffering was deep enough to touch their hearts. That was how the Holy Spirit helped glorify the Lord's name that day.

Thirumeni was always concerned about us. When Thirumeni came once he tried to comfort me saying, "Don't you remember the famous picture "God's Footsteps" where God comforts us by carrying us?" But I was defiant. I said, "If it is so, why don't I at least feel His arms around me?" I could say that to Thirumeni honestly, for he would understand my plight. Thirumeni was constantly in touch with us, visiting, caring, advising, and sharing our suffering. When we went to Anchel, to George Vaidyan's village for treatment, through Prashant's friends Kurien Thomas Achen and Kochamma's advice we stayed in a little village, surrounded by very poor Muslim families, where all of them kept goats. It was a remote place near Anchel. Yet one day Thirumeni came there all the way. I can still see him walking down to the unfinished building where we stayed in a wretched condition. It was all because of the "greater love he had for us". Immediately after that Thirumeni phoned Billy in Australia and said, "You must tell Molly to return to Mavelikara. More treatment in that place is not going to help". Thirumeni knew enough was enough. But there was no one to help me take a decision and I had gone on, just hoping. It was Vinod Victor who reached us with whatever we needed there. In fact when we came to Anchel we stayed with them overnight in Trivandrum before proceeding, to Anchel. The meals in Anchel were just "Kanji" and dried fish (unakka meen). I had become so lean that later we would say, "If you want to reduce weight, just follow the menu in Anchel!"

Mariamma, Sunny's wife would constantly call me from Saba, Borneo, where Sunny was surgeon. There was only George Vaidyan's land phone. I had to reach there by the time she called again. I always think of it as such a caring gesture that reveals the way she was brought up by Saramma Kochamma (Mrs. B. F. Varghese), her mother, who was Bishop Benjamin's sister.

Before coming to Anchel when once we were in Bangalore, all of us together went to Bombay to stay with Vinitha. Achachen and I stayed there with the girl we had as helper and Vinitha gave up her job to look after him. She took up the whole responsibility and made me totally free. The Tata Flat in Powai had enough open space with a garden. It was there I happened to read Philip Yancey's book, "Where is God when it hurts?"

My life had ended the day Achachen suffered a stroke and I had written in a diary later on – "I have only a past: I do not have a future. There is nothing to live for, nothing to hope for, nothing to strive for." I hadn't read anything till then. But this book made me realize I still had the ability to read and understand. It was a turning point. Philip Yancey relates so many instances of innocent people, young people, suffering undeserved disasters. It was so comforting to read, and think with Philip Yancey. In all this innocent suffering God was nowhere there. And we do not find any answer to the question "Where is God when it hurts?" till we reach the very end of the book. We do not find God even there. But at the end of the book Philip Yancey gives the answer, again as a question – "Where is the Church when it hurts"?

The Church is the Body of Christ and is the presence of Christ on this earth. Christ can act only through His body. Christ has no hands, legs and body except that of the church. And where is the presence of the church where people suffer? That is the church's failure, says Philip Yancey.

Philip Yancey relates another of his experiences. He had a friend who had to pass through difficult times because of many problems, including a divorce. On top of it, he suffered a mental breakdown and had to be confined to a home. Every week Philip Yancey visited him and just sat with him, without speaking. It went on for months. Finally the young man recovered. The first thing he said when he saw Philip Yancey was – "You are God, you are God".

Yancey said, "I am not God. But it is God who has healed you". The young man replied, "When I was in total distress I saw only you. You were here by me every week. And if that was God's presence, I saw it in you".

Philip Yancey's eyes welled with tears. The church does not often act like Philip Yancey. When Achachen fell ill, our church's women leaders said, "Why did this happen to such a good man?" They came to the conclusion, "It is not his fault. It is due to the fault of his wife".

Before we criticize a drowning person, it would be more proper to throw at least a straw to him so that he can clutch at it and not sink.

After Thirumeni came to Anchel I too felt we must go home. So I phoned Prashant. When we were in Anchel, Achachen would make loud noises the whole night. He would not sleep. The noise disturbed the quiet of the village. I was afraid what people would say to all this noise when we reached Praikara. But to our surprise, Achachen never made a sound once we reached home. The noise was perhaps his way of communicating that he wanted to go home.

Rev. Jacob Daniel was the vicar of Christ Church at that time. He knew Achachen but not me. He said to me, "Teacher, we must have a communion service every month, in the house". That was a good suggestion. I made the room ready, dressed Achachen, invited close friends and immediate neighbours. I was particular that as refreshments they should be given only good things. This continued and I used to buy good things from "Anne's". I also made cake. That was how I learned to make good cakes quickly. That communion service was of very great value. In fact we had communion service on February 17, 2008 on Achachen's 72nd birthday, a month before he died. Though Achachen was not physically healed, the communion service brought great healing to our home. The presence of these friends too, was a great help. Whenever I needed help to transfer Achachen to bed in the evening,. I would call Babu. Babu himself had gone through suffering through Bessy's loss, Bessy being my student, colleague and a close friend. On February 17th Ninumol, Kunju and Alexkutty came here unexpectedly. I have never forgotten that it was Kunju and Alex who helped me transfer him to the bed that evening. Slowly, I learned to live with our suffering. Every Sunday I would hear the sound of cars and scooters leave for church. Here, I was in the house as care-giver, facing constant problems. At that time, some unusual thoughts would come to my mind. I could not remember it after a few minutes. So I started writing them down. Later I collected some of these thoughts and sent it to, "Health Guild" of which we were members, to be published in the magazine. It was titled, "From a Senior Citizen's Diary" (thoughts of a senior citizen, while looking after a sick husband). It was received with great appreciation. Each thought, though very simple, was enough to make the reader think and put it into action when the moment came.

One day I felt I should find out the great prayers in the Old Testament and write down a meditation on each of these prayers. So whenever I got time, I found out the prayers myself. The Interpreter's Bible, other commentaries, dictionary, everything was spread permanently on the dining table. I wrote the meditations whenever I got time. When I started writing this, my life became purposeful, and as a result, looking after Achachen was no longer a burden. My mind was wholly focussed on the meditations. I enjoyed writing it. Vinod Achen gave me a lot of encouragement. After finishing the work, the Bible passages, the meditations and my thoughts written in a Senior Citizen's Diary, all together was made into a CD which my friend Rajan, manager of the C.M.S. Press, took pains to do. I had to go only once to Kottayam to finalise it. It was Thirumeni who wrote the foreword and Vinod Achen got it printed by ISPCK. He gave it the title, "Neerum Velakalil". The book was released in November, 2007 in the chapel of the Women's Hostel of Bishop Moore College. Potha P. Kochamma and Ammini were a great help to me as usual. They made all the arrangements. Kochamma welcomed the gathering. The main talk by Thirumeni was on, "Understanding God through suffering". Bishop Sam Mathew released the book and gave a copy to Thirumeni, and Thirumeni gave a copy to Leelakochamma, Sister Rachel John. There was a choice audience of very close friends, relatives, colleagues, sisters from Bethel, and a few people from the church. Achachen was sitting right in front. He listened to everything and understood everything. After the meeting, a friend said to me – The meeting was more appealing than a whole week's Maramon Convention!" So the book was a positive outcome of our suffering.

Even today, people beyond church divisions tell me – "Whenever I face difficulties, I read some portion from the book." It is still a great help to people who undergo pain. I thank God that the Lord used my suffering to console others who are in pain.

In those days the Shalom channel on TV had very encouraging sermons by really eminent priests. Achachen would be in the drawing room and I would switch on these programmes. Though he could not speak except by sign language by lifting his hand, he had good memory and could understand everything. The stroke had made him very emotional and the only means of expressing his feelings, was crying. We had no visitors at all because word went round that we did not allow anyone to see him. Everyone knew what was happening here though we did not know what was happening around us. That is the way of the world.

Yet I cannot forget Susie kochamma and Ammini kochama wives of two respected priests, who prayed incessantly for Achachen's recovery. It was their habit to call me every week, talk to me for at least forty-five minutes, encouraging me, supporting me and loving me. This is a great example that others can emulate.

God said, "Fear not", and it is written 366 times in the Bible one for each day of the year. Gradually the Lord wiped off fear from my heart, as from a slate, and when people asked me what I would do if an emergency occurred at night, I was not afraid. At that time I had only a part-time servant, Sujatha. She was of great help to me in every way and looked after him very well. There is no great teacher like suffering, I must say.

Achachen died on March 15, 2008. On Monday, he vomited in the evening and I quickly phoned the doctor and gave him medicine. But his weakness increased. On Wednesday I called our friend Dr. Bela and she came in the evening with Mammen Varkey sir. She herself gave him medicine and she felt there was nothing alarming. They left only by 10 o'clock. On Thursday morning, soon after Sujatha came he suddenly became worse. Desperately I called Jeby, Potha P Kochamma's son whom I had called the previous day to bring Dr. Bela. So I had his phone number on the table. He came with a friend and we took him quickly to V.S.M. Hospital. Achachen's head was on my lap. The hospital was efficient then, and he was admitted to the Cardiac ICU which was empty as that department was closed, and we were given a room next to it.

Vinitha was then in Switzerland and she regularly phoned to speak to Achachen, and I had to sit there putting the receiver into Achachen's ear. Vinitha called home immediately after we left for the hospital and Sujatha informed her what had happened. She quickly informed Anila who was in Doha, and Anila arrived the next day. There was great help in the hospital from teachers and friends. Thirumeni came on Friday evening and went to the ICU and prayed. Thirumeni told me – "Baby recognized me, for he made the familiar sound he makes whenever I speak to him." A little later Sam Mathew Thirumeni, Kochamma and Christy arrived. It was the 14th of March. Meanwhile, Prashant had an important meeting in the office with foreign officials of the company. He phoned me in the evening when it was over. I said, "If you want to see Achachen alive, you must come immediately. Tomorrow is the day just before Hosanna Sunday."

For, five years ago it was on the Saturday just before Hosanna that he fell ill. So I sensed that he would be gone the next day, again the Saturday just before Hosanna Sunday. Who else except God, can make such perfect calculations!

Prashant came at midnight. Monie, our dear car-owner was of immense help. He went to the airport and brought each one of them. Visitors were pouring in. Prashant and I went to the ICU at midnight and saw Achachen. He looked very peaceful but his oxygen level was going down.

Vinitha in the meantime, had come to Bombay and was to reach by noon. We went to the ICU again in the morning. He was the only patient in the ICU. I held Achachen's hand and said the same prayer I had prayed holding Mama's hand just before she died.

"Lord support him all the days of this troublous life, until the shades lengthen, the busy world is hushed, the evening comes, the fever of life is over, and his work done. Then Lord in Thy mercy, grant him safe lodging, a holy rest, and peace at the last."

As I stood looking out of the balcony of our room, I said to myself, "Now Jesus Christ and His angels must be coming to take Achachen home." Suddenly I felt a great feeling of joy surge into my heart.

By 12 o'clock, as we were standing at the door, they quickly called us from the ICU. Achachen was sinking. As we stood by him, he took his last breath. Then Anila noticed that Achachen looked as if he was smiling! It was true. He had never been able to smile ever since he had this stroke. The muscles did not work. But just now he had a smile on his face. He must have seen someone whom he knew and loved as his soul departed to heaven.

He had fallen ill at the age of 67, and died just after celebrating his 72nd birthday. Vinitha, Soman and Sourabh came immediately after he died.

The funeral took place on the 17th. Achachen's body was brought home on the 16th evening. Throughout the night we kept vigil. Early morning people started coming in, for by 10 o' clock the service at home would begin. Biju brought Namith from Bangalore.

At first the body was kept in Peet Memorial Training college where he had been lecturer from 1960 and Principal from 1986-1996. He was given a warm farewell there. Thirumeni and Sam Mathew Thirumeni led the service in the church. Many people spoke, including Thirumeni and Sam Mathew Thirumeni. Just as Thirumeni visited our house when Achachen was sick, Sam Mathew Thirumeni too would create occasions to visit us. So both of them knew how well he was looked after.

Though it rained heavily in other places, there was just a quick shower when we were in the cemetery, which stopped within three minutes. It was

Bethel Sisters - Sister Susie Oommen, Sister Chechamma George, Sister Rachel John

as if Nature herself was shedding tears to honour such a well-lived life. It was indeed a grand farewell.

After everything was over, Bavakutty and Annie, my friends told me that from the Monday he fell ill, till the Monday when the funeral took place, everything went off perfectly as if planned by an architect! The emergency to take him to hospital happened only after Sujatha came. It was God who informed the children. True, I was alone and didn't even own a cell phone. But God took care of everything. He who made me fearless and taught me to trust Him, was by our side.

After Achachen's death, the children had to go away after a week and I was alone here till June. I was desperate. Vinod suggested that I write some of my experiences in poetic form and I did write a few poems that were published in November 2008.

It was the year Achachen died that I became seventy. In June Prashant's new flat in Petra Radiance, near Cox Town was completed. It was Sahanam Achen, their vicar who conducted the house-warming.

For the grandchildren, Achachen's illness and death was an irreplaceable loss, for he was a person who adored children and played with them like a child. Every person who leaves our life creates a great void, some, leaving a chasm.

CHAPTER XI

ENGRAVED MEMORIES

Valiammachy still lives in my heart and her memories are so alive in me. During the war, Mama was in India with us two little children. A daughter who is married, always gets support from her parents who know the difficulties she has to face in her in-law's house. So very often we stayed in Thalavady with Valiappachen and Valiammachy. Thankammama and Ammini Ammama were not yet married and Kunjoochayan was also there to love us. Once when I was very small, I started crying and would not stop. I would not tell anyone why I cried. Finally, Achen Uncle came and asked me and I said with great hesitation, "Will I go to heaven or hell?" He said, "Mol, you will go only to heaven. Don't cry." Thus I found my peace.

After Mama left us in Nicholson and went back to Malaya, our only refuge was Chathenkary and Thalavady. We loved Thalavady more for Valiyappachen and Valiyammachy were there and they were our security. Except for Achen Uncle who was away, all were at home.

Valiammachy would give us only nutritious things to eat. She did not like to spend much time in the kitchen but she used to cook tasty dishes. Her "meen pattichathu", "pavakka thoran", "chicken curry" etc are without rival. We always had a cow in the house which supplied milk. The cows and calves had names. One was "Karambi pashu" and another was "Kombi pashu". I have heard that when the great journalist T.J.S. George married Amminikochamma, she had to be re-named Ammu in her husband's home, for their cow's pet name was "Ammini". After the milk was boiled, Valiammachy would beat eggs and then pour the hot milk into this, stirring continuously so as not to curdle, and then add sugar. It was very delicious and everyone at home drank it and relished it. We would eat eggs and drink milk everyday.

Valiammachy was very scientific in her thinking. She entertained no superstitions or false beliefs. She loved to read, and read every magazine that came her way. There were only Christian magazines then. All of us enjoyed "Pazhanganji" with curds and "meenpattichathu". Sometimes Kunjoochayan would come back from the paddy-fields and he would start losing his temper. Then Valiammachy knew what was wrong and with a smile she would call him and say, "Kunjoonje, you come and drink some "pazhanganji." He would immediately become calm. All her children loved her and the very word "Ammachy" that came affectionately from their mouths proclaimed how much they loved her.

Valiammachy was a great gift of God to the family. Since she was born in "Kuzhiyathu", in the house of Abraham Malpan, she had that heredity and earned respect. Besides she looked elegant and stately and always had a smile on her face. She was greatly loved and respected wherever she was. Once Panampunnayil Thomas Thirumeni who called her "pengal" (sister) saw me at Karippuzha. Uncle introduced me to Thirumeni. Then Thomas Thirumeni said, "Do you know, where her grandmother is from? She is from "Kuzhiyathu". The word "Kuzhiyathu" brought to Thomas Thirumeni's mind Abraham Malpan, his two sons who were Bishops and all history connected with the church. Thomas Thirumeni too was in many ways related to this family.

Valiammachy had a deep attachment to Avarachayan, her brother, when his wife died young, leaving the children behind. Valiammachy and Sarammakochamma stayed in Ampatt for some time. Whenever they got ready to go back to their own homes, the sorrow on the face of Avarachayan often made them change their clothes again and drop their plans. Valiyammachy was a very caring lady. She cared for whoever had a little difficulty or weakness. Avarachayan's children always regarded her with great affection. She had great concern about her brothers and sisters and their children and often would sit alone telling us about them as if in a soliloquy. That was how I had this great interest in Valiammachy's family members.

Nobody had asthma in Mama's family but Mama suffered a lot from asthma, mainly because of her anxiety about Papa who had early heart problems. It was Valiammachy who helped Mama in every way possible. She had great sympathy for Mama and stayed with Mama whenever she needed her. Valiammachy enjoyed good health till the end of her life. She was only worried about her eye-sight for she had glaucoma which was hereditary in Palakkunnathu family. Her father had been blind for ten years and suffered a lot.

Because I loved Valiammachy very much I had a fervent desire to bring Valiammachy here to stay with us. I had to plead with Achen uncle because he thought it would be a blot on the sons' prestige. Anyway, we were lucky to bring Valiammachy to stay with us twice, three weeks at a time. I was working, but it was such a joy to have her here. Mama too was with us. I would make good coffee and take it to her early morning and she relished it as she drank it. It was Achachen who brought her and even took her to Manganam once when Mama was with Alice. Valiammachy loved Achachen because he was so gentle, loving and caring about her.

During the Maramon Convention, Valiammachy and Saramma kochamma would plan ahead and stay in Ambatt the whole week. Everyone remembers that they would be talking throughout the night for they had a great deal to say and a great bond to one another. Whenever Avarachayan sent Thomaskuttichayan, Valiammachy would go and help him by staying with him. Valiammachy was the last person to die in her family, exactly two weeks after Avarachayan's death in October 1987. We asked Valiammachy if she would like to go to Maramon and see Avarachayan. But she was so upset she said she did not want to go. I went for the funeral, and Amminimama was there. She told me to buy some lime and take it to Valiammachy. The next day was Sunday.

I bought some lime and went to Thalavady. Valiammachy was lying down and seemed perturbed. So I sat by her and sang the songs she loved, like "nin sannidhi mathi ha eshuve", "ente deivam mahathwathil", and also read strengthening passages from the Bible. I remembered what I had read two days back and told Valiammachy, "Valiyammachy, tell God – Lord I am not strong enough to hold your hand. So please hold my hand". Immediately Valiammachy repeated – "Lord please hold my hand; please hold my hand". After that her face changed. All worries disappeared, and there was light on her face.

Then she said, "Here nobody reads the Bible, sings or prays". Immediately Kunjoochayan came in and said, "Ammachy, I will hereafter do it in this room. Don't worry".

I came away in the evening. Valiammachy's condition was slowly deteriorating. She sat by the table for food, and could go to the toilet by herself but she was slowly getting weak. By that time, Mama, Thankamama and Amminimama came. They all stayed with her. Valiammachy had strictly instructed Amminimama that she should always be there if ever she needed her. I went to see Valiammachy again twice. I asked, "Valiammachy, when should I come again?" She just said, "just as is convenient."

By that time close relatives were coming to see Valiammachy. Some people came on Thursday and in the evening, Valiammachy said, "Don't call me again if anyone comes". For visitors would always go to the dying person and ask, "Do you know me?" It was just a habit.

Valiammachy didn't want to be disturbed. After saying this, she turned over to sleep. On Friday, she was talking in her sleep. She said, "Avaracha, Saramme, come here. Please hold my hand," as if she were going somewhere with them. On Saturday morning I was quite upset about Valiammachy though I had visited her on Wednesday. I got into the bathroom and cried a lot. Then Leelamma's son came here from Thalavady. I asked him about Valiammachy. From him I learned she was getting worse. I set out at once for Thalavady. When I got into the bus going from Neeratupuram to Arthissery, I heard someone say, "Kandathil Achen's mother has died".

That is how I heard of her death. I reached the house within minutes and Amminimama was bathing the body. She was surprised how I got the news so soon. It was God who sent me then. Both Achen uncle and Kunjoochayan were not home at that time. Valiammachy never exhibited her religious strength to anyone. But she always walked with God. It was a strong but silent relationship. It is really a blessing if one can die like that – just walking over to the other shore with her beloved siblings.

Valiammachy died on November 7, 1987. The funeral was to take place the next day. We had to beg Achen uncle to have a photographer to take pictures of the funeral. He was adamant but at last he agreed. He disliked it only because he thought it was against Christian practices. We did not have any picture of Valiappachen. And we did not want that to happen in the case of Valiammachy.

Everyone came, especially all the family from Maramon. Valiammachy wanted to be buried in the Evangelical church, for then only, Achen uncle would be able to participate. She saw it beforehand and used to attend the

Valyammachi

evangelical church though Valiappachen was buried in the Mar Thoma church close by, and she herself grew up in the Mar Thoma church. Valiammachy was a very sensible person and never gave trouble to her children.

We gave a loving farewell to our precious Valiammachy, who stood tall in every way, among the women of her time. Once Namith asked me, "Ammachy, who do you regard as your ideal except Jesus Christ?" "My grandmother; and my teachers," was my reply. This is the immortal place Valiammachy has in my heart. For I love her, admire her and adore her. She gave me unconditional love and made me secure. She was my shelter. So the absence of my parents in my childhood and teenage did not affect me at all.

Mama spent her last years with us. Mama often stayed with us whenever she wanted and Leelama and family would stay here then. All of them came quite often. But wherever Mama was, I went to see her and stayed with her for I could not live without it. Most of the time she would be with James in Vellore. Once James phoned me saying that the college had allowed him sabbatical leave for two years to go to Australia, but he did not know where he could leave Mama. I said to him, "You bring her here." So just before he left for Australia in 1994, he brought Mama. She seemed to be in a very weak state for he said she was so worried about them leaving that she would not even eat properly. When he left the next morning Mama did not seem to recognize him.

Gradually Mama improved. She would walk around the house and close the windows in the evening with the stick in her hand. Sourabh was here as a little one and enjoyed frightening Mama with small tricks and Mama did not find that amusing.

In the meantime it was time for Santhwana's birth and we had to repair our bathroom also. So Leelama had to look after her for just a few days. Yet Mama was in a hurry to come back and I went to Thuruthicadu. Mama was very happy to see me.

James, Bharathy and the children came back from Australia in January 1997. They came to see Mama on February 12th which was her 81st birthday. Mama was eager to go back but unfortunately their house was not yet allotted. Mama preferred a single house where she could walk around in the courtyard. She did not want to live in a flat.

Four generations

So the allotment took time and Mama was a bit anxious, for Vellore was a secure place for her with the hospital. Maybe, because of this anxiety, she slowly grew a little weak. Sometimes she would call me at night as she came out to go to the toilet. She could still look after herself but found it difficult to drape a saree and take out the correct medicines in the morning. Yet she would not allow me to do it.

When Mama called me at night my sleep would be disturbed and I would fall asleep early morning. But by that time I would get calls from James and Leelamma, for STD charges were less before 6 o' clock.

At last James informed me that he would come on June 10th and take Mama by an ambulance on June 11th. That was Papa's 27th death anniversary. A servant was arranged through an agency and they departed on 11th morning. By the time they reached Trissur, Thankamama's place, her health had declined and she suffered incontinence. It worsened further by the time they reached Vellore. I phoned often and was really upset about Mama. So I booked my tickets for July and asked Leelamma if she was coming. She came with me and we reached Vellore. We stayed with Mama for a couple of days and returned.

But everyday Mama's condition was slowly deteriorating. As Bharathi and James were very busy in the hospital, Mama was totally in the hands of the helper. Alice visited her during Onam but Mama did not recognize her. Mama said, "I know I have children, but I do not know who they are." Mama had not seen her for a long time.

I continued to be anxious about Mama. James said, once she fell from the cot and so was now sleeping on the floor. At that time Leelamma phoned to say that she and Alice had booked tickets to go to Vellore on 22nd October. I said I was not coming. Sourabh was having fever and there was no help in the house. Vinod and Prashant happened to be here then. Both of them and Achachen knew how much I wanted to see Mama. They simply forced me to go and went on insisting it. Finally I said, "Alright, if I get tickets I shall go." I did not think tickets were available. But they lost no time going to the railway station and booked a ticket for the 15th. I reached Vellore early morning, the next day. Mama was lying down on the mattress and the servant was there.

She turned to Mama and asked, "See who this is"? Mama looked up and said, "Mummy!" Mama recognized me. Mama sometimes called me

"Mummy" when she spoke to Sourabh! The servant was surprised Mama had recognized me. But Mama had been with me so long and I am sure I was in her heart.

I spent time with Mama. I knew she was slipping away. I constantly held her hand and prayed the prayer I knew by heart from the days in UC College. – "Lord support her all the days of this troublous life, until the shades lengthen, the evening comes, the busy world is hushed, the fever of life is over, and her work done. Then Lord in thy mercy, grant her safe lodging, a holy rest, and peace at the last, through Jesus Christ our Lord and Saviour. Amen".

When I said, "her work done", I remember wondering what work was left for her to finish! There was nothing. Everything had been done. I stayed there on Thursday and Friday and caught the train on Friday night. Before leaving, I repeated this prayer, holding her hand, and bade good-bye to her. I kissed her but Mama was sleeping.

I reached Mavelikara before noon. Sunday was a holiday for James and Bharathi. On Sunday 19th, Mama's condition worsened. She could not swallow anything. She was immediately admitted in the hospital for fear there might be an obstruction. But it was only the last symptom before a person's death. She died in the early hours of the morning of 20th October 1997 four months after leaving Mavelikara.

The funeral was to take place on the 22nd. They reached Chathenkary on 21st morning. 22nd was the day Alice and Leelamma had booked tickets to go to Vellore. God has always been very kind and considerate to me, I never miss seeing a loved one just before his or her death. That was why He forced me to go to Vellore. God knows our hearts and He always acknowledges our love.

Mama's funeral was very grand, for an Achen and Kochama who had known Papa and Mama well, saw the news of her death in the papers and came for the funeral. He spoke very warmly in the church and gave leadership. So did others who knew Papa and Mama. Thirumeni was not here at that time. Kunjachayan invited a prominent Achen from Tiruvalla, Rev. A.C. Kurien. But he happened to be my junior in Tambaram and was happy that he could come unexpectedly. Santhwana was only one and a half years old. Sourabh was with me. He loved kissing anyone who died.

He was in my lap kissing Mama several times. When Puthenmadathil Ammai died Sourabh came with me and gave Ammai a kiss. He then turned to me and said, "Ammachy, when you die, I will give you a kiss". That is the loving Sourabh.

CHAPTER XII

A SHOCKING FAREWELL

It was December 2015. 2015 had not been a good year for Thirumeni. 1st May was the 35th anniversary of Thirumeni's consecration as Episcopa of the Mar Thoma church. Sabu Achen's wife Asha Kochamma was in the Mission Hospital, Tiruvalla after a hysterectomy. She was to be discharged soon. May 1st was also Sabu Achen's birthday. Both Thirumeni and Achen exchanged greetings in the morning and Thirumeni re-assured him of his prayers for kochamma. But disaster struck all of a sudden. Ashakochamma died unexpectedly. There was a rumour then that the nurses had missed giving her an essential injection and she had a sudden cardiac arrest. Thirumeni went to the hospital immediately, but he could not even say a word. The body was kept in Kallissery Mar Thoma church before being taken to Kottarakara for burial. I went to Kallissery to pay my last respects. Thirumeni later told me that he could not even read a line of the service. Thirumeni and Sabu Achen had a close bond to each other ever since Sabu Achen came to work in Thirumeni's office in Adoor. Asha Kochama was endeared very much as a person.

Before Thirumeni got over this loss, Beena, Thirumeni's niece who had suffered earlier from breast cancer, suddenly became ill and was in a hopeless condition in a hospital in Chennai. Thirumeni phoned me to say that unless a miracle happened, Beena was on the verge of death. I was shocked. Thirumeni had been to Chennai to see her. Beena died very soon. As soon as I read about it in the morning newspaper, I phoned Thirumeni. He said that he was about to inform me. I went for the funeral at Kottayam Jerusalem Mar Thoma church. The church was filled to overflowing. Thirumeni led the service and Rajan kunju spoke. I could not come back without seeing Thirumeni. But when I went to the vestry the vicar prevented me from going up to Thirumeni. Finally Thirumeni's driver Raju intervened and I walked up the steps to see him. Thirumeni was in an exhausted state. But he never allowed anyone to know about his problems. He came here later and we talked about Asha kochamma's and Beena's deaths.

After my birthday in June that year I was suffering from a sort of depression. I felt so much alone and used to get very upset. I remember visiting a woman near our home who had suffered an accident and sitting there and crying because of my loneliness. When I became desperate, I decided to join a tailoring class conducted by Sreeja Electronics in Puthiyakavu. I loved stitching but never learned much. I wanted to get out of the house to ease my loneliness at least by being able to interact with the young girls who came there. So every morning I went to Puthiyakavu. Often I did not get time to phone anyone in the morning.

The depression continued though it eased a little. I wanted to phone Thirumeni on November 7th for it was the death anniversary of Ammachy. But somehow I couldn't make it. Thirumeni too was very busy with all his projects in the diocese. Whenever he came here he used to talk about his pet project Tharangam. I could not contribute anything because it was a vast project and I thought that even if I gave twenty-thousand out of my low pension, it would only be a drop in the ocean. I once gave him a month's salary for Shantigiri when I went there with Kochu Susan my classmate and family.

One day in November, Raju came to say that Thirumeni was having lunch close by after visiting homes of the aged in Mavelikara parish. I quickly donned a saree. The courtyard was a bit wet because of a drizzle, and the Audi could not enter through our gate. So Thirumeni had to walk from the gate to the house and Thomas George Achen was there to help him. Quickly I ran to the grill and held Thirumeni's hand as he reached the step and helped him all the way to the usual place on the settee as Achen sat on the other settee. I happily received his "Kaimuthu".

He talked about his programme, visiting elderly who were staying alone. He then said he had an appointment with Bishop Joshua Mar Ignatius in Punnamoodu. I wanted to ask him, "Have you stopped taking a little rest after lunch?" But I didn't, because Achen was there.

Thirumeni asked me how I spent time. I said, "There is some work in the house and then I read." I continued, "Recently I grew very distressed.

So I joined a tailoring class in Puthiakavu to learn a few things. At least I can get out of the house and meet a few people."

He asked me what I learned. I showed him a few embroidery stitches I was learning. Our main conversation was about Sourabh. He had come back from Canada and had joined a college in Baroda for BCA. I was upset about him and I asked Thirumeni if there was no one in Baroda who could give him good counselling. Both Achen and Thirumeni responded there was. Thirumeni was very caring about Sourabh because Vinitha kept him up-to-date about him. I feel that after all these ups and downs, Sourabh still has reached a reasonable position in his life because he was always in Thirumeni's thoughts till the end.

When it was time for his visit to Punnamoodu, Thirumeni was about to get up to pray. Instantly, as a sort of reflex action, I quickly went to his side smiling, held his hand and helped him to get up. Achen stood on the other side. I stood near him as he prayed. After prayer he blessed me with his right hand. Usually I kiss his hand but I did not do it that day because a stranger was there.

Then I held Thirumeni's hand and together with Thomas George Achen, I walked with Thirumeni up to the grill. Achen helped him to go down. I walked by his side, exclaiming, "Please be careful, don't slip, please be careful." I was scared because the concrete was still wet. I went with him up to the car till Thirumeni got in and sat down in the front seat. I stood by smiling as he waved, and the car slowly moved forward. It was the last time I saw Thirumeni alive.

When he came I ran to grasp his hand and help him in. And again I went to him to help him get up and held his hand all the way. I believe that it was because it was the last farewell and God made me do it to help me at least remember the affection I was able to show him at the end. God has His own ways to remind us of His loving concern and care about us, as we suffer the departure of a loved one, without knowing it.

Vinitha, Soman, Sourabh, Prashant, Megha and the children and Santhwana and Sruthika were to come here for Christmas. I was still mentally and physically worn out to respond to my responsibilities. Anyway I stopped going to the stitching classes on the 10th because Sourabh was coming on the 18th. Vinitha intended to ask me to phone Thirumeni and take him to meet him but she forgot. Later we learned that

Thirumeni left for Muscat on the evening of the 18th. Muscat was the first of a hectic programme he arranged, to visit various places in the Middle East. It was because the Metropolitan had transferred him to Kottayam. So Thirumeni was desperate to collect funds for Tharangam. Muscat was under the Kottayam diocese, and he wanted to see them. Later, Sabu Achen said in a meeting in Shantigiri, "One day Thirumeni said to me, "Achen, I don't like going to Kottayam, I don't like it at all".

Achen said, "Yet Thirumeni did not want to go against the Metropolitan though Thirumeni as Suffragan, was second in command of the church." That was Thirumeni.

Thirumeni does not seem to have been well enough for such a programme in the Gulf, but he wanted to do everything to make Tharangam possible. He also saw to it that Timotheus Thirumeni would be put in as his successor in Chengannur – Mavelikara diocese. When Timotheus Thirumeni said to him, "I am not capable of constructing something huge like Tharangam", Thirumeni assured him, "I will be close by, and give all help". It was a pet project he held close to his heart.

Vinitha would first visit Liza in Thommenkuthu and then come home. Soman was coming from Gujarat. Prashant was to come by car on the 27th, after a halt in Palakkad. I phoned him just before 7a.m. on the 26th of December, just before they started. We talked for ten minutes. A few minutes later he called me and said, "Mummy, there is news that Thirumeni who was coming from Muscat to Thiruvananthapuram, became unconscious on the flight and was taken to KIMS hospital".

Thirumeni had led Holy Communion Service on Christmas day and gave communion to five hundred people. Since Thirumeni was weak they requested Thirumeni to take rest, but he refused. Once the service was over he went back to the parsonage and fell asleep. The vicar of that parish has written about Thirumeni's last days in the book "Ormakalum Darshanangalum". Thirumeni had to see a doctor because he was having pain in his arms. Since the doctors suggested only rest, Thirumeni requested Achen for a physiotherapist. Later he was taken to the hospital, where again the doctors found nothing wrong except exhaustion. Yet he had pain on his shoulders and arms and the same physiotherapist was called. But after the communion service he was so unwell that they advised Thirumeni to cancel the ticket. In fact they did it without Thirumeni's knowledge. But when Thirumeni came to know of it he said, "I must go. I have important things to do on Saturday". So finally they agreed. But his health was very bad and even after Thirumeni was issued the boarding pass, Thirumeni vomited. Thirumeni was allowed to board the plane only on the intervention of a high official of Jet Airways. Thirumeni said to the worried Achen, "Everything will be alright once I board the plane".

The moment Thirumeni occupied his seat in the business class, he fell asleep. In fact Thirumeni had become unconscious but no one knew. There were Malayalees in the same class, even a doctor, but all thought that Thirumeni was sleeping. When the plane landed in Thiruvananthapuram, someone tried to wake him up, and then they came to know that he was unconscious.

I was alone here when I heard the news. Soman and Vinitha were in Sam's house for they had come for a relative's wedding. I had a great desire to dash to Thiruvananthapuram at once, but I did not want to go alone. I sat down and just continued to pray. I committed Thirumeni into God's Hands. I knew he was very serious. Prashant gave me more details. Sanju had said it was haemorrhage and very critical. I only prayed that he would not return to life half alive. For only recently a person in our church suffered haemorrhage and though he was operated upon he suffered a lot before he died. I simply went on praying, committing Thirumeni into the Father's Hands. I felt as if God our Father was holding him close to himself like a mother holding a child. On the 27th, Soman, Vinitha and Sourabh were going to Ernakulam for Christine's child's baptism. I did not know what to do. Finally I went with them, for being here alone was even more difficult. In the afternoon Vinitha's smartphone gave news that "Thailabhishekam" was going to be conducted. Thirumeni was on ventilator and the haemorrhage showed no sign of subsiding. It had started in Muscat and Thirumeni had pain and discomfort in his arms but even the doctors did not find out that it was haemorrhage.

I came back from Ernakulam with Prashant. On the way V.P. Rachel Ammini informed me that Thirumeni had died. Her brother Joychayan is married to Thirumeni's sister Missie. As we passed SCS junction at night, there was not even the light of a glow-worm in the compound. I was surprised, for Thirumeni's body would arrive there that very night.

Vinitha and Prashant were getting information on their phones. At 11 o' clock, Vinitha said that they would soon come to Chengannur Bethel

Church. So we went to Chengannur. We met Thirumeni's secretary Thomas Mathew Achen. Many had come to pay their respects. Finally, when Thirumeni's body arrived, the Metropolitan who was leading the whole way in his grand Mercedes Benz, refused to allow Thirumeni's body to be kept in the church so that people can pay their respects.

He was adamant. Finally the youth of the church took away the keys of the ambulance and still it was after an intense argument that he allowed Thirumeni's body to be brought into the church. Three of the bishops were standing in the compound staring at what was going on.

We came away after they proceeded to Thiruvalla. The mortal remains of Thirumeni were to be kept in the St. Thomas Mar Thoma church for people to pay respects.

We went in the afternoon to S.C. Seminary. People were pouring in. I do not know how I entered the church and had a look at Thirumeni. We went and sat down with Rajankunju and the rest of the family. We were there till evening. The funeral was to be held next morning.

We left home at 7o'clock. Since Prashant told those at the entrance that I was Thirumeni's classmate and could not walk from a remote parking space, they allowed us to go in and we parked by the side of the church.

It was a very painful, distressing experience. The one who had been our everything had left us all of a sudden. Again we paid respects and sat with the family. The evil Metropolitan had his way in everything and everyone obeyed him. He started the "nagarikanikkal" early and we walked in the procession to the S.C. compound. The problem was getting a seat. The front rows were reserved for the Sabha Council members. One Achen allowed me to sit at the end of one of the front rows, but when another came he made me get up. Prashant even broke into an argument with him. The tension was that much. Finally we settled into some seats.

The Metropolitan's behaviour during the whole period is condemnable. The moment Thirumeni breathed his last, he revelled. Mathew T. Thomas who was the Transport minister wanted Thirumeni's body to be taken in a procession by air-conditioned Volvo bus that belonged to KSRTC. But the wicked man refused. He brought in an old match-box ambulance that belonged to Kumbanad Fellowship Hospital which had little space and no air-conditioner. Then he piloted the ambulance in his Mercedes-Benz. Everywhere on the way, people stood by the side waiting to have a glimpse of Thirumeni. They tried their best to make him stop. They even appeared as traffic inspectors. But this man refused. Finally even at Chengannur where Thirumeni had been bishop for the past ten years, and from where Thirumeni had travelled hardly a week ago, he was senselessly adamant. We were able to have a glimpse of Thirumeni only because the young people were bold.

He created a lot of disturbance even in Thiruvalla. He would come to the church now and then and give orders. Everyone feared him and obeyed him because he was the metropolitan. The Synod consisting of all the other bishops did not speak out against his misbehaviour. Rev. Oommen Philip, Sabha Secretary, Prakash the lay secretary and the clergy secretary did everything to worsen the situation, obeying his senseless orders immaculately and putting in their contribution. It was Thirumeni who had helped Rev. Oommen Philip to rise to this height in the church. He had been Thirumeni's secretary in the American Diocese. Thirumeni once flew to Hyderabad just to conduct his daughter's wedding. Thirumeni had lifted him in every way. Yet the manner in which he connived with the Metropolitan to dishonour the mortal remains of Thirumeni, deserves no forgiveness even from heaven.

The family was not given any right to pay their last respects to Thirumeni. When many kidney patients and others from all over Chengannur – Mavelikara diocese came for the funeral service, the Metropolitan roared from the temporary altar, giving strange orders and marring the solemnity of the service. He shouted, "I know Mar Thomites don't make noise and crowd around". What he meant was that these people who out of the love of what they received from Zacharias Thirumeni came to pay their last respects, were not respectable people. The person that least deserved any respect that day was the crony Metropolitan.

He continued to shout when Athnasius Thirumeni was giving the sermon. This man began the service early and finished the service early so that when Bishops from other churches came, the service was almost over. When the time came for the last farewell this man simply stared at Thirumeni and pretended to touch the body with the cross. But when Chrysostom Thirumeni was brought to the "Madbaha" to bid farewell to this beloved person, Thirumeni leaned forward, put both his arms around Zacharias Thirumeni, and hugged him. All the congregation wept with him. Not an eye was dry. That was the greatest moment when love conquered all, and compensated for the immense hatred and evil that reigned supreme till then.

I can still see the procession moving towards Thirumeni's last resting place. We stayed in the pandal with Kochamma, Missy, Usha and Rajankunju. Even when Thirumeni's body was being lowered into the grave, the Metropolitan was shouting un-liturgical words. As written in Mark 1: 23 – "It was a man with an unclean spirit" that led the service in the church that day.

I have ever since wondered why when the head of a church runs amok there is no one to make him stop it. There are bishops, priests and laity, all appointed by God to serve the church righteously and bravely, upholding the Truth. They are there because Christ appointed them and they are to be loyal to Christ and not a deranged man. If good people get together, evil can be prevented. It is because the good are silent, that evil flourishes even in a place that should be the abode of the Holy Spirit. The question that has ever disturbed me is this – there were so many people who loved Thirumeni and could have got together to prevent the Metropolitan from using the match-box ambulance. He was only one man; the laity should have got together if they had any respect and love left for Zacharias Thirumeni. The calamity all the way to the grave could have been prevented if people took the initiative to stand for the right thing. Truth had lost its value.

After some time we walked with Thirumeni's family to the grave to put "Kunthirikam." As I walked past the open grave with tears, and came to the courtyard of the church I remembered how, thirty-five years ago, on the day of Thirumeni's consecration we had walked the same steps to climb into the church's courtyard and receive his first "kaimuthu" inside the church. But today Thirumeni was not there. He had gone to his Father while we stayed behind and mourned his loss and paid respects for the last time.

Usually bishops in the Eastern churches are buried in "Kunthirikam" (Frankincense). Here the Metropolitan used metal chips and then sent a circular to churches all over the world asking them to share the expenses of the "Kunthirikam". Money is the root of all evil, and no amount of money could satisfy the Metropolitan's greed. That is why Jesus Christ plainly proclaimed – "You cannot serve God and Mammon". No matter what robes you wear, take care whom you serve.

All of us were here, except Anila and Vinod, when Thirumeni left us. He belonged to us, the priestly Father of our family, and we belonged to him. God did not leave me alone at such a moment. Vinitha, Soman, Sourabh, Prashant, Megha, and the children and even Santwana and Sruthika were brought by Him for such an unexpected time like this. Our Father provides for our every need, even when we are not aware of it.

There is one thing that still hurts me. How can the spiritual head of a church give such treatment to a "brother" who had completed forty-nine years of service in the church, of which thirty-five years was as bishop? Thirumeni as Suffragan had stood as mediator to tide over difficult situations he created during Mandalam and Sabha Council. Thirumeni never uttered a word against him.

Teachers in Nicholson School remembered how when Alexander Mar Thoma Metropolitan died in Kumbanad Fellowship Hospital, his body was brought in an open, decorated vehicle from Kumbanad to Thiruvalla so that people on the way could pay respects to him. When Thomas Mar Athnasius, Metropolitan of the Orthodox church died unexpectedly in a train accident, near Ernakulam North Railway station, the church authorities brought his body with great respect. On the way, the body was kept in various churches including Parumala church so that people could come and pay their last respects. Then it was taken in procession to Puthencavu, where the burial took place.

A man can never be a follower of Jesus Christ when his heart is filled with jealousy, hatred and vengeance. This is the tragedy of today's institutionalized church. Genuine goodness is threatening to those at the other end of the spectrum.

It is my conviction that if the worst criminal in Poojappura Central Jail were brought to pay respects to a brother or neighbour, he would have behaved with greater dignity. What we saw, was something worse than the worst.

CHAPTER XIII

SUCH A MAN DID LIVE

I was deeply distressed after the sudden loss of Thirumeni. Every moment was too painful. My only conversation was with God. It was even more difficult to bear the insults showered on Thirumeni by the Metropolitan and his coterie from the moment Thirumeni breathed his last. Thirumeni had been a unique person. No one could ever replace Thirumeni. Yet the evil that reigned after his death was too much for any sensible person to bear. The Sabha Secretary and the lay secretary tried to justify all that the Metropolitan did. The S.C.S. compound was full of flex boards with Thirumeni's pictures, set up there as tribute by various churches and institutions. The Metropolitan whose rage did not subside with all the insults he showered upon Thirumeni the previous two days, made his followers throw all these boards into a ditch that very evening. He could not bear hearing the name of Thirumeni. He couldn't stand seeing his picture. He reacted violently to the Niranom Jerusalem Mar Thoma Church, Thirumeni's own parish, who asked his permission to conduct an elocution competition in the Sunday School in memory of Thirumeni. Niranom church was in his diocese.

So no one uttered the word "Zacharias Thirumeni" in front of this man. Even Raju, Thirumeni's driver made a U-turn as he wanted to secure the job he had in the church. All the people who genuinely loved Thirumeni were greatly hurt by the venom spurting from this man. But all the people who had used him all these years for their prestige and gain, forgot him. A friend told me "I get some comfort only when I think that Jesus Christ had to endure so much insults on this earth!"

Thirumeni had been a highly respected and valued priest and bishop all his life. But the Mar Thoma Church crushed him under their feet from the moment his soul departed from his body.

The very next day after the funeral on the 29th, I wrote a letter to Geevarghese Mar Athnasius Suffragan Metropolitan expressing my grief at the senseless way in which Thirumeni had been treated. I wrote it in Malayalam. I said, "The church can never survive unless there is at least one martyr who stands for Truth and Justice".

I did not receive any reply. So a week later, I wrote a very detailed letter to Chrysostom Thirumeni. I did not get a reply from him, either. I continued to pray to God unceasingly, pleading for justice and righteousness.

The Maramon Convention was duly conducted in early February. Thirumeni had been a speaker at Maramon till the previous year. Yet the Metropolitan didn't even mention his name in the "pandal" or conduct a condolence meeting. Athnasius Thirumeni was the only one who spoke a sentence to remember Thirumeni just before his sermon that Friday.

The church did not conduct a condolence meeting of the whole church in their headquarters in Thiruvalla. Instead this man presided over a condolence meeting in Chengannur-Mavelikara Diocese which Rajankunju also attended. The Metropolitan with his absolute authority, silenced every one. His coterie later came to the Chengannur Aramana to formally open Thirumeni's room and inspect his belongings. They burned Thirumeni's valuable manuscripts. Thirumeni had written some Malayalam poems called "Kunjunni Kavithakal"! He was eager to publish it. When he came to Bangalore once, he showed them to us and even read out a few. Prashant then gave Thirumeni some money to publish it. But after these men ransacked Thirumeni's room, the manuscripts disappeared. Perhaps they burnt it with the diary in which Thirumeni had written songs, giving the date and context of each one. It was Thomas Mathew Achen who pulled out the diary from the funeral pyre. In fact I had phoned Rajankunju many times asking him to take away Thirumeni's things before the Metropolitan burnt his valuable belongings. But the room can be opened only by the church and Rajankunju was helpless. The Metropolitan continued his vengeance.

I used to pray a lot in those days, pouring out my heart before the Lord. One day I suddenly recalled a particular thought we had read in the "Upper Room" when Thirumeni came for the first time to visit us. It was on 9th November, 1980, six months after his consecration. I couldn't find the "Upper Room" anywhere. At last I discovered it in Appachen's cupboard. I read through it. The meditation, written by Caroline S. Wilde, Wisconsin was about a re-union. "The thought for the day" had struck us then. It was, "True friendship lasts forever". Ever since then we had cultivated and nurtured a true and lasting friendship with Thirumeni all these years. But here I was reading the prayer given for that day's meditation. It read – "Thank you God for the glimpse of heavenly re-union we'll some day share". As my friend Ammini told me later – "God had in fact come down as it were from Heaven, to console me with this assurance".

Towards the end of February I read from "Everyday with Jesus" – "You must repent if you do not know three things. One, God loves you and you can trust him for everything. Two, Jesus is your brother. Three, God has a universal purpose for your life."

When I read the third one, I said to God – "What purpose can you ever have for me now, at this end of life?" I was confused.

One day in February or early March, I phoned Rajankunju, Thirumeni's brother. I said – "Should we not publish a biography about Thirumeni?" I was thinking of a biography like the one written by the author Katherine Frank on Indira Gandhi. I had read it. It was really a classic.

Rajankunju only said, "Alright. I'll think about it." He told me later that he knew nothing about publishing a book because he was only an expert marketing manager. He said that just to satisfy me.

Immediately after speaking to Rajankunju I phoned Prashant, told him about the book, and asked him to contact Vinod who was then Vicar of Melbourne CSI Church. Prashant contacted Vinod. Vinod said, "A biography can be written at any time. But now people's memories about Thirumeni are fresh in their hearts. So we must ask people from all walks of life to write their remembrances about Thirumeni and we must publish such a book".

That was a marvellous thought. So I spoke to Rajankunju about it. I told him how Vinod was behind my first book "Neerum velakalil" and he and Prashant would help him. Prashant introduced Vinod to Rajankunju and they decided to collect articles from various people – bishops, priests, WCC, friends, classmates and relatives, in fact, people from a wide category. Vinod would contact people outside India, those who belonged to WCC and other ecumenical bodies while Rajankunju would contact people here. So together they started the valiant effort. That is how Rajankunju, Vinod and Prashant later became editors of the book.

I contacted my classmates – Billy and Heather, Sumithra, Kunjamma and Kuruvilla Mathew. By June, even after a lot of effort, we were able to get only twenty five articles. We could not print a book without at least fifty.

Ever since the idea of the book germinated in my heart, I used to sit on the mat ever spread in the drawing room and pray. I prayed as I have never prayed before. I read about the writer N.V. Krishna Warrier who wrote with a pen filled with the ink of fire! I prayed to the Lord everyday that every word that was written would burn like fire and be imprinted in the hearts of people.

Slowly the articles began coming in. Vinod and Rajankunju kept in touch with people. It was very difficult for me to write about Thirumeni. It took immense effort to write an article.

Meanwhile Vinod said, "If there are articles in Malayalam, Auntie can translate it." I was surprised, but I was happy to do it. Later on I translated twelve articles into English, including two speeches by Thirumeni, delivered immediately after the consecration and a few days later. I found it a joy to translate. I read in The Hindu at that time that the best translation is one where you cannot distinguish the original from the translation! When I translated Kunjamma's article, Govindankutty Chettan and Sumithra wanted to read it. I sent it to them. Immediately Chettan said to Sumithra – "Tell Molly to start translating books!". It was a great compliment!

I specially remember translating Shaji George's article. He wrote beautiful Malayalam and was very unwilling for his article to be translated for it would certainly lose its grandeur. I translated this one when I was with Vinitha in Switzerland. It was really tough! I just prayed and translated. It was a transforming experience. As soon as I read a sentence, words would come flowing in to make it a beautiful sentence in English. I said to myself – "It is like the dew falling down from Mount Hermon." I was thrilled. I was able to do it like the definition for the best of translations! I thought to myself – " How many talents are dormant in us which God gave us when He formed us!" Age is no barrier to using our talents.

The editors hoped for only seventy-five articles. But the God who blessed the little boy's five loaves and two fishes, brought in a hundred articles.

Prashant was to be in charge of the printing. I told him that when we print the book it should be done with perfection, on good paper, using the best of printing technology. There should be no compromise about that. He had to find the best printer. I asked him to pray about it and God would show the right printers. At that time, Mathews George Chunakkara suggested that the book be printed by CSS. But I was adamant and told Vinod it must never be printed in the press that belonged to the Poolatheen. Then Mathews George suggested a Delhi publisher and both Vinod and he wanted to entrust the printing to them. Prashant discovered that the Delhi printer could not even write a correct sentence in English. He had to argue for one hour with Mathews George to prove why he would not give the job to them. Finally, with God's help he found Notion Printers who turned out to be very dignified, helpful and maintaining a very high standard as Printers and Publishers.

When most of the articles arrived, Prashant told me that the press was willing to do the proof-reading but they would have to be paid for every word. So Vinod had told them that they had a good person to do it and entrusted the job to me! I was flabbergasted! Prashant said, he would teach me "tracking changes" and I could do it on the computer.

I had to learn a lot of basic things, not just, "tracking changes" to be able to handle these new responsibilities. Prashant taught me "tracking changes" through Skype but still I had all sorts of doubts. Pranoy, Ponnu's son, and our neighbour was my great stay. He was there for every little obstacle that came during my work. He would always come whenever I needed him.

I read each article thrice and did the corrections. It was Prashant who edited the articles before sending it to me. It was a gigantic effort, but it was such a joy. I wondered – "I had only thought of contributing an article for the book. But here I was, doing the translations as well as the complete proof reading. It was God's way of saying that he did not want anyone else to touch the book except people who loved Thirumeni.

The corrections after the lay-out was made when I was in Baroda with Soman and Sourabh in November. I asked Prashant also to scrutinise it carefully. Sourabh was there to help me with the computer. It was after the lay-out of the book did I understand that the very minute corrections are left out even after three readings. There were a large number of very small errors. Usually the press limits the number of corrections they do after the layout, for they expect the work to be almost perfect. Prashant had a good rapport with the press and so they entered all the corrections so that when the book finally came out, there was not a single mistake. I believe that God sent His angels to make the book perfect. It would not otherwise have been possible.

What Vinod did first when we planned the book, was to decide the date of release. It was an act of faith. Unless a date is fixed, the book-release would go on indefinitely. So Rajankunju contacted Timotheus Thirumeni and fixed the date as 1st January 2017, immediately after Thirumeni's first death anniversary. January 1st was going to be celebrated by the diocese, as Founder's day. It was very important that the Metropolitan should not be in Kerala, for no one could predict what he would do if he came. January 1st was a safe date. The book was to be released by Shri. P.J. Kurien. The Orthodox bishop of Adoor, Zacharias Mar Aprem Metropolitan was also invited. We wanted Vinod to introduce the book but it was impossible for him to leave his parish on New Year's Day. So Prashant was entrusted with the duty of introducing the book. He would speak for ten minutes.

Thirumeni had died at the age of 77. I became 78, the following June. It was when I was seventy-eight years old that God entrusted me with the work of this book which was our tribute to Thirumeni. I thought of the Lord of the vineyard in Matthew 20. The Master came to his vineyard and employed labourers at the third hour, sixth hour and the ninth hour. But still there were a few people standing there when he came at the eleventh hour. They were thought to be useless people, old and not fit for work. But the Master employed them too in His vineyard.

I always think of myself as a person employed by the Master at the eleventh hour. Not only did the Master employ me at a very late hour, but. He also gave me every skill necessary to do my job to the utmost. Age is no barrier when we are called upon by the Master.

It was Vinod who found the title for the book, "Such a Man did live." We ordered a thousand copies. The finished books were to arrive in Santhigiri before Christmas. They sent the books on time. It was printed perfectly and each copy was neatly robed in a transparent plastic cover.

The release of the book took place on the first of January in the open-air theatre made by Zacharias Thirumeni himself in "Tharangam". Timotheus Thirumeni had various choirs presenting Christmas songs. Rajankunju invited relatives and Thirumeni's friends. The authors of articles were given special seats in front. For the first time after Thirumeni's sad demise, I went with Prashant to S.C. Seminary church to lay a bunch of flowers at Thirumeni's last resting place, before paying him this loving tribute of a book. He would have loved it if he were here. I can see Thirumeni's beaming smile as he holds the book lovingly in his hands.

The function at Tharangam went off warmly, lovingly, immaculately. Everyone there was happy that a book was being released for they all loved Thirumeni very much. Where the Mar Thoma Church stood still and paralysed, God had His own ways to honour this beloved son who had been so good and faithful to Him in little things and big things. I am so proud and thankful that God was gracious enough to use us as small instruments in His mighty Hands. We did that fearlessly and with great pride for Thirumeni who was given to our family as God's gift, and whom we loved and cherished immeasurably.

Prashant began his speech with a song that reverberated in the quiet of the river and the stadium. It was a song he learned when he attended a conference for High School students in Kottayam while he was staying with Thirumeni. He introduced the book impressively and then requested the Rajya Sabha Deputy Chairman Sri P.J. Kurien to release the book. Sri. P. J. Kurien released it by giving a copy to Bishop Zacharias Mar Aprem. Then he made a very impressive speech.

Though Rajankunju had been fearful all the while about the function, it was as if Timotheus Thirumeni had organized it just for the release of the book. Timotheus Thirumeni's love, courage and support at that critical juncture must be greatly appreciated and written in letters of gold. Thirumeni was a saviour at that time of crisis. It was because of Zacharias Thirumeni's special request that Timotheus Thirumeni was made his successor in Chengannur-Mavelikara diocese. God never makes mistakes. For that was the right place for the release of Thirumeni's book.

Skariah John Achen who was the secretary of Santhigiri, came down to introduce himself to us. Achen did not send us away without having dinner. I also met Timotheus Thirumeni who said he was waiting to see me. We received everyone's affection, including everyone from Thirumeni's family, and it is an unforgettable episode in our lives.

The executive members of Santhigiri who till then used Thirumeni for their own ends, suddenly turned against Rajankunju. Rev. Oommen Philip and the rest of the Santhigiri committee mocked him for releasing a book without any article in Malayalam. The Sabha secretary was in a rage because the book had been released without his article. Rajankunju had sent him a letter requesting an article, but he did not care to send it. He thought that such a book would never be published. He had been Thirumeni's Secretary in U.S.A. and also held powerful position in the Church now. But it was K.Y. Jacob Achen who had written about the North American diocese. He immediately found out a silly mistake in a date mentioned in that article, and wrote in the minutes of the meeting that Santhigiri cannot publish any more copies of the book without correcting this mistake.

That naturally upset Rajankunju. All of them were after him like wolves on a deer. I was in Australia then. He wrote to me that he would like the book to be published by CSS after adding Malayalam articles from these men. A long argument followed. It was very difficult to convince Rajankunju because he was cornered by men who were mean enough to do the worst. This was the treatment that a book on Thirumeni got. Finally I had to write a letter to him in the strongest vocabulary possible, to dissuade him from this misadventure. They were free to publish a book of their own on Thirumeni. But they had no right to touch this book. Thirumeni's book was not even announced at the Maramon Convention in February 2017, in spite of many requests. The Metropolitan went on announcing even cookery books at his proclamations but not this one. He prevented Yuyakim Mar Coorilose too, who was the President of the "Suviseshasanghom."

These are only a few of the obstacles we had to face, even after publishing the book. When I spoke about this to Joy (Dr. Jacob Cheriyan) my cousin in Brisbane, he told me, "Mollymamachy, Santhigiri may not publish the book. But nobody can prevent you from printing more copies at your expense."

Sumithra and Govindan Kutty Chettan

That was a relief. I had to get Rajankunju to agree to that. I had already given money for the publication of the book and Thirumeni's museum, and he did not want me to spend more. I prayed to God everyday that when the thousand copies were sold, we would be able to print at least five hundred more. After long months of prayer, Rajankunju called me one day and said, "Auntie, we shall print another five hundred copies. People are asking for the book."

It was God's Hand. So Prashant gave orders for another five hundred, and I had the privilege of paying the bill.

When Thirumeni died I always had a regret that I was not able to contribute anything to Tharangam. But I was able to do all I could when he needed it most – after his departure – for there was no one else to do it except Rajankunju, his own brother.

Kuruvilla Mathew, being our classmate, and close friend of Thirumeni, and for years now in Australia as a strong pillar of the church, was trusted to be the main distributor of "Such a man did live" in the parishes in Australia where people still valued Thirumeni. It was immediately after the release of the book that I went to Australia, Heather insisting on it. Only when I reached Australia did I accidentally discover that the people in Australia knew nothing about the book. Nobody had told them about it. Kuruvilla Mathew had conveniently taken his copy and ordered two more. That was all. People heard of the book for the first time, from me. When they asked for copies, I had none. Years later, perhaps because of the first book, Kuruvilla Mathew took the initiative to publish the second book "Ormakalum darshanangalum", which came to light only because of the hard work of Rajankunju. So when months later he came to India I asked Kuruvilla Mathew to take at least ten books to Australia. He said, "The book was announced in all the parishes of Australia, and all who wanted were given copies of the book. Not a single copy more is required." He lied to my face. I told him I knew exactly what he had done, for I was in Australia. He could not fool me.

If a person like Kuruvilla Mathew who had pretended to be close to Thirumeni for the past sixty years could act like that, using Thirumeni to promote his status in the church and flowing with the Metropolitan when he found Thirumeni had lost favour, this is the touchstone of friendship. No wonder, I thought, Billy ever disliked him!

Heather, Billy's wife, though an Australian, stood by me in all this. She loved and valued Thirumeni as much as I did.

I remember a letter Heather wrote to me after sending their article for the book.

She wrote – "Molly, we wanted to say that we used to get quite cross and indignant when Thirumeni visited, because it was such a battle to be able to offer him rest time with us. People here all wanted him to do things, never a let-up, pressure all the time, pressing rich food on him, (out of care, of course) but selfish in terms of ultimate disregard for his health, I think. But at least we were able to cajole a few days each time and offer him the peace and quiet we felt he needed. It was very special for us that he took such delight in the gardens and birds and wild life that we were able to show him in a low-key fashion. He is such a gracious, generous spirit. We were deeply concerned last visit, for we felt that his health was being overtaxed with the relentless travel. How can Christian people be so mean-spirited and well, simply blind?"

This letter shows how people all over in the Mar Thoma church used Thirumeni for their own selfish ends with utter disregard for his health. They manipulated Thirumeni's gracious and generous spirit and speeded his end. If this is not mean-spiritedness, what is?

CHAPTER XIV

THE BEST THINGS IN LIFE

Sometime after Achachen's death, Prashant asked me to renew my passport, for I had a great desire to travel to Israel. When I was in Bangalore he bought me two boxes, one for check-in luggage, and another, for hand luggage. Just a few months later P. J. Mathew, my friend and classmate now staying in Melbourne, suggested that I make a visit to Australia. Kuruvilla Mathew, another of our classmates was in Perth. Kuruvilla Mathew became the sponsor and I got a visa for three months, without any difficulty. Prashant offered to pay the airfare while Vinitha and Anila contributed towards my expenses. My pension then, was very low, only four thousand rupees.

In Australia, summer began in December. So I was to travel first to Perth, stay with them for three weeks, and then go to Melbourne and be with Billy and Heather for three weeks. Tickets were booked and I was to travel from Bangalore by Singapore Airlines. It was my first journey after a long time and I prayed and trusted God and took the flight. Singapore Airlines was a narrow-bodied flight from Bangalore and took off at an odd time in the night and landed early morning. This prevented me from getting a wink of sleep. There were one or two persons sneezing constantly. Since the aircraft was narrow, all passengers breathed this infected air.

By 6 a.m. we were in Changi Airport, Singapore. I had help to board the next flight. As I flew over Australia, I was filled with wonder and pleasure as I looked down at the distant view of the Australian demography. I thanked God that he was enabling me to see another continent!

I landed in Perth where Kuruvilla Mathew and his wife Valsa who was my student once, welcomed me very warmly at the airport. Somehow, from the same evening, I had a slight loss of appetite and an infection in the upper respiratory tract. Because of my inexperience I had not taken any basic medicines from India which would have been a great help. For, seeing a doctor or getting a prescription was very complicated in Australia. Nobody had told me that I should have medicines handy, in case of small emergencies. Kuruvilla and Valsa took me to a farm where we collected peaches. On our way back we visited a Malayali family.

The lady was a doctor. I had the least appetite. She checked me and said to Kuruvilla Mathew – "You must give her a strong antibiotic because her upper respiratory tract is infected." Unfortunately, no medicines were bought. Christmas was approaching and one day after bath, I could hardly breathe. So immediately we went to a doctor of Malayali origin. He prescribed Amoxyllin which was very mild and I was feeling no better. Next day we visited him again, and after examining my chest he said I must be taken to a hospital.

So very unexpectedly, I had to be admitted in an Australian hospital where investigation would begin from scratch. At first they suspected tuberculosis and I was isolated. Health care workers would come wearing clothes that looked as if they were on a visit to the moon. When tuberculosis was ruled out I was shifted to a big room with two other ladies who had more complications.

Every morning a lady came to help me have my bath. Food in a hospital in Australia is something you can get only in a five-star hotel in India. A very friendly nurse comes every day to jot down each one's preferences from the rich menu for the day. The lady next to me was very friendly and kind and sometimes gave me lovely red Australian grapes which her visitors had brought. I used to get phone-calls every day from the children and from Billy. Kuruvilla Mathew came to the hospital without fail. Billy, himself a scientist, always spoke to me positively. He said that the swelling on my feet was only because I was not walking. But my haemoglobin was low and the hospital made a great fuss about it. I even felt, may be, I was having leukaemia. Kuruvilla Mathew's friend, the doctor I saw earlier, even said I would have to go to a good hospital like Vellore for investigation. I had never been in a hospital except when my children were born. And here I was, in a foreign country, with all sorts of complications.

After two sachets of blood transfusion, we waited anxiously for the next blood test. By God's grace the blood count rose steeply and there was nothing wrong.

Kuruvilla Mathew was advised to get me discharged from the hospital that day itself, for if a new physician came and wrote down some investigation, I would never be able to get out. So finally he got me discharged and we reached home. Valsa had very kindly and lovingly made a lamb soup for me, to help me regain my strength. But as if to culminate everything, the soup created a disastrous stomach upset!

Time was drawing near for me to travel to Melbourne, because the itinerary was fixed at the time tickets were bought in India. Kuruvilla Mathew was doing all he could to send me back to India for he feared the medical bill, as there was no coverage of insurance. Billy insisted that I proceed to Melbourne as planned and Kuruvilla Mathew was dead against it. I could not make up my mind. Finally Prashant consulted Kochamma, a doctor, and she advised me not to return to India immediately. Since I was weak, they might even send me to quarantine in Singapore. So, that was settled. We bought medicine to be taken for an emergency in case the stomach upset aggravated. God gave me courage to travel. In Australia, those who come to see you off can come right up to the door of the plane. It was a three-hour flight from Perth to Melbourne. I was very weak but I put on a brave face. Finally when I reached Melbourne Billy was right where I stepped off the plane. As soon as I saw him I held his hand and did not leave it until I got into the car.

We reached Billy's house. I hadn't eaten anything on the flight. So when Billy asked me if I had had lunch, I told the truth. They were surprised. But Heather gave me yoghurt with ripe mangoes in it. I ate it ravishingly and from that moment I started to recover. They also gave me yakult which contains good bacteria in concentration from yoghurt. Every moment I spent in their home was also a moment of recovery. I am ever thankful for it. Heather knew exactly what she should feed me. I recovered day by day, and though we could not travel to Sydney as planned, we were able to travel to other places where in one place we were joined by Heather's nephews, and we had a barbecue.

Billy took me to a goldmine. Australia became rich because of its goldmines. Good governance, together with riches, made the country prosperous. We went to the Botanical gardens with Selena and saw the native trees of Australia and its ancient flora and fauna. Heather also took me to the zoo where for the first time I saw a real kangaroo. It didn't come up to my expectations because pictures of Kangaroos had created a creature of more beauty in my mind.

I enjoyed walking in the park and around Victoria. Though Billy and Heather stay in a modest house, the place is in the heart of the city with the University and many institutions of importance around it. Their small home is actually a heritage structure. Billy played golf every morning and dinner was his speciality. Once he bought some dried fish bones and made a soup saying it was good for my recovery. Everyday he makes soup that consists of all nutritious things and a side dish of meat. I was no stranger to Heather because during the rare occasions they were in India, both of us had the pleasure of being with them in Kalloopara and also in Santhigiri with Thirumeni.

On my way back I was to stay with Sindhu and Shibu in Singapore for three days. Sindhu is Baben's daughter, and Shibu, happily was my student. As I landed in Singapore and came to the exit in a wheel-chair, a handsome young man came to me and asked, "Do you remember me?" It was Ajit, Sunny's son, a very loving, fine young man. He had come to Singapore from Hong Kong and was supposed to go back the next day. So he had volunteered to come with Shibu to the airport to meet me. It was a great joy staying with Sindhu and Shibu and their two children. The daughter is an expert in violin and the little son was enamoured of frogs and other small animals.

While staying with them I contacted Kuttimon, my friend Maymi's brother who is a journalist in Singapore. Kuttimon (Mathew K. Thommen) picked me up and we went around the little island of Singapore, which brought back nostalgic memories of the place – especially the causeway connecting Singapore and Malaya. We went for lunch to a farm-house where you get only healthy food like papaya salad, the flower-stalk of plantain and other nutritious things. It was a joy being with Kuttimon who was a late-comer, born when Maymi and I were room-mates in Tambaram. So I had seen him growing up from the time he was a baby.

Finally I caught the flight back to Bangalore and was relieved to be back. Prashant and Megha were at the airport. All of us were so thankful that after all the unexpected emergencies, God enabled me to travel according to the planned routine and reach home safely. It had been a twelve-hour flight from Melbourne to Singapore by British Airways, which was going to London. The food and service was excellent. On the other hand, the Quantas I flew from Singapore to Perth had served horrible food. I was able to get a taste of different airlines. After sharing Heather's traditional, fantastic Christmas cake with them and other things, I flew back to Kochi. Since the internal flight allowed only 15 kilos, I had to pay extra to take my whole luggage home.

Vinitha and Soman had given me a hundred U.S. dollars which I didn't spend in Australia. So Soman bought me a Dell computer. That was the beginning of my computer education.

As Vinitha was in Switzerland, I always dreamed of going there. At first she was not very encouraging. Finally I was able to go with Soman from Bombay. It was early December and Sourabh was already there after his tenth. From Berne we went to Germany to spend Christmas with Barbara, Gottlieb and their two boys Morritz and Felix. They lived in a far corner of Germany. First we went to Basel and from there changed trains again at Frankfurt and Munich. Finally we caught the train that goes to Furth-im-Wald. That was my first experience of Germany after going to Berlin in 1971. I have no words to describe the wonderful time we had with them in a quiet little village. Barbara has her lovely garden where she grows vegetables and fruits and even keeps chickens! All produce comes from the garden and the residents share potatoes and other things which they have. There is a forest nearby where every morning we went for long walks with the dog. Since it was winter, there were icicles hanging from trees. Skiers came down from the hill. The children enjoyed throwing snow-balls at each other.

Barbara had a small party for friends when we cooked Indian food. But there were plenty of salads and fruits from her own garden. Barbara's mother too came for a visit. All of them enjoyed their quiet life in the villages. They do not boast about huge houses; generally Europeans live in smaller houses when the children leave home. Once we also cultivated our own food and vegetables, milk, meat and eggs and then decided it is easier to buy. Then we bought ill-health with it for everything came with pesticides. Whether winter or summer, Europeans enjoy the outdoors. They love walking for long distances and being one with nature. As upstarts our values are different and we have even decided to destroy nature in the name of development. Every person in Germany is conscious about their country and keeps it clean and healthy. They do not allow a tourist to put even a piece of paper in the wrong place. They do not give importance to political leaders; they, the people are very responsible.

Back in Berne, we also visited Peter and Chris with whom Vinitha stayed on rent when she first came to Switzerland. Peter is a farmer and keeps a herd of cows that graze for days in summer, in the forest. Peter's son, though very small, was bent on becoming a farmer like his father.

Peter said, "If everyone sits at the computer, who will produce milk and dairy products?" Chris belongs to Denmark and met Peter in Switzerland. She had to learn everything to become a farmer's wife, otherwise she would lose Peter! Peter's mother had come to take the children for a week to her home. As she was leaving she said to me, "Auf Wiederschen", which means "Good-bye:"

When the farmer and his wife get old, they move to a smaller house on the farm, and his son takes over. The farmer also has a safe place to keep valuable things to protect them in case of a fire. Peter's little son already had a small room so arranged as a farm with animals and other equipments. Thus he grows up loving the life of a farmer; "catch them young", say the wise.

Children in Kerala grow up on the smart phone and computer without stepping on the earth. If parents take interest and teach them while still young, to enjoy the wonder of creation and cultivation, they too will grow up doing useful things.

After enjoying the beauty of Switzerland as much as we could, Soman and I flew back to Bombay.

I went to Switzerland many times since that visit. I learned to travel on my own via Abu Dhabi, Dubai and Muscat. Of course I felt tense though I had wheel-chairs until I boarded the flight to Zurich. But in Zurich I always alighted with the other passengers and managed on my own.

The Emirates was the best flight I travelled by. As a surprise Vinitha once upgraded my flight from Dubai, in business class so that I would get the feel of its luxury. I really felt at odds, but it was very kind of her.

Vinitha has stayed in Hartwig's and Fiona's house on rent, for years. Whenever I reach Zurich or depart from there, Fiona and Hartwig always come with us. Not only that, they have joined us to travel to various places in Switzerland. Since they know my love for places, they have on their own taken me to various locations. We have always felt as a part of the family. Fiona is Scottish and Hartwig comes from Hamburg, Germany. When Vinitha is out for work and I am in the house, Fiona calls me from downstairs, "Anna". We talk, or I have a break in their house or Fiona fixes a time for us to go out. Travel makes the world smaller and your hearts bigger and you come to regard humanity as your family. People look different, speak different languages, and have different traits. But there is this universal language of love which binds the world together. I have always loved meeting people, interacting with them and loving them. So I have been loved in return and there is a bond with people I meet, wherever I go.

Dorothy is an older friend of Vinitha. She is English and married to a Swiss. She and her husband were teaching in the university. Dorothy loved taking me to unique places close-by and described the significance of each place, walking around and enjoying the natural beauty that Switzerland is blessed with. After that we always had coffee or ice-cream and something to eat. Later when her husband died, aged 92, she still continued living at home and her children and grand-children came to help her. She loved reading and told me she read Swiss and English books, setting apart time for reading.

Rosemary was another of Vinitha's friends who helped me enjoy Switzerland. She is a devotee of the Hebrew Bible and goes on constant visits to Israel to study it. The Swiss have a perfect system of public transport. So even a rich man need not have a private car. Hence the traffic is thin and pollution nil. Those using public transport have equal rights and convenience as those travelling in their own vehicles. There are very frequent buses and trams which are punctual to the minute. There are also very convenient stops, pedestrian crossings, and broad pedestrian walks on either side. One does not have to wait long to cross the roads because signals turn green at constant intervals.

I had a great longing to visit places in Europe. With a Schengen visa it was not difficult. Though I paid for travel, Vinitha had to take responsibility of the expenses there. She needed a lot of persuasion, coaxing and pressure to take me anywhere. I would not give up only because of my great love for places.

Austria was one of my dreams ever since we saw the "Sound of Music". So one day we went to Bregenz which was the nearest point from Switzerland. Wherever we go there are beautiful lakes and mountains and cable cars, and with knowledge of German, Vinitha was able to manage well.

I once told her I wanted at least to step on the soil of France! So she took me to Lausanne and from there we took a boat to Les Baines. The boat-ride takes a little longer when you are going towards your destination, but it took hardly thirty minutes to come back. Once we step on to French soil the climate suddenly becomes warmer. Hartwig told me that it then becomes the Mediterranean climate.

It was a quiet fishing village down there, with fishing nets let out to dry. The fishing boats were all anchored in the small port. Just a few minutes down the village road a French woman accosted me in a blue saree saying, "Namaste" with folded hands! She had been to India and it was just a coincidence we met in the same dress. We climbed up to the road and walked to the old castle that sells a famous wine. On our way back we bought the loveliest ice-cream I have ever eaten, two balls, with the real taste of fruit!

On another occasion we went to Avian, whose mineral water is served in five-star hotels in India! We went with Hartwig, Fiona and Braidie (their dog). Braidie himself had a passport! There is a good market in Avian on certain days, and Hartwig wanted to buy some meat he liked. We spent the whole day in Avian, and took only the evening boat to Lausanne.

Earlier Vinitha took me one day to see Lausanne itself which is a beautiful place with the lake, swans and various sights. On that trip we took a boat-ride to Montreaux. The boat would stop at different places and people would get in. The blue of the lake, the blue of the mountains, and the lovely scenery on either side, merged into a picturesque delight for the eyes. We met Andrea, a Lativian girl, by chance, and she was with us all along, until we parted company at Montreaux. As we landed at Montreaux, there were lots of shops under umbrellas, at the ferry. It happened to be a festival.

In the North of Switzerland they speak German, and in the Southern most part, Italian, for it is close to Italy. But in places like Lausanne that lie close to France, they know only French. If you go to Geneva, English is easily understood and in the Eastern part they have Romansch.

We went with Hartwig and Fiona to the Southern part where we get Italian food and people speak Italian. When we came back the train went through parts of Italy, and there is such a contrast between people who dwell there, and those who are luckily part of Switzerland. The Italians are not well-off like the Swiss. We saw a procession being taken out in a small church and I was reminded of the processions we have in Catholic churches here.

One day Fiona planned that we go and see a glacier. We went to Eggishorn which is at 2869 metres. It was very cold and there was snow everywhere. We had taken the small Panoramic train. The view on either side with flowing streams, pebbles and small bridges together with tiny cottages sparsely seen, are so picturesque and one drinks deep of the unspeakable beauty of nature.

I had borrowed a warm cardigan from Vinitha and with two cardigans and so much excitement, I forgot all about the cold. As the clouds cleared, the glacier was glittering in the sun. After spending some time there, we came down to Fiesheralp which is at 2212 metres. We had lunch there and then took the cable car to Fiesch (1049 metres). We sat in a restaurant and ate a whole lot of ice-cream. Then slowly we walked from the cable-car station to the railway station from where we caught the small panoramic train back to Brig, going through Lax (1039 m.) Belken Tal station (826m). Morch (759m.) and then Brig at 676 metres. Wherever we went God cared for us in every way, giving us fine weather.

Initially Vinitha was not at all interested in travel, a trait she might have inherited from Achachen. But slowly she started enjoying the pleasures of travel. So one day we went to Stresa, a small place in Italy, very close to the Swiss border. The train was going to Milan! We took a boat ride to three small islands in the lake – Isola Bella, Isola Madre and Isola Pescatori in Lago Maggiore. There was so much to see in all these three islands. Many Italian tourists were with us. The Italians are very handsome, very fashionable, big-built and family oriented.

The next morning we went for a trip to the famous Santa Caterina (St. Catherine), a monastery situated on a steep rock. There are at least fifty steep steps to get into the monastery. After walking around, we took the

Billy and Heather

boat back to Stresa. It was magnificent – the blue of the mountains and the sea, dotted with red brick buildings and a large number of boats all around, magical it seemed.

Soon after Thirumeni left us in December 2015, I felt so desperate here, that I told Vinitha I would like to come and stay where there was one more person in the house. Work on Thirumeni's book had begun. Vinod and Prashant had given me the responsibility of translating all the Malayalam articles into English. When my visa was ready, I flew to Zurich via Muscat. I thought this time God had taken me through Muscat for that was the last place Thirumeni had visited, from where he came straight to Trivandrum and then to the hospital, in an unconscious state. In Berne I was busy translating the articles. But Vinitha had plans to go to Barbara's place in Germany. So both of us went on a lovely trip to Furth-im-wald.

It was summer and we had regular walks in the forest when Barbara collected various types of mushrooms which are not seen in India. We also visited Barbara's mother "where the blue Danube flows." The blue of the river is to be seen to be believed! We picked acorns from an oak tree which was a thousand years old!

We went to Passau where we can see three rivers united. The colour of each river is different and we can clearly distinguish it at the place they become one. Danube is an exciting blue! One can see three domes of a Cathedral, and on the other side is Austria. It is just fifteen minutes' drive. On the other hand, Vienna is just three hours' journey from Passau.

Both Vinitha and I had planned to go to Prague and it was close from Barbara's place. Tickets were cheaper when we bought them from Domazlice, a place which belongs to the former Czech Republic. Domazlice was just a few miles from Barbara's home. The journey to Prague took only two and a half hours. From the hotel Ibis we took a guided tour with a good Czech tourist guide who took us round to so many historical places. Then we came down for the boat tour where he explained the importance of the beautiful, majestic, historical buildings around. Prague is a majestic city and has old buildings of historical importance everywhere, that attracts a large number of tourists. He said, "Luckily they were not demolished even at the time of the occupation by Soviet Union. Only one thing was demolished", he said, with regret – "the Jewish ghettos". That was the only valuable structure destroyed like what the Americans do!

There are statues everywhere in Prague. The Saint of all the bridges was a priest of the Cathedral who was thrown by the Emperor into the river for not obeying him, by revealing a "confession secret!"

Next day during our breakfast in the hotel, a wonderful thing happened. We met a Jewish lady who had come from Israel to Prague with friends, for a Jewish wedding. She came to us and asked, "Are you from South India?" We said, "Yes."

Are you from Kerala!" We said, "Yes!" Then she said, "Do you speak Malayalam?"

When we said "yes"; she replied – "I too am a Malayali" and she chatted away in wonderful Malayalam.

Her great-grandfather had come to Kochi at the time of the Spanish Inquisition. She, her father, grandfather, all were born and brought up in Kochi. She is a gynaecologist who studied in Trivandrum Medical College and was teaching at Calicut Medical College. She did her post-graduate degree in Egmore, Madras.

They had migrated to Israel and was now living near Gaza, where there are constant problems with Palestinians. I asked her, "How can you speak such good Malayalam?" She replied unashamedly, "It is our mother tongue. We speak Malayalam at home."

Compare this doctor with the Malayalees who take pride in proclaiming they do not know Malayalam! She said, "Kochi State was very lenient towards the Jews. 'Yom kippur', Day of Atonement, and one New Year's Day were very sacred for the Jews when they never touched books. So no examination was conducted on these days by the government. She spoke with great warmth and eloquence about their foster country.

We returned from Prague (Praha) by "Alex" (name of the railway company) that was going to Munich. The train passed through Czech Republic when the stations were announced very clearly in Slovak, English, and German. The final Czech Station was Domazlice and the next one after twenty minutes was Furth-im-wald!

Just before we returned, Barbara presented me with three books – Ken Follett's Trilogy – Fall of Giants, Edge of Eternity and Winter of the world. She said once I started reading it I would not stop! It was true. That way I was introduced to Ken Follett.

A very interesting thing happened when we were returning from Furth-im-wald. We had to change trains at Schwandorf and Nurmberg and reach Karlsruhe to catch the train to Basel. The German ticket inspector who came to inspect our tickets on the train to Basel said, "Namaste" when he saw us. When he learned that we were from Kerala he said, "Malayalam parayan ariyumo?" And again, "Namaskaram, Sukhamano?

He had been working with a young man from Kerala forty years back, and he learned it from him. He was talking and laughing with everyone and making them happy, cracking jokes, singing after playing music on the phone, all the while, doing his work! I felt, "Can't we all make others happy while doing our work! Why don't we give up our sullen faces?"

Next day we went to Chur (Pronounced koor) in the Eastern part of Switzerland. The beauty of the place is indescribable. The Zurich lake, which is so big, was full of tourists and boats. Just before my journey back to India, Rosemarie met me at Barenplatz tram station and took me by car for a drive along the most beautiful villages with many farm-houses, cows, sheep and little old houses. The landscape looked like framed paintings. We reached her friend Anna Maria's little house which had two flights of wooden stairs. It was made of wood in the ancient way. We had tea in the balcony of the kitchen which had a view of grandeur, the blue mountains so close by, a lovely hut and two other tiny houses and a vast stretch of green. Living so close to nature can purge one's soul.

Next, we went to a tiny old church right near the mountains, with the tiniest cemetery all decked with flowers. In the backdrop was a little stream coming down from the mountains "with a soft inland murmur." The parson lived in a beautiful tiny house near the church. I wonder why in Kerala, we have mansions for ourselves and the pastors!

This is just a short account of the wonderful travel in Switzerland with Vinitha. What a delight it is to stay in such a beautiful country where everything seems to be in order. Awareness of citizens is very important. The countryside, rivers and lakes are so clean! The way even cemeteries are kept beautiful, gives such peace and joy. One can sit in any corner of

Cable car, Switzerland

a park, alone, with no one else around and walk along forests where you may meet no one on the way! But how safe it is! Patriotism should be proclaimed in this way, not through empty slogans!

In 2017, Heather wrote to me from Australia – "Molly, I would like to see you at least in 2017!" It was January, and we had just released the book on Thirumeni. Heather said I could stay with them for two weeks. Summer was not over yet. Heather sponsored me instead of Billy, for as she is an Australian, there would be no hitches. So I immediately applied for a visa.

In the meantime, Vinod Achen who was then vicar of St. Matthew's CSI church, Ashburton, Melbourne, came for the book review organized in Santhigiri in March. As soon as he heard I was coming to Australia for two weeks, he insisted that I should stay with them for two weeks. Thus began my plans for a month's stay in Australia.

The visa was delayed a little because of Passion Week. It was to come towards the end of April. But unfortunately towards the end of March, as I climbed a steep step to Geetha Medicals, the ligament of my left leg suffered injury and I had great pain when I walked. I went to two doctors, one after the other but the medicine I got was just pain killers. If I cancelled my travel then, it would never take place. Time was running out and so I booked my tickets by Air-Asia, via Kuala Lumpur. Any cream applied to soothe my pain near the left knee, immediately created allergy. Anyway I came to Alwaye to stay with Maymi for the night, for Davy said he would kindly take me to the airport early morning. But only when I came to the Airline's counter was I informed that the flight would only be in the evening. They did not have the courtesy to inform a passenger. That created a lot of inconvenience to me, Maymi and Davy. I missed my connecting flight from Kuala Lumpur and all were to be informed about the change.

There was a long delay at the airport in Kuala Lumpur. By sheer courage that comes in critical circumstances, and by the sole help of God, I finally landed in Melbourne airport after multiple difficulties. The ordeal in the airport was even worse. There were different queues for coloured passengers. Finally I came out. Billy and Heather were there to meet me. Billy had grown a little anxious because of the delay.

We reached home and I confided to Heather about my leg. She gave me a herbal ointment and was very kind and considerate to me throughout my stay. We went out for walks in the Royal Park and also Whetland Park. We visited Selena and Billy took me to Heather's sister's place, a long way away where they made wine for export. Heather had a small party for the neighbours and I went to church with them.

Billy and Heather invited Vinod, Molly and the children for dinner one day and Billy made a lovely cake for the children. Heather made apple trifles.

We talked about Thirumeni and the book. I hadn't brought any copies because of a misunderstanding about Kuruvilla Mathew's sincerity. The Melbourne Mar Thoma church was very near to Billy's house, in fact, right by his doorstep. Yet we had no books to sell there.

Billy and Heather invited two Malayali couples and together we had dinner in a nice Indian restaurant. One couple really belonged to Mavelikara, Freddy and Mariamma both doctors settled down in Australia. Another, Kunjannama, a very friendly lady, knew Zacharias Thirumeni very well.

With Fiona and Vinitha

Later when I was in Vinod's house I sadly realized that except for the copy that Vinod kept in his drawing room, not a single copy had reached Australia. Even an Achen who was in Thirumeni's diocese before coming to a parish in Australia dared not speak about the book. The fear that had spread by word of mouth, could be seen in that church.

Kuruvilla Mathew could easily have sold at least two hundred books. This was the crocodile love he had for a classmate who was his close friend as a student, priest and Bishop.

I have not been able to forgive him this utter falsehood and deceit. When he made Rajankunju take the initiative to publish "Ormakalum Darshanangalum" he collected a lot of money from India and Australia as pre-publication discount. When he lied to my face and lost all respect, he wrote to me later, "It is sixty years of friendship, and it should not be cut off." But not a slender thread remains for this utter ingratitude.

On 12th May when the two weeks was about to be completed, Billy was down with a severe cold. He feared it was flu and it may affect me. So I cut short my visit two days early and went to Vinod and Molly. Autumn had begun, and it was cold weather. Australia does not have central heating like Europe, only a system of air circulation and electric heaters. Hence I found it really cold.

My stay with Vinod, Molly and the children was most enjoyable. The young CSI congregation consisting mostly of people from South Kerala was very warm and loving, as if they were one family. It was a great joy to be with them.

Mother's Day was celebrated in Ashburton with great fanfare. Not a person was left out. It was followed by barbecue for all. Quite to my surprise I met P.C. George who had worked in Bishop Moore College Office in 1964. There were two people from Chathenkary! That was the most surprising part of all, Anitha, Ashok and Renjju. Anitha is married to Anand and they have four well-brought up children, the eldest Anne being the organist.

I met many wonderful Malayalis while staying with Vinod. Thirumeni's first cousin Georgekutty and Jolly have all their three daughters in Australia. We were invited for dinner by Beena who is the wife of Varghese Chandy, son of the famous neuro surgeon, Dr. Jacob

Lausanne Lake, Switzerland

Chandy. Their son is married to Kunjannama's daughter and all of them live in Melbourne. It was Molly's birthday on 19th May, the first birthday after her mother's death. Yet she made mutton biriyani and pudding for a few people. Molly is a very good cook and cooks very fast. She is also an efficient driver.

Vinod had told me earlier that he would give me an opportunity to speak about the two books – "Neerum Velakalil" and "Such a man did live." But I was totally unprepared when he announced during the Communion service on 21st May that I was going to speak to them. I was utterly taken by surprise and did not know what to say. It was the first time Thirumeni's book was being announced in any church. By God's grace alone I was able to present my thoughts well.

As soon as the service was over Suma, a church member came to me. She took me to the hall where lunch was kept and said to me, "Auntie you must visit Pragyud and Vidhu". She had heard me talk about my acute experiences with stroke and she wanted me to share my experiences with a young man of forty who had a stroke and was still suffering the severe after-effects. He could not speak and could not move around. His wife Vidhu was an innocent lady from Thalassery. They were supported by kind souls like Suma and Renji. Suma was in the re-hab centre and was of great help. Later Renji took me to their house and I was able to share with them my experiences and encourage them to hold on to the Great Physician who would not abandon them.

That incident was the beginning of my warm friendship with Suma who is always bubbling with humour but a great cook and professional. As Sreekumar, my student and friend told me once, "Teacher, when older ones desert us God keeps on giving new people to love."

Anand took Achen and me to Maru Koala Park where I had a wonderful time feeding the kangaroos. I didn't know they were so friendly, friendly enough to eat from our hands. From there we drove back to Anand's house where Molly and the children joined us. Anitha cooked a wonderful dinner. Anju, Anitha's daughter, was always giving me compliments. First when Achen made me speak about the books during the sermon, she said to me, "It was so powerful". Again at the study and birthday dinner a few days later, when I had to field questions Achen raised on marriage, she said, "All older people may have knowledge. But you have wisdom!"

The congregation gave me a gift and a card when I was about to leave Australia.

It was also a joy to meet Jenny, Thirumeni's niece and Missy's daughter, and Joe her husband. Joe happens to be my classmate Emily's cousin's son. I know his mother Lucykutty kochamma very well. They came all the way to Melbourne to see me.

Later, Joshua their son came to take me to their home in Tatura which is about 250 miles away from Melbourne, though in Victoria State. They were all very happy to have me in their home. From there Joe connected me to Joy my cousin in Brisbane and I was able to talk to him about the book. Joe also called Emily and she was surprised. They have a greyhound, Rocky, who did not mind my presence at all.

Next day Jenny and I went with Joshua further up till Lake Victoria, which was nothing like a lake, compared to the lakes in Switzerland. We also visited the "Moooving Park" where they display all kinds of figures of cows.

Joshua is a fine boy and is working as tutor in the Melbourne University. His brother Joel too is in Melbourne studying for engineering.

After returning to Melbourne I went with Molly and Vinod to Cokes, which is the biggest supermarket in Australia and bought jam, biscuits and a toaster to take home. It was all very cheap because of discount.

Renjju and Ashok wanted me to stay with them for at least a night but there was no time left. They belong to Valiayaparambil, Chathenkary. All in the Ashburton Church were very loving, caring and generous.

I was to leave on Tuesday. On Saturday Heather phoned Vinod saying that one of them would come and pick me up on Sunday afternoon. They wanted to make up for the time I had lost with them on account of Billy's flu.

So Billy came, and he was not quite pleased about the weight of my box. Heather was simply overjoyed to see me. Billy cooked good dinner on Sunday and Monday.

Early morning on Tuesday, Billy and Heather drove me to the airport. It was an eight and a half hour flight to Kuala Lumpur and a four hour flight to Kochi. I had to spend five hours in transit. But the young man who took me in the wheel-chair was very kind and wheeled me right to the door of the aircraft. And finally I landed safely and happily in Kochi where Devarajan was waiting for me.

"To God be the glory

Great things He has done!"

CHAPTER XV

PEOPLE WHO TOUCHED MY LIFE

Shakespeare has written:-

"All the world's a stage,

and all the men and women merely players.

They have their exits and their entrances

and one man in his life plays several parts."

So many people were an integral part of my life during the past eight decades. Many played their parts and made their exit. New people then made their entrances. I would like to write a few words about a small number of them.

Kokkaparambil Ammachy, Papa's eldest sister, was married to a hard-working Appachen. Ammachy had a special place in her heart for me because she said that both of us were born under the same star "Thiruvathira". Whenever we went to their home, Ammachy would cook all the delicious tuberous roots and with good chutney we enjoyed it. All this was the sweat of Appachen's labour. They also fried cashewnuts, and the nuts came fresh and warm into the plates. It was typical of the generosity of people in those days.

In her last days she lived with her youngest son in Tiruvalla. One day Kunjummamachy told me that Ammachy was ill. I was about to go to the Maramon Convention. I cut short the afternoon session and came straight to Tiruvalla. Everyone was standing around Ammachy's bed for she was sinking. I too gave her a little water to wet her lips and within minutes she breathed her last.

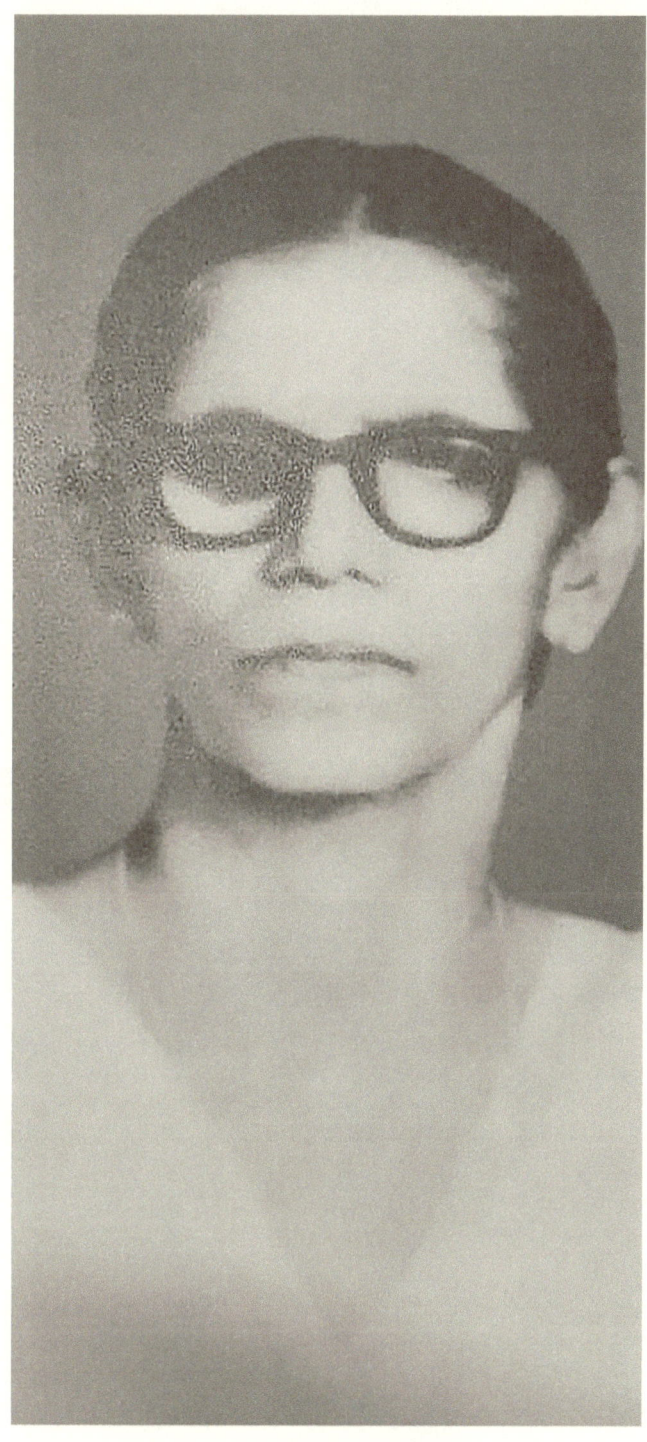

Chengannur Kochammachy

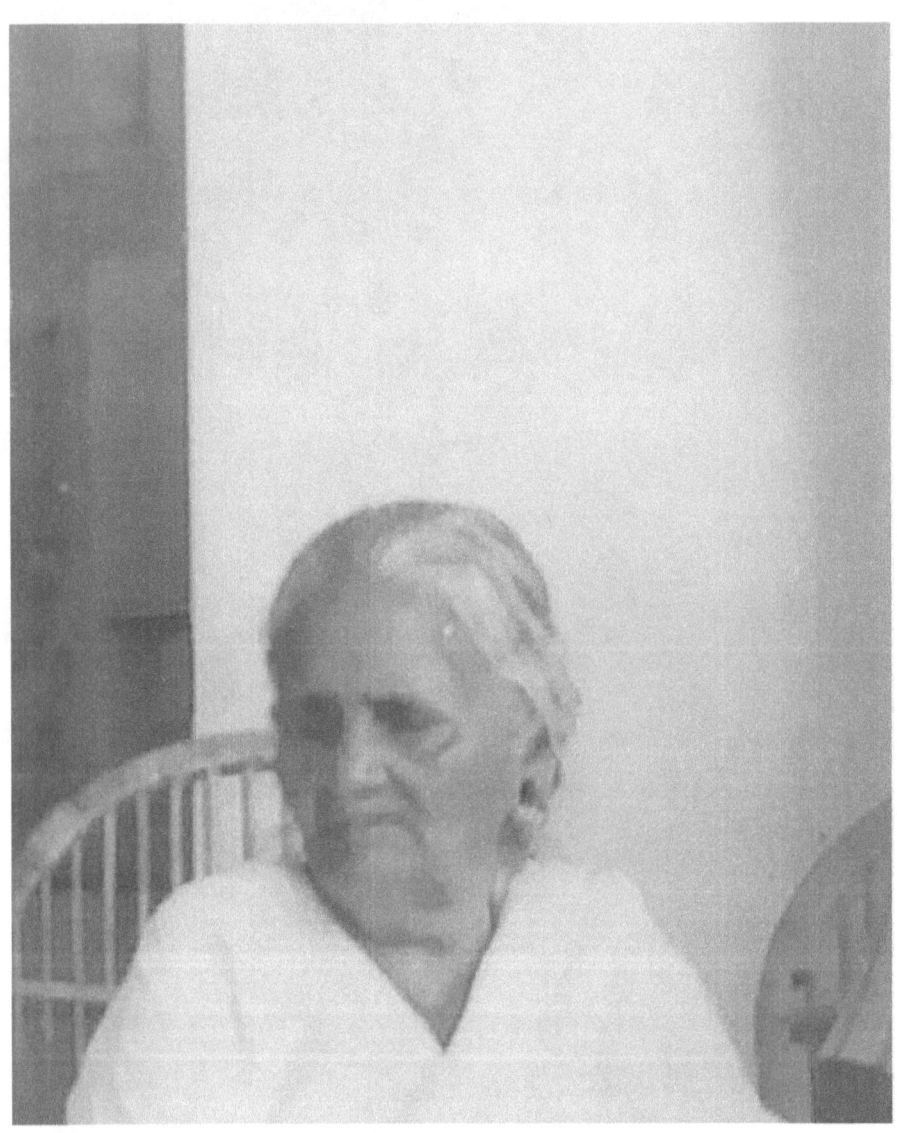

Kokkapparambil Ammachi, Chengannur

Kochammachy, Kunjeliamma, was Papa's second sister and was married to Kochappachen of Payalippurathu. He was a small farmer. Both sisters were neighbours. Ammachy was very lean, extremely generous and caring, and fed others even when her own stomach had to remain empty. Amidst all her responsibilities, she would walk all the way to Chathenkary to look after Valiyammachy. She cared more for others than for herself. Hence her children and grandchildren are today bound to one another with a special cord of love.

Sosamma, whom we called Vallimamachy was the one who stayed at home. When Kunjumamachy died while staying with Baben in Trivandrum, she could not bear the grief. As Kunjumamachy was far away she could not even visit her. At home she asked me to sing a few songs. She went home to Chathenkary immediately after the funeral and fell ill

Kunjachayan and Kochamma

the same night. She died in the wee hours of June 14th, hardly two days after the death of Kunjumamachy. Both of us were at the hospital when she died for Kunjachayan had phoned us at midnight.

I was very close to Kunjumamachy because I was close to Karippuzha. I used to visit her often and enjoyed her hospitality. We spent joyous hours together. When at last she left for Thiruvananthapuram with Baben for that Christmas in 1991, she told me she would return within a few days and then come and see Sourabh who was born on December 6th.

Unfortunately, she had a fall in their dark bathroom and never came back. I visited her whenever possible and used to write comforting letters to her. She kept those letters under the pillow, re-reading them and trying to find comfort from my words. Once as I was leaving, I said, "Ammamachy, shall I pray?" And instead, Kunjumamachy prayed a long prayer herself. I remember the very humble words with which she referred to herself when she spoke to God.

Finally when she died, I happened to be in Thiruvananthapuram for a meeting in the University.

She was on her death-bed. Her beloved grandson Ajit was there. I wanted to stay there if Kochummamachy or Vallimamachy had come. But they had been there the previous day and left in the evening. So I came back unwillingly and asked Anila to visit her in the morning. She died next day at 9.30 in the morning. It was 11[th]June, Papa's death anniversary. Both of them died at 9.30.

Kochumamachy was an extremely hospitable person and fed good things to all who came there till our stomachs burst! But in her last days she stayed with Kochumon's wife Susheela in Kesavadasapuram. I visited her often. At the end she had a tumour in the brain and lost her ability to speak. But on my last visit soon after this, she burst into conversation with me. Omana was surprised for she had just come to see her mother from Bombay, and Kochumamachy was not able to speak. At last when she was in hospital we were in Trivandrum. I remember standing by her side with her children as she breathed her last. She used to tell me, "When I die you must be the one who comes to sing and read the Bible." I remembered that, as we sat in Thalavady, and I did everything I could as she wished.

Kunjumole Kochamma, Kunjachayan's wife is only four years older than me. I have to make special mention of Kochamma because during a very critical period in my life after Achachen's death, when I was marginalised by those who ought to have loved me, Kochamma became my shelter and my refuge. I had to endure it during Achachen's illness and death but it reached its zenith when I lost him. Kochamma understood my predicament and she was very concerned about me. She would often ring me up and say, "Molly, come tomorrow morning and spend the day here with me."

This became a constant routine. At Easter and Christmas I was never allowed to be alone. I very much needed it for I was broken-hearted. Kochama understood my feelings and poured balm over my wounds. In those days I learned to cling to God whatever happened. He gave me strength beyond man's imagination. The Japanese have an art called "Kintsugi" to make a broken bowl whole, by joining the pieces together with golden seams. It is a golden rejoining of fragmented parts. God will give us the greatest view through the broken windows of our lives.

Kochamma is not one who boasts of her religious devotion and "bhakti." But she was the human presence of God for me when I needed it most. I am ever indebted to her for the love she gave me during this dark episode in my life.

Though Kochama's children are spread all over the world, they are by her side at all times. All children should emulate their example. Christians have to learn a lot from our Hindu friends. They literally follow the dictum –"Matha, Pitha, Guru, Deivam." The Bible teaches us – "Honour your father and your mother".

Even those who do not love their father and mother as they ought to, profess they love God. The Hindus are totally different. They value the blessings of parents and elders and teachers. Especially in Brahmin families they are taught from their birth to touch the feet of elders and receive their blessings. In my colleague Anantha Siva Iyer's house I have often seen them prostrating before their parents and gurus, and humbly paying their obeisance. Once when after a long time Sreekumar my student, came to see me, he prostrated right in front of me! A blessing goes out from you immediately. It is also true that the moment a father or mother is pained by a son or daughter, the very moment they create a pang in their hearts, Heaven takes away God's blessings until he or she turns back in repentance.

Another experience I want to share is this. Whenever a dear one nears death God's unfailing love takes me there. This happened at the death of Puthen-madathil Ammai, Angelekochamma and Achayan later on, Papa, Mama, Kunjumamachy, Vallimamachy, Kochumamachy, and both Ammachys in Chengannur. It was also true of Valiammachy and Appachen and Ammachy here. I can affirm without any hesitation that God sees through our hearts and is partial towards people who love.

This came true in the case of Ammuttykochamma, Sister Susy Oommen also. Leelakochama (Sr. Rachel John) Chechammakochama (Sr. Chechamma George) and Ammuttikochama of the Bethel Ashram were very close to my heart. That bond began years ago when they invited me as the chief guest of Bethel Day. It became stronger and more intimate when Achachen, whom they all loved and respected, fell sick. Bethel Ashram prayed for him every morning and evening all these five years without fail. They were a great support to us. It was just like "seeing God who is invisible", the motto of Bethel Ashram.

All three of them came from good families and set apart their lives to serve the Lord. Leela Kochama and Chechama Kochama were the daughters of two of Bishop Jacob's brothers. Ammutty kochama was from Kaniyamkulam and her father was a highly employed person. Though I did not deserve the love and friendship of such eminent people, God gave them to me. I loved them with all my heart. I used to visit them regularly in "Home of Peace." After Chechama Kochama's death, Leela Kochama and Ammutty Kochama kept up this warmth.

Later on Ammutty Kochama, a great woman of character, became very close to me. She confided in me as in a friend, prayed early morning for me and cared for me in every way. She shared with me the problems Bethel faced and asked me to pray about it. She had great love for all the orphan girls who grew up in Bethel Ashram and was very concerned about them. I phoned Kochama every week, wherever I was and we used to have long conversations. She needed a friend to unburden her heart and she chose me lovingly.

I loved visiting Bethel regularly and whenever I flew to Switzerland and other countries, these 'Kochamamar' prayed for me and waited eagerly for my return. I used to give a small help for those in "Home of Peace." Ammutty kochama sent regular letters and cards to strengthen me.

I specially remember one verse she wrote from Isaiah – "You are precious to me, and I love you." Those words were enough to hold me in my deep trials. Today I have regular help in the house because Ammuttykochama was very anxious about it whenever I told her I had no outside help and she used to pray with great concern.

Ammuttykochama was particular that I should come for every Bethel Day. I used to sit by her on the veranda of the chapel till the last Bethel Day we attended together.

Kochama would inform me everything that happened in Bethel and in her family. Ammuttykochama was deeply attached to Biju, her sister Grace kochama's and Bishop Benjamin's younger son. The older son Benji had died when both of them were alive. Biju's wife Shobha too was a very caring person. Biju died all of a sudden, after a few days in hospital and Ammuttykochama did not have the strength to bear that. She would talk to me about it. She did not go for the funeral but that incident always stood as a question mark in her mind. One day she said to me – "Kunjoonju and Jiji (Biju's sister and husband in the U.S.) came to see me. Kunjoonju said, "We only know that God loves us. We know nothing else."

Biju's death was ever in her mind and she was trying to accept it.

It was the annual meeting of Health Guild in Bethel Ashram on 9th March 2018. I went with Babu, Y. Oommen. I intended to see Kochama and spend some time with her. But because of the length of the meeting I could not make it. So when the meeting was over I made a quick visit to Kochama. She was having lunch. Kochama said she had been to hospital and as usual it was Neela who took her and spoke to the doctor. Neela was from Parakkal and has been here for a long time and Kochama cared for all these girls.

Then Kochama gave me a packet of chakka chips. I said to Kochama, "Kochama, I will come soon to see you and we will spend some time together." I gave her a little money to be used as she wished for "Home of Peace".

I was eager to keep my promise. Since Achachen's death anniversary fell on March 15th, I decided to go on the 14th. It was a Thursday. I went by bus early. I would come back only in the evening for I planned to visit Kunjumol kochamma.

Again Kochamma shared her thoughts about Biju. She also told me that she had written on a piece of paper that if ever she should fall ill she should never be shifted to an ICU or put on ventilator. She must be allowed to die. The funeral too must not be delayed for there were not many relatives who could come, for many were far away. She had given the letter to the Mother.

We spent a lot of time together and she was happy I had come. I told her I would go back only in the evening from Kochamma's house, so there was no hurry.

Then we parted. On Friday and Saturday, Kochamma sat there as usual. On Sunday morning she did not wake up. Neela discovered that she was not conscious. They took her to Believer's Hospital and she was admitted to Intensive Care Unit. I was informed by my young friend Sr. Molly Devassia. Kochamma was shifted to the room on Tuesday but was still in an unconscious state.

I decided to go to the hospital on Wednesday, early in the morning when visitors are allowed to enter. She was in the room as if sleeping peacefully. Sisters from Bethel, Rajamma, Gracey and Aleyamma were in the room, looking after her. I was there for some time and then came away, praying that God would call her to His eternal home where there would be no more suffering or sorrow.

I had booked tickets to fly to Bangalore on the 26th. I knew God knew. I was praying. I got news from Molly everyday. Kochamma's condition remained the same. They feared she might remain in an unconscious state for a long time. But on Saturday evening, by 5 o' clock Kochamma slipped away into eternity. She died a very peaceful death. It was the 23rd of March.

The funeral was to be held on Monday the 25th. Kochamma loved flowers. Molly bought a lovely wreath of white roses for me which remained on her feet where I placed it till the coffin was put in the vault. I reached Bethel early morning before Kochamma was brought to the Ashram. I remained there till the very end. I have no words to thank God for that great life of service and the way God gave me such great love from a great friend. I can only say I don't deserve a thing. But God's infinite care for us evidenced even in minute things in our life, is indescribable and the sum of His thoughts about us, are truly precious!

I flew to Bangalore the next morning. Kochama's face is imprinted in my heart. I can still see her, sitting at the entrance of "Home of Peace," caring for everyone around her with a great responsibility – including the orphaned workers serving there, the mentally disturbed, the orphaned children of the school, and the retired sisters of Home of Peace, loving them like a mother, and caring for them in every way possible, saying – "Who else do they have to love them, except us?" Kochamma was to be ninety on May 31st of that year.

Dag Hammarskjold was the second Secretary General of the United Nations, and the youngest, for he was only 47 when he became Secretary General in 1953. He died in an aircrash in Northern Rhodesia while en route to cease fire negotiations during the Congo crisis, in 1961.

He is the only person in history to be awarded Nobel Peace prize posthumously. He wrote in his famous diary "Markings"--

"When you were born, everyone was happy; you cried alone. Make your life such, that in that last hour, all others are weeping and you're the only one without a tear to shed. Then you shall calmly face death whenever it comes."

These famous words have stayed in my heart for ever, from the moment I read it in **Markings**.

I met Thampichayan, M.C. Andrews when I was sixteen and stayed in the YWCA with Aleyamma Kochama. I loved him ever since and he was as much a part of my life as Aleyamma Kochama. His tall, handsome demeanour, is ever impressed in my heart. When he was Deputy Director of Agriculture, he fell out with K. R. Gouri who was Minister and resigned his job. Ninumol's son Alexkutty was born on September 30th 1984, and when I went to Mallappally, Thampichayan was rocking him in his arms, singing a funny song – "Chandi Mappila, choondayittu.." That day, before I left, Tiji took a snap of Aleyamma Kochama, Thampichayan and me. That was the last picture of Thampichayan. He passed away two weeks later, of a sudden heart-attack. He was only 54.

When Aleyamma Kochama was in the hospital for the last time, I visited her the day she was discharged. She spoke to me, though she was weak. Ninumol and I went to the canteen and had lunch. Finally, when

I was about to leave, I held her hand. She asked "Molly, are you going to leave?" I said, "Yes." She was very calm and peaceful and I left thankfully though I knew I would not see her again. She left us within two weeks, on March 7th. She was in Jikky's home and since he caught chicken-pox nobody was able to visit her again.

I do not know how to express my love for Thampichayan and Aleyamma Kochama. She was always a mother figure in my life and a very close friend and elder sister. My life has become richer in the ocean of their love which has not ended with their death. Though the children were born long after I met them, Ninumol is still like a daughter to me. We have stayed with Thampichayan and Aleyamma kochama wherever they were transferred and Aleyamma Kochama's long loving letters, scribbled in beautiful hand-writing like Mama's, are still with me.

There are two precious friends I still have, whom I met when I became Chief Editor of "Kudumbapriyavadini." One is Kunjamma Kochamma, wife of Bishop Sam Mathew. I haven't seen such a humble lady, who despite the position she held in the church as a bishop's wife, did all her duties as for Christ. She is a great woman of noble character and a model for wives of priests and bishops, if they care to learn from her.

Rajan, Rajan Ittycheria was manager of CMS Press when I took up the responsibility of "Kudumbapriyavadini." The manager of CMS Press is a coveted post and highly esteemed. Rajan brought the press from loss to profit. Rajan is an expert editor and manager and there is none to excel Rajan's talents. At the same time there is none to excel the warmth with which Rajan loves ordinary acquaintances like me. Reena and Rajan keep a high regard and affection for me even today. Rare are such gems in our Christian society.

Another person who cannot stop loving me is Pochen, Prof. C.O. Philip who as a young lecturer, joined the English Department of Bishop Moore College. He was in the choir, had a golden voice and enjoyed his life here. He was sent away unjustly from Bishop Moore College because, the then head, a retired man Prof. D.G. Isaccs could not understand his accent.

He did very well in CMS College, Kottayam and settled down in Kottayam, his wife Latha being YWCA Secretary for many years. But still he misses all of us here, and we are still bound to one another by the golden chords of love. Such people who come into our lives are sent by God, people who never forget you and whom you can never ever forget. May God bless all of them, that is my only prayer.

Sometimes you get lasting tributes from very unexpected places that boost your life and give meaning to your life. Achyamma Thomas, much younger than me was my colleague in the English department. The college published a souvenir to commemorate its golden jubilee, and we were all asked to contribute articles. Achyamma concludes her article, "Life with my long-lost friend," like this:-

"Before I conclude this short account, let me mention two great persons of the community who have left indelible marks on my mind. One is Rev. K.C. Mathew, the founder principal of the college. His fore-sight, optimism, trust in God and trust in himself have given the college a local habitation and a name. The other person is Prof. Anna Verghise, lovingly called Mollykochamma. She has been a brilliant teacher and a strict disciplinarian. She is a storehouse of cheerfulness and self-confidence. A good wife, a good mother, a good teacher, a good servant of God, she has won over the hearts of her colleagues and students with her dedication and fortitude. I take her to be a symbol of Indian womanhood. Persons like Rev. K.C. Mathew and Prof. Anna Verghise are the salt of the earth. I consider it a proud gain having worked with them. The impact of such people in the community is too great to lose. May they continue to be sources of strength and inspiration to many".

I have faced undeserved indifference in my life. But what is written down in indelible ink by Achyamma here, is ever an oasis in my heart. I have no words to thank Achyamma for these beautiful words written in kindness and love. I am overjoyed that my life and career have not after all, been in vain. My blessings go to her and I remain ever indebted to her.

It was a great joy, the English Department, with all my colleagues. Though we were a motley group we made one another's sorrows halved and joys multiplied by our spontaneous love and laughter. There were celebrations in the department for everything and teachers from other departments would come there wondering how we made it special. P.U. Jacob was a great teacher, having Grecian looks, who sadly left us early. I have to make special mention of M.I. Itty sir, an old student of Alwaye who was a great friend to the end treating me with great respect because while a student, I had just come to UC as a lecturer. His sincerity and

Thampichayan and Aleyamma Kochamma

regard for both of us is unparalleled. He was also a unique teacher, very hard-working, who loved his students more than he loved anyone else. My heart flows out to all my colleagues in the English Department and other departments from whom I learned many things and who enriched my life making it worth living.

When Vattapparambil Gopinatha Pillai a brilliant Malayalam teacher and scholar turned 84, the Malayalam department decided to honour him. He had also lately got the Matha Amrithanandamayi award. I went for the meeting early. When Gopi sir came in with others we all stood up with folded hands to greet him. As soon as he came near me I greeted him.

Rajan Ittycheria

Bishop Sam Mathew and Kochamma

He was so happy to see me, and as an expression of happiness he hugged me. It was an affirmation of the long years of camaraderie we cherished as teachers. It surprised everyone but I am thankful for such a gesture of love after so many years.

A word about my beloved friends Syamala and Susheela of the zoology department. They are much younger than me. We regard them as Tom and Jerry and even as Pachu and Kovalan. They are a unique pair. If you have any worries you only have to give a call and your worries will vanish into thin air. We stay together at times, mostly in Ernakulam at Syamala's residence. Then you burst into splits of laughter all day that your ribs really need some hot-water treatment. Asha and Suja add to the flavour. We have had wonderful days together which the green-eyed monster Covid with its deadly fangs has taken away.

Achakuttychayan was the eldest in Achachen's family and he always had a rough exterior. When we first went to Kozhikode immediately after our wedding I feared to talk to him. He simply boasted about being an atheist but always supported the church. He was the person I loved most in the family. He used to come and stay with us quite often on his visits to these parts and taught the children wonderful action songs when they were young, and told them stories. Anila was three when he taught her the action song-

"Oru mazhu erinjappol aa maram kulungi".

Finally when it came to "aa maram veenu" Anila would simply fall down flat like a tree and we all enjoyed it. There would be laughter in the house always when he was here. He spent his retired life in Ottappalam when he became a great farmer. We loved visiting Ottappalam and staying there with every bounty that the earth provided.

During his last days we went to see him in Ottappalam. He was lying down and we stood around him. Kochamma introduced Achachen but he could not recognize him then. Then Kochamma uttered my name and immediately he burst out crying. He was so warm a person, very straight forward and dearest to my heart. So was Kochamma who came into the family when Achachen was eight years old.

After Achakuttychayan's death, the family shifted slowly to Palakkad. Kochamma was very well taken care of by the children. She loved both of us very much. After Achachen's death she insisted that our photographs be kept on top of the cupboard in her room so that she could see it. It was always kept there till her death.

Georgekuttichayan was very friendly to all but he was not a steady character. I want to mention one incident to warn everyone. One day he decided to sell the plot and house that he had inherited from Appachen. With Peelikutty's help he sold it to a man who belongs to the Orthodox Church. He never asked Achachen, and I knew about it only the night when all the things in the house were being taken on push-carts by people around to their own homes. I cannot describe my shock. Appachen's bed, Ammachy's meal-safe, the wooden cradle that had rocked all the children for a hundred years were all given away. Achachen had known about the sale but kept quiet. In the morning I was very angry and that was how the only things left, Appachen's old Almirah and Ammachy's "Kaalppetti" came to our house and are still kept here with pride. Georgekuttichayan was always very friendly and we would have meals together but no one expected this as he was a faithful soldier of God's army for years, holding the top post of Gideons International in India.

There is a saying among the wise – "An inherited family property should never be sold outside the family." This whole plot that belonged

Achakuttychayan and Kochamma

once to Ammachy's father was only less than forty cents, and we were at one end on eighteen cents! This land that should have been sold to us because we lived in the same plot came into the hands of a stranger because of Georgekuttichayan.

Later, when Achachen was bed-ridden, this new owner filed a complaint in the municipality asking us to cut a few small branches that leaned over to their plot. He had houses and plots everywhere and this was only a symbol of his immense wealth and authority. I came to know of it when the man from the municipality came with the legal notice. I said to the man, "Do you want to see the owner who should get up and cut the branches? Come and see. "And I led him straight to Achachen's bed.

Whenever I look out of the window, I always grieve about this half that was given to a stranger to torment us eternally. The house there was more than a hundred years old and all the children including the eldest who died five years before Achakuttichayan was born, grew up in this house. The place has many stories to tell. There are stories about everything there, the "elanji" with its sweet smell in the flowering season making the whole place fragrant, the well with its rich supply of clear water, the fence, the people who came there, and the experiences of each child who grew up there, married there and went away to build their lives in new lands. Even I who came here last have fond memories of Appachen and Ammachy, Pillachen and Aleyachedathi, and every grain of sand.

Alexikochama of Kumpalampoika was Valiamachy's youngest sister's daughter who lived in Nellanikunnu. I knew about "Alexi and Ammini" long before I met them because Valiammachy loved them and always spoke to herself about them, sharing her thoughts with us when we asked.

I came to know Alexi Kochama personally only after Anu her youngest daughter came to teach in Bishop Moore College. We became very close and I experienced the immensity of her unbounded love. I would often visit her, especially with Anu, and I also got good things from her home that she gave me like a mother. She enjoyed reading all that I wrote in "Njananikshepam" and "Kudumba priyavadini" and was very proud of me. There is a sentence in the liturgy of the Mar Thoma Church – "Lord beautify our women with the unfading ornaments of gentleness and modesty." She was the epitome of gentleness, modesty and love. I thank God He gave me the great good fortune to know Alexi Kochamma, and taste the sweet riches of her blessed qualities.

Grace Amma (Angele ammama) was an angelic person who loved me very much. It was such a joy whenever she came to stay next door with her father. She would share the lovely curries she made and was so loving. Whenever she came there she would visit us and make us happy with her loving ways.

Unfortunately she fell ill and was confined to her home for a few months before her death. I made it a point to visit her regularly, when I would sit by her side and just talk. Once I thought of praying before I left. Then Ammama said, 'Do you want me to pray' and she prayed a long and loving prayer to our Lord our Father and Maker. She told me while in bed, 'My only regret is that I have not been able to bring you here to stay with me.' She was Achachen's first cousin's daughter, but was much older. Age or in-law relationship is no barrier to loving. Let us love others in such a way till there is just no more love left. That was the love Ammama gave me.

Of Mama's two brothers, Achen uncle affectionately addressed as "ichachen", lovingly by his sisters, had God's love in him. He had a great caring mentality and would regularly visit all his relatives wherever they were, and help them in their needs. His great mistake in life was that he left the traditions of the Mar Thoma Church that was reformed by his great-great grandfather Abraham Malpan and became one of the founders of the Evangelical church. When Abraham Malpan reformed the church he reformed it from within. He did not leave the church though he was very close to the missionaries. Good tradition must always be valued, honoured and kept.

Achen uncle was always a respected priest wherever he was for he was very sacrificial. But the decision to leave the church has always remained as a blot in his priestly career.

Kochamma too loved us much. She was Vinitha's godmother, the others being Ammama and Papa. She came for Vinitha's confirmation with home-made delights and stayed with us. Annie too came with her. All their children are close to our hearts and so are we to them.

Papa became Vinitha's godfather just by chance. Valiammachy, Papa's mother, was bed-ridden for a long time. It was believed that she was waiting to see her beloved son before going home. So Papa came for a short visit to be with Valiammachy. Vinitha's baptism took place at that

Achen uncle and Kochamma

Kunjoochayan

time and thus he happily became her godfather. Valiammachy died soon after that at the age of 80.

Mama's younger brother Kunjoochayan inherited the ancestral home. He married Sally kochama from Kainakary. Her father was well known by Achen uncle for he belonged to the Evangelical church. I remember Koshy Achen, Vallyamachi's first cousin conducting the prayers before we left for Kainakary by boat. He sang " Inni mangalam shobhippan karuna cheika, ennum kanivulla deivame" – not a well-known song, but he was a great singer.

Sally kochama was educated in great Christian institutions like Nicholson School and UC College. I have seen her as a very senior student in Alwaye. I believe that when a girl is married into a Christian home she should be like a lighted lamp in the home, keeping the good traditions of the family and also bringing in good traditions of her own ancestry. Education and Christian training are of no use if we cannot live it. Then we will spread only darkness wherever we are.

This is exactly what happened in the home where the five children of Valliappachen and Valliamachy grew up like lodestars. Kunjoochayan died only at the age of ninety, long after Sallykochama's death. But by that time the family was in a disastrous state. Sally kochama never valued the home she was married into and least respected Kunjoochayan and Valiyammachy. Kunjoochayan stayed in Kozhencherry for he was teaching in St. Thomas College, and came home only during the week-ends. He had to obey everything that his wife said and had to borrow money for her spend-thrift ways and the wayward lives of the children that Sally kochama encouraged. Only the daughters were gentle.

We had a neighbour Mathu and he and his brothers lived in little plots of land next to our compound. Mathu was an avaricious man who created border disputes with Valiappachen for no reason except his desire for gain. When Sallykochama came she knew he was not a well-wisher. She only wanted to create a good impression on her neighbours. So Mathu was welcomed into the home and from the time the children were a little old enough to play cards, he put them in his lap and taught them the game so that they lost all interest in education and learned gambling. He did it purposely to destroy our family and she paved the way for it. That was the beginning of the great decay that befell our family and Kunjoochayan's three sons. Kunjoochayan always had cows that yielded twelve litres of milk. While she distributed the milk freely she never allowed Valiammachy to have a little milk or curds that Valiamachy had, and valued all her life. When she fried fine fish at home she did not care to give it to Kunjoochayan who did not have an indecent heart or a strong hand to control her. All this has so accumulated before the throne of the Almighty whom we call upon each day that it has fallen like the sword of Damocles.

Everyone in Thalavady had great regard for Kunjoochayan. But they wondered why a saintly-man like him had to suffer so much. There is no answer. We now know that he should have been more assertive as a husband and father for when God puts us in charge of a family it is a great responsibility. Kunjoochayan was extremely kind, patient and generous. Yet when consequences come we cannot say to God, like Adam, "The woman you gave to be with me, she," is responsible.

As a young man, my picture of Kunjoochayan is praying whenever he got out of the house to do anything. In his latter life when he lived with his beloved son-in-law Thampi and daughter Lalu, he spent a lot of time praying for all, loving all, and caring for all. Valiammachy's photograph was always on a table near him. All of us loved him deeply and his prayers were a refuge for us. He remains a saint in our hearts who was too good for the world's wickedness.

The ancestral land and home we loved are almost gone. This happened in the short span of one generation, before our own eyes. Will a redeemer come like Boaz, for deliverance?

Thankamama, Mama's younger sister, who resembled Valiappachen suffered a lot after her marriage, for Uppappen, a handsome young man and an only son, thought only about himself. She, with her good family traits faced it with great dignity. She faced all her adversities with a lot of time spent in prayer and with fortitude and good humour. All her children are blessed now and even Uppappen was able to enjoy the money that his children sent him.

AmminiAmmama, the youngest in the family was pretty but not highly educated. She was a great help to Valiammachy whenever she was needed. Uppappen and Amminimama lived a very long happy married life for Uppappen died only when he was 94. They lived a thrifty life for their two girls. Amminimama who is just eight years older than me, is

Amminimama and Uppappan - Ranni

the valuable remnant we still have to remind us of our beloved Mama, Valiammachy and Kunjoochayan and all we loved in Thalavady.

When I came to Mavelikara as a young bride, an elderly person, stout and serious came one day to our house to see Appachen. His voice was enough to make you tremble. He said to Appachen, "Where is your new daughter-in-law? Let me see her."

I appeared. Vallichayan, whom I have most affectionately called all my life, later said to me, "I came to say something rude to frighten you. But when I saw you, I was reminded of my niece Kuttiyamma and immediately, affection flowed from my heart."

Ever since then Vallichayan loved me.

Vallichayan, M.M. Samuel of Mammoottil house was a person of high intelligence, education and capabilities. Since he had a loud voice that carried far, he used to repeat the speeches of great speakers at the Maramon Convention for all to hear, for there was no other sound system. Gracey, my colleague and classmate was later married to Oommachayan, Kuttiamma's brother and they stayed with Vallichayan in that big house. Kuttyamma and I were classmates and we stayed together in the YWCA in Alwaye and thus Ammama, her mother too had great affection for me. Since Mama's home was in Thalavady, Ammama who stayed in Kunthirickal, near Edathua knew them.

Vallichayan had only choice friends, friends who could speak on an equal par with him. When Papa died, Vallichayan came home a few days later and said, "I have come to congratulate you for not crying before others. When my mother died I did the same thing. At times, without anyone seeing it, I would squeeze my nose." Vallichayan had problems with his wife who was no match for him but he was very much attached to his mother.

I said to Vallichayan, "When Papa died it was my responsibility that came to me. That is why I could not show my feelings in public".

I would often go to Vallichayan's house to see him and talk to him. He loved it. Gracey would say, "Vallichayan loves talking to Molly".

As a good conversationalist he was choosy about people. That was indeed a great compliment for me. Sometimes Vallichayan would give me pineapples to take home. I used to meet Ammama whenever she came to stay with Vallichayan.

I spent the night in Vallichayan's home the day Vallichayan died. Years later when Ammama was staying with Gracey, she had a fall and as treatment was delayed she slowly became bed-ridden. Ammama's older son was a doctor, and it was a family of doctors and they waited for Pappachayan's children to come for Pappachayan had already died.

I used to visit Ammama just to be by her side and talk to her. Gracey and Oommachayan did not like it. Even Kuttiyama was not allowed to come and look after her. Ammama who said that in her home in Edathua, as soon as they got up, neighbours would come to their fences and talk to one another lovingly, was left on a bed in a small room, her only view being the ceiling.

Gracey died the year after Ammama's death, before she retired. But Kuttiyama nursed her in her illness, and also looked after Oommachayan when years later he fell seriously ill. Kuttiyamma still lives in Kothamangalam, a benevolent person loved by all.

We must learn lessons from life's experiences. Then only can we live a life as God designed us to be.

CHAPTER XVI

LOOKING BACK

When I look back over the years that have gone by, I see that the hand of God has guided me in life. I have put my sole trust in God just as my parents and teachers taught me and tried to be true to them and true to myself and above all true to God.

I remember when Achachen died, Skaria Abraham achen who knew him well was then vicar of Thazhakara Mar Thoma church. Achen came twice to the house. I will never forget a sentence that he prayed that day – "It is because teacher was brought up in a Christian home by Christian parents that she has been able to look after sir so well with such love."

Even at that moment, the credit went to my parents. I thank God for Christian homes and Christian parents.

I have never liked display of Bhakti or religiosity. I have even told my children – "Do not count me among the righteous people. I prefer to stand with the sinners, for Jesus walked with sinners."

People had much more love in our days and that love was lasting and sincere. I cannot forget Thankamma kochama who became Physical Education teacher in Nicholson School when I was in 6th form, the year I completed schooling. We became close friends years later when I went back to Nicholson and became Old Girls' Secretary. Her home in Ancherry where she lives with her brother and sister is always open for me. She is a very precious gift of God to me and to the school. Even today she takes great interest in keeping the school as it was in olden days, preserving its ideals and tradition.

And so are Saramma and Susamma retired Principals of Nicholson school and the younger teachers Susan, Lizy and Ammukutty all of whom dedicated their lives in God's service and in working in the school.

I had a great surprise on my 82nd birthday. A large number of students came to know about it and phoned me from different parts of India and the gulf. It was a great gift for my birthday. My own children did not get slots to call me in the morning! I have to make special mention of Moncey and Shobha. I stayed with them in Delhi and also in a beautiful flat in Kochi built right on top of the lake as it were, with such a view of grandeur. They give me loving calls from Bangalore where they are now. Alex and Betty and Aniyankunju do keep in touch regularly.

Another niece who constantly keeps in touch with me is Sheelamol, Achakuttychayan's daughter. She has all the caring qualities of her mother and father. She became a widow when quite young. After Joy's death, one day she called me when I was in Bangalore and talked to me for a long time. She was thinking of her future when she would be alone. I tried to help her with a few suggestions and encourage her to use her talents and live life abundantly. She said to me, "Mollymama, my desire is to be like you." No one has told me that! Not even my children! She is a great caring person and my valuable friend. Two grand-nieces are very close to me and they give me great joy, Sheelamol's daughter Inna, and Alex's daughter Mini.

Achachen & me

I get unexpected compliments from many of my former students at times. One day when I was standing in the organic vegetable shop in Puthiakavu, a young lady walked in with a school-going daughter. She introduced herself to me and then said to the daughter – "this is the teacher I talk to you about, the teacher who taught me English." Her daughter had great interest in English literature. She told me the child was born ten years after her marriage; then, as directed by her mother the girl came to me, and touched my feet to receive my blessings!

On another occasion I was standing with Gopi and his autorickshaw in front of the chicken shop. A car came from the west and parked on the other side of the road. The owner got out of the car and came straight to where I was standing. He introduced himself to me. He had been my student in Bishop Moore College and had just retired from Mar Thoma College, Tiruvalla. After talking about the good old days and the attitude of students now, he just hugged me as a token of his love and appreciation!

There is a verse in the Bible – "Cast your bread upon the waters, you shall find it after many days." "(Ecclesiastes 11:1)

Teachers are a class of people, who, if they have sincerely given of their best to their profession, will benefit in greater ways in the future, with affection, respect and appreciation from students.

There are two sisters, Valsala and Vijayalakshmi who call me regularly from Bombay. They are past sixty, but they haven't forgotten me. The list is long, including Jayakumar and Sanal, Vinitha's classmates, who are at hand for any help; Sreekumar who is a close friend; Usha, Alex, Isacc, Sam, Suma, Reji, Gopi, Mathew Ninan and a host of others who keep in touch. Some say they became English teachers because of me! For all this, and more, I am really thankful.

I believe that a Christian life is to be L-I-V-E-D, and you and your home must become the true Temple of God. We must be the gospel that others read – especially our children, others in the family and people in our workplace. I have learned in life that unless God's love is first implanted in our hearts we cannot love others with God's love. God's love should first flow into our hearts. What matters at the end of our lives is how much we have been able to love and how much we have been able to serve.

Selwyn Hughes has written that there is a creative spark in Jesus and we too have that spark of creativity in us. Age is no barrier to making good use of this creativity. It is the Indian concept that makes us believe that we cannot make our lives useful after retirement. As the Westerners do not have this stigma about age, they travel, learn new skills and use their talents in every way they can. There is no limit to what we can do at any age with God's help. As Valson Thampu, writer and thinker and my student, exhorts – "Jesus came to give us life, and life in abundance. We have only to seek it."

I am grateful to my children for helping me accomplish my great love for travel, seeing the world, as Hardy says. After Achachen's death it was Prashant who encouraged me to renew my passport and bought two boxes for travel. I have stayed in Club Mahindra many times, in many places. It has been a very unique experience. My 80th birthday was celebrated in Club Mahindra in Pondicherry when all my children and grandchildren came to make me happy. It was Prashant and Megha who took me to various destinations of Club Mahindra. I went with Anila and Vinod too when they visited Club Mahindra. Anila and Vinod took me on a nostalgic trip to Singapore and Malaya because they could not take me to Doha. I could never have dreamed of staying in Taj Hotels in Cochin and Bombay if not for Soman, Vinitha and Sourabh. I have lost count of the number of times I have visited Switzerland. I paid only my airfares. Vinitha looked after everything else. I thank all my children for this love for making my dreams become a reality; and God has abundantly blessed each one of you. May He continue to do so.

God has given me good grandchildren whom I treasure. They love me very much and I value their love. My request is that they love one another as if they are one family, and be a sister and brother to one another all their lives, bound by the unbreakable chain of God's love.

You will see new things in life, new technology, new values. But always remember to walk straight, never to swerve to the right or left. (Joshua 1:7). "Nec dextrorsum nec sinistrorsum" which is the motto of Namith's and Shobhith's school Bishop Cotton – neither to the right nor to the left. When life's tempests come, God's word alone will be able to guide us, for His faithfulness knows no end. As young people I want you to remember these words when you come to the crossroads of life.

Jeremiah 6:16 – "Stand at the crossroads and look; ask for the ancient paths: ask where the good way is, and walk in it."

We had two Mahogani trees at the back of our house. Two small saplings were brought by Prashant from school as a part of the social forestry scheme. They grew into huge trees. One became much bigger than the other. When it was cut we found that the main root of that tree had gone deep down into the wetland just next to our plot. Even in extreme heat, the tree had plentiful supply of water. In the same way we must be deeply rooted in Christ.

Blessed is the man that trusteth in the Lord, and whose hope the Lord is. For he shall be as a tree planted by the waters and spreadeth out her root by the river. Her leaf will be green and she will always yield fruit" Jeremiah 17:7,8.

I have loved the story of Solomon. When Solomon became king over the vast kingdom of his father David, God appeared to him in a dream in Gibeon and said, "Ask what I shall give thee."

Solomon knew that God had showed unto his father David great mercy as he walked before him in truth and righteousness and in uprightness of heart. And now he was chosen as the king over these great people that cannot be numbered.

Solomon humbled himself before the Lord and said, "Give therefore thy servant an understanding heart to judge thy people, that I may discern between good and bad."

God was pleased that he had asked not for riches or long life but for understanding and discernment. And God gave him a wise and understanding heart so that there was none like Solomon before him and none like Solomon after him. (I Kings 3:1)

None of us have Solomon's responsibilities. But we need wisdom and discernment every day. Pray this prayer that Solomon prayed; let it be a chant in your mind as you face each responsibility. God will give you the discernment that he gave Solomon, and you will live successfully.

I conclude with the words of King David, uttered in great gratitude to God in II Samuel 7:18

"Who am I O Lord God, and what is my house, that Thou hast brought me hitherto? "

"Now unto Him that is able to do exceeding abundantly above all that we ask or think, according to the power that worketh in us,

Unto Him be glory throughout all ages world without end."

Ephesians 3:20, 21.

Family tree

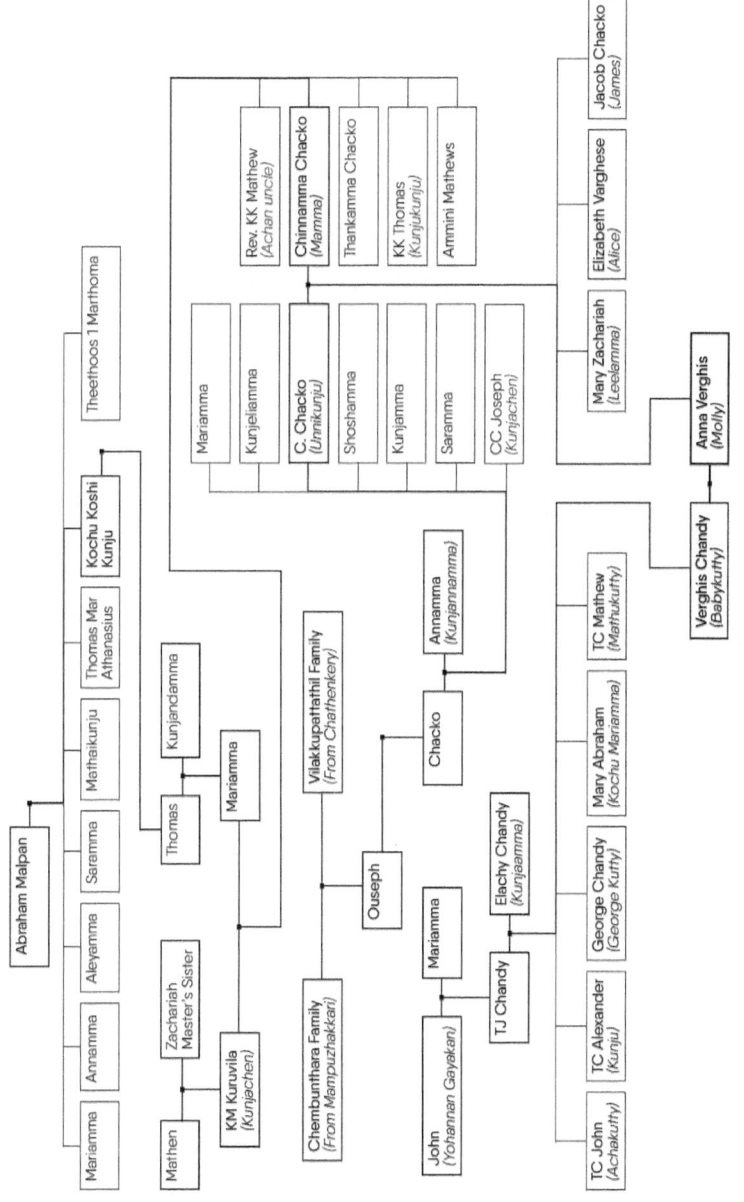

Family tree